Also by Ben MacFarlane

*Holiday SOS*


Praise for *Holiday SOS*

'It's terrific' *Independent*

'A barn-storming account' Libby Purves, *Radio 4*

'An eye-opener for any holidaymaker' *Now Magazine*

'Will have you engrossed' *Sunday Herald*

'Hugely entertaining' *The Lady*

# BEN MACFARLANE

## The Life-Saving Adventures of a Doctor at Sea

HODDER &
STOUGHTON

All patients' names have been changed in order
to protect doctor-patient confidentiality. All characters are
composite characters.

First published in Great Britain in 2010 by Hodder & Stoughton
An Hachette UK company

2

Copyright © Ben MacFarlane and Neil Simpson 2010

The right of Ben MacFarlane and Neil Simpson to be identified as
the Authors of the Work has been asserted by them in accordance
with the Copyright, Designs and Patents Act 1988.

A CIP catalogue record for this title is available from the British Library.

ISBN 978 0 340 91977 4

Typeset in Rotis Serif by Hewer Text UK Ltd, Edinburgh
Printed and bound in the UK by CPI Mackays, Chatham ME5 8TD

Hodder & Stoughton policy is to use papers that are natural, renewable
and recyclable products and made from wood grown in sustainable
forests. The logging and manufacturing processes are expected to
conform to the environmental regulations of the country of origin.

Hodder & Stoughton Ltd
338 Euston Road
London NW1 3BH

www.hodder.co.uk

To the family and friends I still see too little of when I'm travelling. And to all the doctors, nurses and medics around the world who help put dream holidays back on track.

# CONTENTS

# Part One

# Setting Sail

# CHAPTER ONE

'Do we know his name?'

'It looks like Paco. Paco Robredo,' says Eileen, wiping blood off the plastic identity card that has fallen from the man's belt. He's got deep, messy wounds on both wrists. He's terrified, his eyes are flashing around the room and he's trying to force his way past me and back into the centre of the ship.

'Paco you're going to have to calm down. The door's closed and I'm not going to let you go back out there. If this is a battle then I'm going to win. We can't help if you keep on acting like this. Do you understand me, Paco?'

Ten minutes ago I had arrived at the ship's Medical Centre to introduce myself to Eileen, my new senior nurse. The emergency call had come in while she was handing me a mug of coffee. Two crew members then carried this wild-eyed, violent man into the waiting room. They threw him down in disgust and disappeared. Now Eileen and I are gloved up and trying to stop him from tearing himself apart.

'They're all over me! They're killing me—they're everywhere!' he screams. I push him back on to the bed and he curls his whole six-foot frame into a ball. Then his voice breaks. He's still talking but he's slurring his words so much it's impossible to work out what he's saying. What is clear is that his breathing is speeding up. Between each word he's trying to fill his lungs with desperate gasps of air. His chest is moving fast and he's shivering, even though his T-shirt is drenched with sweat. 'I'm dying,' he shouts, thrusting his head from side to side as if he's no idea where he is or why. Every muscle in his body is tensing and flexing as he tries to pull himself away from the demons he can see all around him. 'They're inside me now! Help me!' He uncoils his body and reaches for his wrists. He starts scratching them so hard he draws even more blood. Then he does the same to his neck.

'Paco, you're hallucinating, there's nothing inside you, there's nothing here and you're in no danger.' His eyes finally stop going from corner to corner of the room and he looks directly at me for the first time since he arrived. Maybe it's time to try some of my Spanish: 'Paco, I'm a doctor. *Soy Médico. Me llamo* Ben. My name is Ben and I can help you.' His muscles relax and, as tears start to run through the stubble on his face, he lets himself flop back on to the bed. His head sinks into the pillow and his eyes close. It's pretty clear that this man is going through an extreme case of alcohol withdrawal – delirium tremens or the dreaded 'DTs', which sailors used to call 'the rats'. 'Stay calm like that and everything will be OK. I'm just going to check you out, Paco,' I say very softly. The room is quiet at last and I know from treating other de-toxing alcoholics that this is an important moment. This man's skin will be hypersensitive to the creatures he's convinced are crawling all over it. He'll only let me examine him if the room stays silent.

That's when the phone rings.

Paco slams his fist hard against the side of my face and throws himself off the bed in panic at the sound.

'They're here – I can feel them!' he shouts, drawing blood when he digs his finger nails even deeper into his neck. He tries to fight his way back towards the door as Eileen grabs the phone.

'Dakila, we've got someone going through serious cold turkey. We need you here right now,' she shouts. She jams the receiver down and Paco lets out another anguished yell at the sound. I manage to force him back on to the bed, but I can see his arms tense up as he grabs the sides and prepares for another burst of fight-or-flight. This man's brain is in overdrive. Everything is alternately confusing and scaring him now. His body is beating itself up from the inside.

'We've got to keep the noise down and the lights up,' I call out at Eileen. Shadows and sudden noises always set people off when they get the DTs. Other distractions can be just as dangerous. 'Can we hide those wires?' I ask. Paco is suddenly staring, transfixed, at the monitoring equipment on the wall alongside him. There is a look of absolute terror on his face. It's as if he's seen pure evil in the tangle of electric cords. Eileen clicks on two bedside lamps and tries to pull some paper towelling over the wires. Paco's mouth is opening and closing in fear. He's swearing profusely, this time in Spanish, but now he's slurring his words even more. His eyes are flashing wildly round the room and I can tell he's going to make another bid for the door.

'We're not going to be able to talk him down from here. Can you get some haloperidol?' I ask Eileen.

'I'll have it in thirty seconds,' she says, rushing out of the room. The good news is that a sedative like this will have Paco acting like a puppy in about five to ten minutes. The bad news is that we'll probably need to inject it into his backside – and I've got a feeling he won't be very happy with the idea.

'OK, Paco, this is for your own good,' I say as I hold him against the bed with one hand and yank his trousers down with the other. Fortunately we act so fast he doesn't know what's hit him or where. Eileen does the business, puts the used syringe in the sharps box and stands back.

'That should do the trick,' she says. But Paco's brain won't let him give in so easily. His eyes are locked on to the green and gold spectacle chain Eileen has around her neck. At first he looks simply confused, as if he's trying to work out what it could be. Then, suddenly, the terror comes back.

Everything seems to go into slow motion as he leans back on the bed. He takes two or three deep breaths to gather his strength, then he lunges at Eileen's neck. He lets out a roar of defiance and throws himself across the room. Both his bloodstained arms are stretched out, desperate to grab and presumably to kill whatever he thinks is around her throat. She screams and falls back against the surgery door. Somehow I get between the two of them. Paco reeks of sweat and vomit and worse. My feet are barely holding firm on the surgery floor when he suddenly crumbles. He slumps into my arms. Eileen has ripped off the chain and, now that he can no longer see it, he can't seem to work out what's going on. There are more tears in this big, angry man's eyes as he looks around.

'You're going to be OK,' I tell him. I'm relying on the fact that the drugs must be on the point of kicking in. But something else happens as I guide him back on to the bed.

His body starts to shake, his shoulders roll forwards and his eyes suddenly look even more afraid.

'Stay with me, Paco,' I say as his first ripples become a surge. But I know that he's already losing control. This is when the nightmare of the DTs goes into its next phase. This is the start of a seizure.

I'm holding Paco's shoulders when the surgery door opens. Two people in sharp white uniforms rush into the room.

'Thank God. It's Kiri and Dakila. They're our nurses,' Eileen says. 'This is our new doctor,' she tells them. 'And this is Paco. He's in a bad way.'

All four of us move to Paco's side. He's pulling his wounded hands up towards his chest. His neck is tensed forward and his body is in the foetal position. His eyes are open and rolling up into his skull as his consciousness drains away. The seizure is taking command and ripping through every inch of him. If he'd been terrified before, he's clearly petrified now. But if he's capable of thinking at all, there's nothing he can do. His body has sent him on a violent, dangerous journey. He can't fight this on his own.

'I'll get some more meds. What do you need?' Kiri asks. Her blond hair is tied up in a ponytail. She's pretty, in her late twenties and sounds Australian. She's also the definition of a strong, calm professional. Within twenty seconds of meeting her I'm hugely pleased she's on the team. I ask for a tourniquet, a cannula and some diazepam to see him through the fit. She disappears to get them straight away.

'Have we checked his head?' This time it's Dakila, a small, thirty-something Filipino man, who proves his worth. He gloves up, moves round to the top of the bed and starts threading his fingers through Paco's hair.

'Can you see anything?' I ask. If Paco's seizure is triggered

7

by his alcohol withdrawal then he'll get through it. But if it is caused by a head injury then all bets are off. At that moment I realise that I've no real idea of what kind of equipment we have on board the ship. If he's had a brain haemorrhage I don't know if we'll be able to save him.

'There's some kind of wound here but it looks new. Where was he found?'

'On his toilet floor,' says Eileen.

Dakila looks across at her, then at me. 'I'd say he got this when he fell. It looks like something from the door frame or the hand basin. I'd not even stitch it if he came in to the surgery like this. It's a head wound, not a head injury. I don't think it's the trigger.'

Paco's shakes are building up. His teeth are chattering violently as his head is thrown back and forward. His body is now entirely out of his control. No wonder seizures were blamed on witches in medieval times. If you believe in the devil, then this is surely the work he would do. I put my hands back on Paco's head to make sure he doesn't swallow his tongue and choke on it. If he deteriorates I can intubate him to keep him breathing. But that's an ugly process. I'm desperately hoping it won't come to that.

'It's been three minutes,' Eileen calls out when I've administered the drugs brought in by Kiri. We're all holding our breaths. There's no average time for a seizure. But there is a point at which they become even more dangerous, and we're getting close to it. A fourth minute passes and all of a sudden Paco's shakes start to weaken. The death mask on his face disappears. His limbs relax. 'The meds have kicked in. He's getting through it. He's back with us,' Eileen says softly.

A couple of minutes later Paco's demons have left him completely. He's going to need a lot more help in the next few hours. But at least the real danger is over. I can sense the three other medics relaxing alongside me as Paco's breathing slows.

'Hello, by the way,' I say to Kiri and Dakila. 'I'm Ben MacFarlane. It's nice to meet you.'

# CHAPTER TWO

'That was quite an introduction to ship's life. I do hope it won't put you off,' Eileen says. She's putting an iced compress on my eye while Kiri and Dakila sit and watch over Paco in the Crew Ward. She's brewed a fresh pot of coffee and we're trying to pick up where we left off a couple of hours earlier.

'It's probably a bit late to change my mind now, isn't it?' I ask, trying to smile. Paco's medical emergency doesn't seem to have stopped the ship's departure and, while I'm no expert, the sound of the engines suggests we're already moving at a pretty decent pace.

'You could probably jump ship in Madeira. That's where Paco will be leaving us if he doesn't pull through this pretty fast. But I do hope that you won't. You handled yourself very well out there and I can promise you that this was a very unusual incident. We do get an awful lot of alcohol-related problems on board. But this is the first time I've seen a doctor hit in the face before we've left port.'

I take the compress off my eye so I can look at her properly. 'Eileen, I was expecting you to say you'd never had a doctor hit in the face at all. I didn't think it was just a matter of time. They certainly didn't mention that in any of my interviews.'

'They probably didn't mention a lot of things. We'd never

be able to recruit any medics at all if we told them the unvarnished truth. So what were you expecting of the job?'

I lean back in my chair. 'To be honest I thought it might be a little bit dull. I thought a floating hotel would be nice and peaceful after two years doing emergency repatriations for holidaymakers. I thought the worst thing that might happen is that someone forgets their blood-pressure medication or falls down the stairs on their way to dinner.'

Eileen shrugs and smiles. 'You're close,' she says. 'But you've missed one key detail. You've forgotten that this particular hotel is staffed by around a thousand lonely, low-paid workers who haven't seen their families in months and tend to walk around in a seething mass of testosterone and hormones and who knows what else? Add to the mix the fact that they're from some seventy different countries, speak fifty different languages and work long hours doing dangerous, manual jobs. Oh, and every night they let off steam on the premises by drinking, fighting and running as many scams as they can find.'

I let all this sink in for a while. 'The brochures don't really mention that, do they?'

'Not if they can help it. They don't mention some of the other worrying things we've got on board either.'

'Oh dear. Like what?'

'Oh, everyday things like the endless array of kitchen knives, steam irons, pans of boiling oil, power tools, wire cutters and bottles of bleach. If a cruise ship was a game of *Cluedo* we'd have far more than a few candlesticks and pieces of lead piping to round up as possible murder weapons.'

'I think I will join Paco and take the first flight out of Madeira after all.'

Eileen is really smiling now. 'No you won't,' she says

confidently. 'I've seen the way you work under pressure. I think you're going to love this job and we're going to love having you with us. Some days this will feel more like a battleship than a cruise ship. But it's still a wonderful, magical place to work. We couldn't operate if everyone on board was at war all of the time. Mostly we rub along very well together. I promise that you'll see more acts of kindness than acts of violence by the time we get round the world and back. Whatever else happens in the next three and a half months I promise you'll never get bored.'

For the next half-hour Eileen talks me through the medical team and the facilities we have at our disposal.

'My background is midwifery though I've been on cruise ships for far more years now than I care to count. Kiri is only twenty eight but she has a background in mental health as well as general nursing. Dakila is on about his eighth year of cruises and takes breaks every now and then to work in ICU wards and in theatre back in the Philippines. He's a whiz on all the new equipment we have down here. I know from your file that you've spent the past two years doing emergency and repatriation medicine, so I'd say we're going to make a very strong team.'

'Can I ask about our senior doctor? I was given the name Doctor Edward Marlborough but I haven't met him yet.'

Eileen leans back in her chair and gives a wide, indulgent smile. 'Doctor Marlborough is a wonderful man: a marvellous, utterly charming and unforgettable ship's doctor. You will probably meet him in the morning. His job is to focus upon our guests. As his deputy you will go by the name of "baby doc". Your job is to look after the crew, though as you'll be on duty most nights you'll see plenty of passengers as well. There are always a lot of late-night calls so I hope you aren't a heavy sleeper.' She stops suddenly, then leans closer. 'If you plan to make a career out of this job then you'll find no better teacher than Doctor Marlborough. But take advantage of him while you can. No-one else knows this but this is going to be his final world cruise. He is going to do a few fjords over the summer and then he's taking early retirement. Will you keep that a secret?'

'Of course.'

'Then let's move on,' she says. 'Let me tell you more about how we work. We have two open surgeries a day – the first from eight to ten in the mornings and the second from five to seven in the evenings. That gives us a seven-hour lunch break, but please don't think we get to sit around and enjoy it. We do our own administration and paperwork and you will spend a lot of time keeping the bridge, hotel management and Head Office up-to-date with your patients. As you know we're all on call pretty much twenty-four hours a day because there's nowhere else for us to be. We also do safety inspections, prepare the ship for all manner of emergencies, lecture the staff on health and hygiene, do crew rounds to check for damage and danger in cabins, help out on shore excursions and even dress up and host tables at all manner of social occasions. You look fit and well, Doctor MacFarlane. I hope you've been told that you'll need to be.'

Kiri interrupts the flow by poking her head around the door. 'I've cleaned him up, bagged up his smelly old clothes and I'm gasping for a coffee,' she says. 'Eileen always has a pot on,' she tells me. 'That's just one reason why she's the best senior nurse in the business.'

Eileen appears to blush, ever so slightly. She's got a mug tree on the shelf beside her desk and picks a big red cup for Kiri. Eileen's got a soft, Welsh accent and I'm estimating that she's in her early fifties. I don't yet know if she's married or whether she has kids at home, but I've a feeling she's going to be a great surrogate mum to all of us. She glances up at the big clock above her door as she gives Kiri her drink.

'We've got just over forty-five minutes before the first safety drill,' she says. 'At some stage before then, doctor, you're going to have to get back to your cabin and change into your uniform. The captain will give you a little bit of leeway because of what just happened, but beyond that he will want you to be properly dressed at all times.' She stands up. 'Kiri, you're going to have to drink that while you walk. Let's give the doctor a guided tour of our world.'

The Medical Centre is one deck below the lowest of the passenger areas. It's far enough down to be one of the most stable parts of the ship but not too close to the waterline to be oppressive. Patients can sit on three small sofas in our main waiting area before being led into one of our four consulting rooms – one for Edward, one for me, one for Eileen and a Nursing Station shared by Kiri and Dakila. Beyond these rooms we've got the six-bed Crew Ward where Paco is recovering. Eileen then shows me the six private rooms we've got for passengers. Among them are a high dependency room and a state-of-the-art isolation room. We've also got an X-ray room, a dispensary, a laboratory area and a drug store. Emergency medical bags are stored in the locked dispensary alongside a rapid-response trolley and all our portable lifesaving equipment.

'Every bit of kit has been photographed and numbered,' Eileen says, pointing to the line of colour enlargements pinned to the wall. 'It's the only way to do it if we need a non-medical person to help us find things. You don't need to ask them to bring a defibrillator, some oxygen and an intubation kit. Just ask for a number three, four and seven and they'll be able to find what you need.'

'It may look like having a job in a medical Chinese restaurant,' Kiri says, 'but it actually works surprisingly well.'

The equipment itself is better than I'd feared. Someone, somewhere, has been happy to spend an awful lot of money on us. Clearly it's a long time since ships' medical centres were staffed by a retired GP or a crew member with a bottle of brandy and a well-thumbed copy of *The Ship Captain's Medical Guide*.

'At the end of the corridor two levels down we've also got the morgue,' adds Kiri ghoulishly as we walk back towards the waiting area.

'On some cruises that place ends up busier than the gym,' calls out Dakila from the door of the Crew Ward. 'Some of the big ships lose so many passengers they factor it into the catering plans.'

Eileen gives him a disapproving look. 'Not in front of the patient, Dakila.' She turns to me. 'That isn't true at all. I sincerely hope we don't require our morgue even once on this voyage. But if we do, then it has space for three unfortunate souls and is, of course, fully refrigerated. And if you do want to know a few more gory details our isolation room is effectively padded and we've plenty of restraining equipment for any passengers or crew who can't be calmed down any other way.' She sends Dakila back to his station and leads me into my own consulting room.

'We're obviously online and Kiri can help log you on to your computer later on. You have a direct-dial telephone. We're linked up to Medline and have tele-radiology and tele-medicine facilities so we can get instant advice and second opinions from shore. We've got most of the standard reference books and we have online subscriptions to most major journals. If there's anything you want that we don't have then just ask. They say if you want to have a heart attack, there's no better place than a big, modern cruise ship. That's certainly true of us. We can be at the patient's side within two minutes of a Code Alpha call. Our equipment is as good as it gets and, all modesty aside, I'd say we've got the best team in the business as well.'

It's been a fast-paced but useful overview. 'I don't think I was told half of all that when I joined,' Kiri says as we step back into the waiting area. 'I was thrilled to discover we've got a set of handcuffs in the isolation room next door.'

Eileen looks set to scold her again when she glances at the wall clock. 'I think we need to cut this short,' she says. 'The full emergency evacuation drill will sound in fifteen minutes, Doctor MacFarlane. If you're not in your uniform for that then Paco won't be the only person seeing his cruise end before it's even begun.'

I can't stop smiling when I step back into my cabin – because it's so much nicer than I'd expected. It's not big but there's a double bed instead of the skinny single I'd been dreading. I've got a desk, a flat-screen TV, a little sofa and, best of all, a pair of double doors opening out on to a tiny private balcony. The table and two chairs set there look the perfect place for breakfast or a nightcap.

Inside the room it's all very corporate and clean. All the surfaces and furnishings are blond or beige and I know it's going to feel more like a hotel than a home. But I'm thanking my lucky stars that medics are treated as officers and get passenger cabins on the guest decks.

The other thing I can't quite believe is that my room has already been cleaned up. I was one of the last people to board because I'd only been allocated the cruise last week and needed to finish off some paperwork at Head Office in the morning. Once I'd cleared security and found my room I'd thrown my suitcase on my bed and pulled everything out to find the information pack about my new job and the names of my new colleagues. I'll sort it all out later, I'd thought. Someone has beaten me to it. All the clothes I'd strewn out on the bed are now on hangers in the wardrobe or stacked neatly in the drawers. My discarded toiletries are lined up in my bathroom, my books are piled up tidily on my desk and even the empty suitcase has been put in a storage area by my door. Clearly I will have no secrets from my room steward, a wiry Filipino man I'd met very briefly when I first arrived.

'I cleared up for you, sir. I hope you had a nice dinner. Yours, Albert,' he's written on a note attached to a fruit basket on my desk.

I stand on the balcony and bolt down two bananas and a handful of grapes. Then I get down to business and try to work out which uniform I need to wear. Head Office has issued me with three sets of clothes, as well as telling me to bring my own dinner jacket for black-tie events. Apparently one of the three uniforms is for daytime, one is for the evenings and one is for shore excursions. But which is the right one for a late-night evacuation drill? I go for the first of the three and try not to laugh when I look in the mirror. For the past two years I've been a full-time emergency repatriation doctor. I've flown around the world to rescue people who have had some kind of disaster abroad. In that job my standard uniform was scruffy black cargo trousers, a dark-blue polo shirt and a pair of trainers. Things are just a little different now. I pull on a gleaming white short-sleeved shirt and look as if I should be sitting behind a car-rental desk in an airport. Then I pull on the matching white trousers. Now I look like an extra from a Medical School production of *HMS Pinafore* or, worse, *Saturday Night Fever.*

Can I really go out like this and keep a straight face? I look at my watch and realise that I don't have any choice. I rush to the end of my corridor. Safety drills were a big part of the pre-cruise briefings I'd had in London. Every member of the senior staff has some degree of responsibility for these exercises. Ultimately we need to make sure that the full 3,000 plus complement of passengers and crew can get to all the right lifeboats in the shortest possible amount of time. My role today is to check people make it safely up the emergency stairs from one deck to another. I've got a yellow high visibility jacket on top of my white uniform and all the passengers are bouncing around in their huge orange life vests. If you're prone to migraines then seeing all this under the harsh emergency lights of the stairwell is likely to add an unpleasant edge to your cruise. Add a sense of urgency and excitement to the mix and it's easy to see why safety drills can feel as if they are anything but. No-one on my stairwell stumbles, bangs their heads, twists their ankles or sprains their wrists today. Fingers crossed it's not just beginners' luck.

My phone is ringing when I get back to my cabin.

'It's Kiri. Now you've survived the first of the drills Dakila and I wondered if you'd like to join us for the rest of the evening. Eileen is staying in the surgery looking after Paco and we've got lots to show you if you're up for it. See you in the Crew Bar in half an hour?'

She runs through some rough directions to the bar. The essence of them seems to be that it's two decks below the Medical Centre and that I'll know I'm close when I hear the noise and smell the booze.

'Oh, and take a deep breath because you're going well below the water line,' are her final, slightly worrying words as I hang up.

The corridor outside my cabin is hushed and empty as I head towards the nearest passenger lift. It's got teak panels and has a red velvet bench alongside its three walls. When I get down as far as it will go I follow Kiri's instructions to a heavy door marked 'Private'. That's where the world changes. No more soft lighting, glossy cream walls and gloriously colourful works of art. I'm now in a world of grey metal and I'm facing the kind of steep, narrow stairwells that you normally see in World War Two submarine films. There's thick green plastic lino on the floor of the next deck and I feel horribly over-dressed in my shiny new uniform. Was Kiri winding me up when she said I needed to wear it? Will she and Dakila be laughing away in jeans and T-shirts when I join them?

I head down the passageway. The whole ship is noisier down here. The corridor itself seems to hum. The ceilings are lower and the temperature is higher – and as I get to the end of the corridor it really does start to reek of alcohol. On my left I pass what I think Kiri had called 'the slops' – the cheap crew store that apparently sells everything from toothpaste to underwear. Then I see the doors to the bar.

I do a double take when I step inside. If the staircases had looked like something out of a war movie the bar looks like the one in *Star Wars*. It's big, it's packed and each group of drinkers seems quite different to all the others. The whole room seems to be divided by age, sex and skin colour as well as by the clothes they're wearing and the way they're acting. Along one wall crowds of men are gathered around a row of video games. Other groups are sitting in front of the dozen or so television screens suspended from the ceiling – all of which seem to be showing different football games. In a smaller room behind the bar I can see a couple of pool tables, a lighting deck and what looks like a small stage. The music is as loud as the football commentaries and everyone in the room seems determined to shout above it all.

'Ben, we're over here!' Dakila is waving at me. He and Kiri are both in their whites and they've saved me a chair.

'A bit of a culture shock, isn't it?' Kiri shouts. 'We ordered you a drink. We thought you might need it.' She passes over a beer and we all clink our cans. 'To our new baby doc. To the first night of the cruise,' she toasts.

'To the best team in the business,' adds Dakila.

'Tell us your first impressions. This is the first cruise job you've done, isn't it?' Kiri asks as we settle down.

'It's the first time I've been on anything except a Channel ferry. I told Eileen I was expecting it all to be like Harley Street-on-sea. She made it sound more like Saturday night down at the local A&E.'

'You've found out early that most of the crew are psychopaths,' Dakila says.

Kiri kicks his leg. 'Well, as the worst of them are having

a drink in this bar right now, we should probably keep our voices down,' she suggests.

'What about the passengers?' I ask.

This time Kiri's face brightens. 'There are about two thousand of them and they're going to surprise you. You need a lot of stamina to do a worldie. Forget all the jokes about ships being full of newly weds and nearly deads. Odds are that the crowd we've got on board today will have more energy than all three of us combined.'

'No-one on a cruise ship ever acts their age. Especially when they've had a few drinks,' Dakila says.

'You'll get some good stories out of them as well,' Kiri continues. 'You'll see some tiny little church mouse of a lady who looks as if she'd never say boo to a goose. Talk to her one day and you'll find out she set up a dressmaking business in the fifties and had an affair with Cary Grant. You'll see a totally ordinary looking couple and you'll find out that they headlined at Madison Square Gardens the year you were born and spent the next twenty years working as lounge singers in Las Vegas. I've been travelling since I was nineteen and I think I've seen a lot of the world. But every cruise I meet people who put me to shame. If you get into the spirit of this you're going to love it. By the time we get back to Britain you'll be hooked.'

The conversation moves on to patients, the way it always does with medics. Kiri and Dakila gossip about some of the passengers they've treated on recent trips and gradually get me up to speed with what life is going to be like on board. I tell them I was originally supposed to be flying out to Miami in a week's time to work on one of the company's ships out there, but got moved on to this cruise when someone else pulled out. They both seem to approve.

'A worldie is the best way to start the job,' says Kiri. 'In the Caribbean all you treat is indigestion. The passengers are just taking a slow boat to a shopping mall.' She looks at her watch suddenly and stands up. 'It's getting late. You've already had a pretty dramatic introduction to the job, but the night is young and Dakila and I have got some more tricks up our sleeves. It's time to show you the most dangerous place on the ship. How do you fancy a trip to the midnight buffet?'

# CHAPTER THREE

'It's only half past ten. How far do we have to go?' I ask as we head out of the bar. We're following in the wake of a group of men in dark-blue overalls who have each bought a six-pack to go.

'Don't worry. Technically speaking the midnight buffet isn't at midnight any more,' Kiri shouts over the sound of an Italian football commentary.

'It's not a buffet either. We had that banned on health grounds,' adds Dakila as we finally stumble out into the corridor. 'Too many dirty hands picking things up and putting them back down again. It was a gastro-bug in every bite. Didn't you Brits have a television commercial about that once?'

'Dakila knows a bit of television trivia from every country in the world,' Kiri says before I have a chance to reply. 'He's been in international waters far too long.'

'So if it's not at midnight and it's not a buffet, what is it?'

'It's a Moonlight Welcome party. Snacks are made to order and it's more about having a nice hot coffee than a life-threatening sugar rush. It's the new fashion and I have to say I like it. When I was on my first Caribbean cruise the midnight buffets terrified me. Put 2,000 car workers from

Detroit on an all-you-can-eat weekend and you'd see nature in the raw. You didn't want to stumble when they pulled back the barriers and let that crowd get a view of the chocolate fountains.'

'You didn't want to be around when their immune systems found out there were nuts on top of the chocolate cake or strawberries hidden in the profiteroles either,' says Dakila.

'One time I had to resuscitate a twenty-stone guy with wheat intolerance and an allergy to shell fish. He blew up like a puffer fish after stuffing his face with prawn toast. I never found out just which bit of the phrase "prawn toast" failed to give away the danger. But I do remember he was back at the buffet every night for the rest of the trip. The medics and I had to load up with vials of adrenaline and patrol the place like lifeguards round the pool.'

'It should be a bit more civilised here,' says Dakila. 'But I always carry an Epipen in my pocket just in case.'

'The other good news for you is that this will be the last evening you can go to any of the ship's passenger decks without being recognised,' says Kiri. 'When people realise that you're the ship's doctor your life will no longer be your own. From tomorrow morning's surgery onwards passengers will discuss their bowel movements with you in the lift. They will show you a rash on their arm while you drink your coffee. You will hear about aches and pains everywhere you go for every minute of every day. No matter how many people there are on the deck tonight, it will still be the most peaceful evening you spend on board.'

We get to the end of the corridor and seem to be on the point of turning into another one that heads right back to where we started. 'How long does it take to learn your way around the ship?' I ask, trying to get my bearings.

'If you get lost just look underneath your feet,' suggests Kiri. 'If you're standing on carpet you're in a passenger area and there'll be a map on the wall to show you where you are. If you're standing on coloured lino or metal then you're down here with the rest of us, and you're basically screwed.'

'Unless you can speak Latvian and can ask one of the maids for directions,' adds Dakila. 'Once ships like this were full of good honest Filipinos like me. Now it's all Eastern Europe this and Chinese language that. It's something I will mention to the Captain next time we chat.'

Kiri throws him a look as we stop by a pair of lift doors. 'The Captain mistook Dakila for someone important at a cocktail party at the end of our last cruise,' she explains. 'The poor man ended up having his ear bent by him for about twenty minutes. If he could have driven the ship into an iceberg I swear he'd have done so just to get away. Dakila, as you will soon find out, has barely stopped talking about it since.'

'I told the Captain my best joke. The one about giving a bear a blow job in the woods. He said he would remember it.'

'He said he would remember you. There is a difference, Dakila.'

The service lift arrives and I do a double take as we step inside. It's vast and contains a tiny Chinese girl carrying a two-foot-long leg of Serrano ham, a man holding a golf bag and two barefoot and fully-costumed showgirls using plastic forks to pick the cherries off the top of a huge slice of sponge cake. No-one speaks or makes eye contact with anyone else. I seem to be the only one who thinks anything about the scene is even remotely unusual.

'Look down and you'll see the lovely thick passenger carpet,' says Kiri. We've stepped out on to a passenger deck, our dirty service lift shielded from view by a floor-to-ceiling glass screen etched with a picture of what looks like Mount Vesuvius. Two minutes later we pass a surprisingly busy internet café and a flower arrangement the size of a family car.

'It's all a bit different to our humble bar downstairs, isn't it?' Dakila says as we walk. 'Remember that you, my friend, are an officer. You have three stripes on your shoulders and can walk these halls whenever you choose. Lowly two stripe nurses like Kiri and me can go where we want as well – but not everyone on board is this lucky.'

'So these things matter?' I ask, touching the red and gold striped epaulettes on my shoulder.

'They matter more than almost anything else,' Kiri tells me. 'Whoever said the class system is dead never worked on a cruise ship. Whenever you meet someone new you'll see they look at your shoulders before they look at your eyes. They want to know where you rank so they know what you're entitled to do, where you're entitled to go and how useful you might be to them. You can tell from the stripes on someone's shoulder if they've got their own cabin or if they share. You can tell what deck it's likely to be on. You can tell where they probably eat their dinner.'

'The only thing stripes don't tell you is how much anyone earns,' Dakila adds. 'If we've got a lot of Americans on board the waiters can earn more in tips than the three-stripe officers. Some of the hairdressers reckon they earn more than the pursers.'

He's running through a list of the best and worst nationalities for tips – and making me feel just a little bit ashamed of being

British – when we reach the entrance to the party. It's a clear, cold night but it's lovely to get a burst of fresh air as we step out on to the deck. Half of it is covered by a huge striped awning and it's dotted with patio heaters, little tables and extraordinarily resilient candles. Pastry chefs with big hats are standing behind little work stations and there seem to be more people drinking champagne than coffee. I've got a feeling I'm going to like nights like this.

'It's magical, isn't it?' Kiri says, reading my mind.

'It's beautiful. I can't believe we're being paid to be here.'

'Paid? Who said anything about being paid?' asks Dakila. 'You must have misread a vital part of your contract, my friend. If you as much as look at a blueberry muffin you'll have ten dollars added to your on board account.'

We find an empty spot on the far edge of the deck and hold on to a corner of the wooden railing. Whatever you do, don't say anything about Kate Winslet and Leonardo DiCaprio, I tell myself. All the old-timers will have heard stupid comments like that a thousand times.

'It's just like Kate Winslet and Leonardo DiCaprio in *Titanic*,' I hear myself say. 'I should have brought my camera.'

'You don't need it. Just smile,' says Kiri. We're suddenly bathed in a flash of white light.

'I'm Bill, one of the ship's photographers. Nowadays we're specifically trained to appear every time anyone says: "I'm the king of the world" or mentions Kate Winslet. If you want it, the picture's already been sent down to the photo store in the galleria. You can have it put on a very tasteful T-shirt or send it to your mum as a fifty-piece jigsaw.'

'I think she'll survive without that, thanks.'

The snapper moves off to a couple nearby and manages to get them to strike the full *Titanic* pose on the bow.

'Ten dollars says you've bought the jigsaw by the time we get to the Panama Canal,' says Dakila.

We grab some snacks and drinks, sit at a table and look up at the sky. The nurses tell me more about the morning and evening surgeries and I explain a bit about my old job doing emergency repatriations. When we've had a few laughs and seem to be getting on well enough I ask a bit more about Doctor Marlborough.

'He's good. We like him. But he can be a lazy old boot,' is Dakila's verdict.

'He's slowing down. But this is his last worldie before his top-secret retirement so he's entitled,' adds Kiri. 'He might miss a few clinics but you'll want him on your side in an emergency. He's an old-school gentleman and an old-school medic. You'll like him. We'll miss him when he's gone.'

She starts talking about some of the other doctors she's worked with and Dakila pitches in with some very indiscrete comments of his own. It's cosy under the air heaters and I yawn suddenly as I stretch out on my chair.

'Hey, it's too early for that, baby doc,' says Kiri. 'I hope you don't think your initiation is over after a few cookies and mug of hot chocolate. Once we're done here we're going to your first pour-out.'

'It's Australian for a cabin party,' she explains as we slip off the passenger deck and head back down towards the water line. 'Down on the crew decks there will be a pour-out starting somewhere on board practically hourly for the entire time we're afloat. The first rule of cruising is that someone, somewhere, is always going off shift and needs a drink.

Pour-outs are a brilliant way to meet other people. You won't want to spend three months talking about the patients with Eileen, Dakila and me. The sooner we introduce you to the rest of the circus the better.'

We walk down a long, wide internal corridor towards the crew section. The floor is shiny green lino and there are about half a dozen pipes running along the ceiling. 'This is the M1, the I-95, the Green Mile or whatever else everyone has decided to call it today. It's the main route from one end of the ship to the other. Watch your toes!' Kiri shouts when a fork lift truck suddenly thunders down towards us. 'The dry-food stores and some of the freezers are on this level. They're the size of Melbourne.'

The world changes again once we've negotiated a steep metal staircase and joined a narrow corridor on the next deck. This is clearly a residential area. Bollywood music is blaring out and I can see up to four bunk beds with heavy curtains through some open cabin doors. I get a pang of guilt when I think of my comparatively vast passenger cabin several decks above us. The hierarchy of ship life is going to take a bit of getting used to. The Bollywood gives way to blisteringly loud reggae as we turn another corner and we need to step over a group of men sitting on the floor and fighting over a computer games console. If Kiri is right and someone, somewhere is always coming off shift that means someone, somewhere is always trying to sleep. I thought junior doctors were the only people who get so tired they can sleep through anything. Cruise staff clearly need the same skill.

'Having fun, Curtis?' Kiri stops at the door to one of the reggae cabins and shouts at a bare-chested man sitting at the head of a very intense card school. 'This is Ben, our new baby doc. Ben, this is Curtis, one of the maintenance boys and

one of our very many resident Casanovas. You'll probably be
treating him for all sorts of embarrassing medical conditions
in a week or so once he's had a bit of shore leave. See you
later, lover boy.'

We walk even further down the corridor. Every now and then
there are metal lips to step over as we pass through watertight
doors. Red and yellow paint marks out 'do not obstruct' areas
on the floor to show where they have to close in an emergency.
On the walls are red levers to close them manually if the
automatic systems fail. The corridor lights, protected by metal
grills, are more yellow than white. Deep within the ship I can't
work out if we are above or below the waterline. I certainly
don't want to find out in an emergency.

'That wasn't the right party?' I shout out.

'Not for your first night. You've already had one nasty shock
about this job but it would be cruel to scare you off entirely.
Curtis would consider it a personal triumph to relieve you of a
month's earnings in the next couple of hours. Gambling is an
obsession on cruise ships. People spend every minute in card
schools when they're off duty. The first thing they do when
they get shore leave is to run into the nearest casino to get
some more of it. You want to watch out for that. Now, if we
head up here we'll get back to a nicer corridor where the next
class of crew live . . . this is our party.'

On this deck American R&B music is bouncing off the
metal walls. Kiri bangs on the door of a cabin.

'This is my boyfriend, Kieran,' she says proudly of the
stocky, dark-haired man who opens it. 'He works in the
casino. We're doing one more year of cruising then we're
going to open a bar in Dublin.'

'Wow, she didn't hit you already, did she? Kieran asks,
nodding to my black eye and wrapping his arm around his

girlfriend's shoulders. He then points to an extraordinary array of bottles in the corner of the cabin and tells us to help ourselves. There are five other people sitting on a mixture of chairs, beds and boxes. Dakila pushes his way in and makes room for me to sit alongside him by the cabin's far wall.

'You'll do a lot of sitting on floors down here,' he says. 'What do you want to drink?'

'Is it OK if we're always on call?'

'Just take it slowly. And you'll need a drink while I tell you more about what you've got yourself in for,' he says. He hands me a beer and smiles. 'Ask me anything. Just like your *Mastermind* programme. Name: Dakila Bautista. Chosen subject: Life on a Cruise Ship. Your two minutes start now.'

'You really do know your British television shows,' I say. 'Well start off by telling me something good. What's the biggest perk? Feel free to lie.'

Dakila smiles. 'The best perks are the ladies: the dancers, the singers, the shop staff, the waitresses, the hairdressers, the spa girls. They all love a man in uniform. They adore a man with three or more stripes on his shoulders. Are you married or do you have a girlfriend?'

'I've got a girlfriend. She's just quit her job and started Medical School. I'm here to get out from under her feet while she settles in.'

'Well, you'll have to decide how faithful you want to be. Most of the officers on board are married, but you wouldn't know that from the way they act once we leave port. Last cruise we had a nasty outbreak of gonorrhoea. The contact tracing took the rest of the cruise. It would have been more efficient to just put antibiotics in the water supply and treat the whole bridge and spa staff in one go.' Dakila flashes me a smile. 'But if you're a decent type then you can be like me. I look but I don't touch.' He pulls a plastic wallet out of his pocket. 'This is my wife. These are our girls. They're nine, eleven and twelve. I'm here to pay their way through school.' He's miles away, suddenly, as he strokes the faces of his children.

'How often do you get to see them?'

'Every year. Well, normally every year. I do extra cruises, sometimes, because that way I can earn my money a lot faster. My wife works as well but three lots of school bills aren't easy to pay. But it will be worth it in the end, my friend. It will be worth it.' He kisses each of the four faces through the plastic of his wallet, then puts it away. His good humour is back. 'You want a better perk. How about the chance to live like a traditional English gentleman for four months? You need your clothes washing? Leave them on your cabin floor and they'll be taken away and cleaned before you've said "Chinese laundry". Your cabin will be cleaned and tidied every day and your steward will bring you tea, coffee or whatever you want for breakfast in the morning. You're a three-stripe officer on a passenger ticket. You can go to the spa or work out in the gym any time, and go to the theatre every night. Just sign for anything you want to eat or drink and it's free. You'll get discounts if you want anything from the shops and don't settle your bill till the end of the month. This is the kind of life people dream about, my friend.'

I'm about to say it's all too good to be true when something in his face tells me to stop. His relaxed, off-duty smile has disappeared. The serious, professional Dakila from the Medical Centre has suddenly re-emerged.

'Oh dear, oh dear,' he mutters as he watches an equally worried-looking Kiri step across the room towards us. She's got what looks like a walkie talkie in her hand.

'That was Eileen,' she says softly. 'There's been a problem in the atrium and another one in the bar. Sorry about this, Ben, but we've got to go.'

# CHAPTER FOUR

'This first lady's name is Mrs Anita Philip. She was found twenty minutes ago in the glass lift in the atrium. She was in her nightclothes, very distraught, very disoriented and by the look of it very dehydrated. Two passengers helped the security boys bring her down here but they had a bit of a struggle as at one point she lashed out and tried to run away. She's travelling alone, she's seventy-six-years-old and the boys say she's as strong as an ox.'

We're in the passenger ward and I look from Eileen to the tiny, pink-clad figure with her head in her hands on the edge of the bed. She can't have been more than five foot four in her youth and probably stands just five foot two now osteoporosis has taken its toll on her spine. I doubt she weighs even eight stone. Strong as an ox? It is proof that in medicine you can never judge a book by its cover.

'Mrs Philip, can you hear me? My name's Doctor Ben MacFarlane. You've had a bad turn but you're going to be fine now you're here. You're in the Medical Centre and we're going to look after you.' For the first few moments Mrs Philip deliberately ignores me. Then she starts kicking at me with the weakest of pale legs. Only when she realises she can't reach does she finally lie still and look at me.

'Mrs Philip, we're going to take care of you,' I repeat. I give her what I hope is a reassuring smile. It doesn't seem to work.

'What's your name?' she demands.

'It's Ben. Doctor Ben MacFarlane.'

She slaps me on the shoulder then bursts into tears.

'Mrs Philip, please don't cry. We're going to make you better just as soon as we can.' Her sobs get louder as I reach over to take her pulse. She grabs my hand when I've finished. Her grip is incredibly tight. 'Everything's going to be fine,' I say, trying and failing to extricate myself from it. Mrs Philip just looks at me. Her tears stop almost as quickly as they started. Her eyes are big and blue. One moment they're sad, the next they're scared. It's hard to know which is worse. I'm about to whisper some instructions to Eileen when Mrs Philip screws up her eyes and lets out a weak moan. She's holding on to me with both hands now – and all of a sudden I can feel something drip on to my shoes. We're going to need a urine sample to help us work out what's wrong with her. I think we've just got one.

'OK, if that's the first lady, where's the second one?' I ask Eileen as I wipe myself down. We've stepped out into the nursing station and apart from Paco's snores the whole place seems quiet.

'Dakila's gone to fetch her and I don't know what's happened to him,' Eileen says, looking up at the clock. 'They said there had been an accident in the Library Bar. With a bit of luck he'll be dealing with it himself, or else it was a false alarm. He'll call if he needs help or he'll be back with a big smile on his face and a bigger story about how heroic he was. In the meantime we've just got poor Mrs Philip to look after.'

We talk through her case and agree she's probably got a urinary tract infection. We can start treating that straight away – and the disorientation and delirium that come with it will hopefully be gone by the morning.

'It's not just the ladies who get confused and can lose control on big ships,' Eileen says. 'We had the most marvellous gentleman on the South African leg of a worldie a few years ago. He was the best-dressed passenger on the ship. He wore a tweed jacket and a tie every single day. Some mornings he even wore bow ties or silk cravats at breakfast. Then one day when we were going through rough seas at the Cape of Good Hope he decided to take some quack seasickness medication he'd read about in a book. It pushed his whole system off balance. That night he started taking all his clothes off at the Captain's Reception. "Cocktail, cocktail – cock, cock, cock!" he kept shouting. By the time we had him stabilised and back to normal the poor chap was so upset he barely left his room for the next three weeks.'

'Well at least we'll be able to tell Mrs Philip that things could have been a lot worse.'

We head back to her bedside. Eileen had discretely collected a urine sample from the pool on the bed and we put it aside to test later. She starts cleaning up while I talk Mrs Philip through the rest of our plans. 'We've decided to keep you down here with us for the rest of the night if that's OK with you, Mrs Philip? We're going to give you some fluids and a dose of antibiotics now to clear up any infection you've got. Both of those things are going to have you feeling right as rain in no time,' I say. I don't get much response. I reach out for her right arm. 'I'm going to put something in your arm here. You've had this done before, have you? Hopefully you know it's over pretty quickly and won't hurt a bit.' She still looks jumpy and angry. Every few moments she starts muttering to herself then spits some angry, barely intelligible words at me.

I find a vein and inject the antibiotics, and the saline starts to flow. Mrs Philip keeps mumbling for a while but her words are getting quieter and at least she's no longer aiming insults at me. Eileen and I finish tidying up the room until the patient starts to doze. We get Kiri to sit with her while we go across the hallway to check up on Paco. He seems to be alternately snoring and moaning so we leave him to it and head back to my office.

'In a minute I'll show you how we log all our patient details on the surgery's computers. Everything has to be recorded and all sorts of people need to be copied in on everything so the sooner I explain how it works the better,' Eileen says. 'But first of all I'll give Dakila a quick ring to check what's going on upstairs.' She makes the call from her own desk and is soon back at my side. 'It wasn't a false alarm and our work isn't over,' she says with a sigh. 'I'll talk you through the paperwork later. Dakila's bringing our next patient down right now.'

The Medical Centre doors bang open and a tall, confident and assured woman strides in. A sheepish-looking Dakila is left well in her wake. The passenger is wearing shiny high-heeled shoes and a purple sequined dress that sparkles in the lights. Her rich dark hair is heavily lacquered and topped off with a jewel-encrusted clasp that wouldn't be entirely out of place at the state opening of parliament.

'My name is Mrs Belinda Coates,' she announces as I step forward to introduce myself. 'I told this young man that I was perfectly fine but he wouldn't have it. He wanted me to sit in a wheelchair but I simply refused. I may be 78, but I can still walk. I was embarrassed enough by all the attention already. Being pushed through the ship like an invalid would have been the final straw.'

Eileen leads the lady into my consulting room as I try to work out what's happened to her.

'I fell.' She says, reading my mind. 'Off a bar stool.'

'Oh dear.'

'Exactly. And to make matters worse they'd only just poured my drink.'

'Well, first things first, did you spill it?' I ask. I get the feeling this lady wants to keep things as light and low key as possible. Her smile tells me I'm right.

'Fortunately I didn't spill a drop. But it was single malt and I was very much looking forward to it.'

'Well, let's try and get you back there before the ice melts. I'm guessing you landed on something?'

'My wrist.'

She holds out her right hand and I take a look. The joint is starting to swell and it's obvious when I touch it that it's incredibly tender. A shadow of pain flits over Mrs Coates' face as I examine the injury. For a moment I wonder if she's going to be sick, but she pulls herself back together. She grimaces a couple more times as I feel the swelling, but she doesn't say anything out loud. It might be bravado or it might be pride, but this is clearly a woman who hates showing any sign of weakness.

'Can you move your thumb for me? Now each of your fingers in turn?' I ask. I check the pulse in her wrist then start a touch test. 'Can you feel it here? And here? Now here?' I ask.

'Yes I bloody well can,' she replies every time.

I can't help smiling as the examination continues. But there are a few things I need to get sorted before I can relax completely. 'Now, are you sure you didn't bang your head when you fell? If you did then this might be a little more serious.'

Mrs Coates pretends to be offended. 'As I hope you can tell I don't have as much as a single, very expensive hair out of place,' she says, lifting her good hand to her head. 'They don't call this style a "Harrods' helmet" for nothing. It can protect me from a lot more than the occasional tumble from a bar stool.'

'Just as long as you're sure.'

'I am. But I'm not so sure about you. What happened to your face?'

For a split second I'm not sure what she's talking about. Then I remember Paco's fist. I touch my eye and wince. 'It's a long story, I'm afraid,' I say. As if on cue Paco lets out a snore that morphs into a moan from the Crew Ward. Mrs Coates looks at me, eyebrows raised.

'It's one of my other patients, nothing to worry about,' I explain, trying to drown out the sound by pushing my surgery door shut. A second, louder moan drifts through before it closes.

'I appear to have stumbled into a scene from a Hammer House of Horror film,' Mrs Coates says dryly. 'I've always wondered what happens in the ship's Medical Centre. Perhaps I was better off not knowing.' She smiles briefly but it's clear that the waves of pain are coming more frequently now. It's late and the time for small talk is over. I check a bit more of her medical history then lead her down the hall to take some X-rays .

'It's a classic Colles' fracture,' I say when the images flash up on the screen. I point to the offending bones, then show where they are on my own arm. 'Some call it a dinner fork deformity. If you look at the shape you can just about see why.'

'I think I'd prefer to use the more formal description.'

'Then Colles' fracture it is. The good news is that it could be a lot worse. Your bones aren't displaced so all we need to do is immobilise them for you. We'll make you an appointment with an orthopaedic surgeon in Madeira to check it over in more detail. But I think you'll be well on your way to recovery by then. We'll have you back in the bar before you know it.'

As the immobilisation and bandaging are going to hurt, Eileen injects Mrs Coates with some painkillers through her thigh and we then add a little extra sedation through a drip in her arm.

'I feel more ridiculous by the moment. No-one must ever know this happened to me,' Mrs Coates says as she surveys the equipment piling up around her. I try to take her mind off it all while we wait for the drugs to have some effect.

'Tell me about the bar,' I ask. 'This is my first time on the ship and I don't know the best places to go.'

'It was only just warming up,' she says ruefully. 'I had only been there about half an hour but the main barman was an absolute hoot. He was cracking some very risqué jokes just the way I like it. I adore that kind of banter. I hate to feel as if I'm missing out.'

I decide to take that as a challenge. 'Mrs Coates, whoever the barman is, I bet he doesn't know any medical jokes.

Do, please, let me entertain you.' She's getting drowsy as the medication kicks in but she's nice enough to carry on laughing at my terrible punchlines as I build the plaster block for her arm. She groans a little when I push it in place and start to bandage it all together. But I take it as a good sign that she groans even louder when I remember the one about the man who comes to A&E after eating too many Christmas decorations. 'Tinsillitis, Mrs Coates. He's diagnosed with tinsillitis,' I say.

'That's quite appalling,' she breathes. 'But do tell me another.'

It's gone two o'clock in the morning by the time I finish up and for all her good humour it's clear that even Mrs Coates has run out of steam. Her face is pale, her eyes are dry and even her hairstyle is starting to come awry.

'I've got a suggestion to make,' I say as she tries to hide yet another yawn. 'We can take you back to your cabin, but if you're happy to stay down here for the rest of the night we'll be able to keep you a lot more comfortable. You'll have your own room – one of us will be down here anyway – and it'll be easier to top up your painkillers if you need us to. Would you like to stay with us?'

'For your information, doctor, it is not a cabin, it is a stateroom,' she says groggily. I decide to take that as a yes.

Dakila is sitting with Mrs Philip and he calls me into her room when I pass. He's holding her tiny hand and trying to comfort her. It's not easy. The anger and aggression of the infection have now started to leave this lady. All she's left with is regret.

'I've started to remember what I did,' she says flatly when I ask how she's doing. Her voice is hollow, broken and very hard to hear over the noise of the engines and the air-conditioning. I lean closer. She doesn't look embarrassed now, just unutterably sad. 'I was in my room and I was so nervous and so lonely,' she says. 'Then I was in some endless corridor and for some reason I ended up getting really frightened. I carried on walking for such a long way and then I was in this enormous, awful area with all these shops and plants and I didn't know how to get out of it. There were people everywhere. I was lost and I think I started to cry. I don't remember anything else until I was in a lift and it was made of glass and I didn't know how to get out of that either. I soiled myself in there, didn't I, doctor?'

'I don't remember, Mrs Philip. I'm sure that you didn't,' I lie.

'I know that I did. Someone has taken my clothes from me. This nightdress isn't mine. I've never felt so ashamed and I can't possibly go out there again.'

She reaches out for my hand now. She holds it very tightly. This tiny, sparrow of a lady really does have hidden strength. 'There's nothing at all to be ashamed of. Nothing terrible happened. This is a huge ship and no-one else will have noticed a thing,' I reassure her.

'So why was I brought here?'

'Because you were a little bit confused. That happens all the time when there's a change of scene like this. If you're used to your own home and your usual routines then the start of a cruise can be a bit of a shock to the system. If you were tired and a bit run-down before coming on board it can make things worse. We've settled things down for you now. You're already getting better and you're going to be right as rain for the rest of the trip. You need a good night's sleep for the medication to do its job. From then on it will start to feel like a holiday, I promise you.'

Mrs Philip isn't listening. 'I can't stay here,' she says suddenly. 'I've been so much trouble and I'm so ashamed. I'm going back to my room now.' She tries to pull herself up off the bed. She moves surprisingly fast, trying to twist herself around so she can bring her feet to the floor.

'Just wait here with us for five more minutes,' I say.

'I'm too ashamed. I have to leave,' she repeats. But even as she speaks a new wave of exhaustion rolls over her. The medication is taking effect and a few moments later she's asleep. She looks even smaller and more vulnerable on this over-sized medical bed.

Eileen has followed me into the room. She lifts up the bed's cot sides and locks them in place. 'I know a lot of people don't like to use these things on land but on ships they're essential. We're protecting people, not imprisoning them. In rough seas we strap people down as well.' She looks down at Mrs Philip and smiles. 'I wouldn't put it past this little lady to try and leave in the night. She's a determined character. We're going to have to take special care of her.'

Once we've got all our patients settled, Eileen pours me a coffee. 'You really have hit the ground running,' she says when we've finally finished logging all the details on the surgery's computer system. 'It's very rare to have three medical beds occupied at any one time. It's almost unheard of for it to happen within twelve hours of leaving port. If the Centre is empty we can do our own thing out of surgery hours and just come running when we get a call. But with two passengers and a crew member to watch over we'll need to get a rota going.'

Dakila is standing in the doorway. 'I'm happy to watch over both of the guests. Kiri can stay with Paco,' he says. 'It's nearly three o' clock in the morning and you've been here all night, Eileen. You should get some sleep.'

I offer to stay but the consensus seems to be that as the new boy I should head back to my cabin as well.

'Who knows what horrors your first morning surgery might bring,' Dakila says with a disturbing amount of relish. 'If we carry on the way we've started you're going to need all the rest you can get.'

# CHAPTER FIVE

'My dear boy, how absolutely marvellous to meet you.' A tall, pink-faced and white-haired man in his sixties greets me the moment I arrive at the Medical Centre the following morning. His rich, deep voice bounces off the walls and he bounds towards me with all the energy and enthusiasm of a teenager. This must be Doctor Edward Marlborough. I can see why Eileen calls him unforgettable.

'Handshakes are supposed to have been banned to stop on-board infections but I simply refuse to comply,' he booms, gripping my hand with both of his. 'I gather you have met my whole team and have already been at the coal face helping out with both our dear passengers and our fine young crewman. Marvellous, absolutely marvellous of you,' he says. If some Hollywood casting agents were looking for the quintessential ship's doctor I get the feeling that the auditions could stop the moment they met my new boss.

'Do follow me into my lair and join me for a chin-wag before clinic begins,' Edward says heading into his consulting room. 'I do believe the wonderful Eileen will be furnishing us with coffee within thirty . . .' At that moment Eileen walks in the door with two mugs '. . . seconds. A new world record, my dear. A podium finish. Congratulations.'

He has a file containing my CV on his desk and he taps it energetically. 'I approve wholeheartedly of your skills and your career to date. I already feel this team will be stronger than ever with you on board.' He's clearly had time to talk to everyone else about the events of the previous evening and to check up on Paco, Mrs Philip and Mrs Coates. 'Our friend from the store room is being very amenable to his treatment. His New Year's resolution was to get off the sauce and I fully intend to help him. The marvellously efficient Kiri is working out a drugs regime for him as we speak. Giving him that extra dose of vitamin B was a good call last night, by the way. It should head off some of the other problems he'll face as he picks himself up off the ground. Anyway, barring any sudden relapse I think we can move him on this afternoon. We'll have him come back here every day to collect his medication until we've got him properly clean. I've had a wee chat with him about some other things he can do and he's agreed to check the staff newsletter for the daily Friends of Bill W meetings. He'll get plenty of support there as well.'

'Friends of Bill W – that's Alcoholics Anonymous, isn't it?'

'It is indeed, and with more than 3,000 people on board it's surprisingly popular. Mr Robredo's twelve-step journey starts now and I sincerely hope he can complete it.' Edward sits back in his chair and brushes a nonexistent piece of dirt off his shirt. He looks as if he was born to wear his white officer's uniform. I wonder if I'll ever feel as comfortable in mine.

'The quite adorably mortified Mrs Philip is also in need of a support group. By all accounts the Friends of Dorothy have a high old time but that may not be quite the place for her. She is very embarrassed about what happened but the antibiotics are doing their magic and she has already regained some strength – both mentally and physically. I think she will be able to leave this morning and I will invite her to dinner at my table one evening soon. I do hope you will be able to join us.'

'I'd love to.'

He smiles his thanks then turns to another file on his desk. 'This brings me swiftly on to the redoubtable Mrs Coates. Quite a character, as you've no doubt discovered. Quite a fan of yours as well, Doctor MacFarlane. She too can be discharged this morning, though she has requested that you call upon her before she leaves. She tells me she no longer believes that your Medical School joke about "never sitting on a loose stool" is the most juvenile she has heard. She has been reminded of an even worse medical joke her grandson told her at Christmas. She wishes to pass it on to you as soon as possible.'

'I was trying to take her mind off the pain with some funny stories,' I say, slightly embarrassed. I hope she didn't repeat the one about the two old ladies who see the streaker in the park.

'Humour is better than medication any day,' he declares, which I hope means I'm off the hook. He asks me a bit more about my career to date and we're talking away like old friends when there is a tap on the door. 'That will be the marvellous Eileen again,' he says, looking at his watch and barking out a strident 'Come!'

'It's nearly eight o'clock, doctor. There are just three people here so far, one guest who wants to discuss her prescriptions and two members of the crew.'

Edward stands and takes a quick look around the waiting area. 'I think this fine young man will be quite capable of handling this session on his own,' he says to Eileen. He shakes me firmly by the hand again and guides me to my own consulting room. 'The marvellous Eileen will be able to reach me if you need me. As you may well have already realised your job here is to be a counsellor, a physiotherapist, a gastroenterologist, a gynaecologist, a dietician, a pharmacist and an oncologist, as well as a GP, an A&E registrar and a diplomat. I am sure you are up to the challenge but do not hesitate to call if you need me,' he says. 'Be kind to the nice new doctor,' he booms out at Kiri and Dakila as he passes their surgery door. Then, like a hurricane, he is gone.

'I think things should be relatively calm in surgery today,' Eileen says just before leading in my first patient. 'As it's our first day we'll have a lot of lost or forgotten medications to chase up for passengers. Then there are the very wealthy travellers on the £125,000 plus tickets who want to meet the medical staff and check we appear competent enough to cope in an emergency. Don't feel flattered by their attention because they'll be making personal calls to an awful lot of other people as well. They'll be passing on their food requirements to the chefs and block booking appointments with the hairdressers and spa staff when they're finished here. This ship is their home for the next four months and they're used to having their homes run well. The only people you won't see much of today are the crew. They are normally too busy getting settled in to need us. We'll be seeing a lot more of them as time goes by.'

She's right about the big-ticket guests. I see one wonderful lady from San Antonio in Texas who says she and her husband fly to England to do the same world cruise almost every year.

'We started in 1992 and we've seen no reason to stop,' she

drawls. 'My husband made a lot of money buying and selling land. Now we spend it all at sea.'

My next patient is a man who has lost his cholesterol pills. He hasn't got a copy of his prescription, can't quite remember what the medication is called but thinks it might begin with an M. Or possibly a D.

'Can you remember what the pills look like?' I ask.

'Well, like pills, really. They're white. They come in a little plastic bottle,' he offers after a great deal of head scratching. This continues when I ask him for the name of his GP. 'It will come to me in a moment. I'm sure it will come to me,' he says hopefully. It doesn't, but we track down a likely address and I promise to get the number, check the drug details, make up the prescription and have it delivered to his stateroom as soon as possible. He leaves, full of thanks, having given me an open invitation to join him and his wife for dinner any night I choose.

'Will it be a low cholesterol meal?' I ask.

'That's all I ever eat, doctor,' he says with a wink.

It's getting on for ten o'clock and I've just prescribed some cream for a Romanian carpenter's eczema when I hear a crash out in the waiting area. I take a look. A middle-aged man with what look like pyjamas underneath a thick winter coat has just slammed his shoulder against the surgery door. It flies open and he almost falls as he stumbles into our reception area. He looks wild-eyed and angry. He looks out of control.

'I need to see a doctor. It's urgent,' he mumbles as I reach him. I lead him into my consulting room and ask his name.

'It's Mark. Mark Neville.'

'Well I'm Doctor MacFarlane. Sit down and tell me how I can help you.' I reach across to close my room door behind him when he grabs my arm.

'I need that left open,' he says. He dabs a handkerchief across his brow and leaves a line of sweat across his forehead. He sits down then stands back up again. He moves to the door, stumbles, looks out over the empty waiting area then trips back to the chair.

'We've got all the time in the world, Mr Neville. Do just tell me what it is that's bothering you,' I say. I'm trying to get a view of his pupils. Is he on drugs? Can this really be my second case of the DTs in less than twenty-four hours?

'I can't breathe,' he says as he tries to calm himself down. I look beyond him out into the waiting area. Eileen, Kiri and Dakila are all there, trying to listen in. But for a while it seems as if Mr Neville has nothing to say.

'Whenever you're ready, sir,' I say as the muscles in his arms and neck pulse away. His eyes are still flashing around the room like crazy.

'I need you to turn the ship around,' he says in the end. 'I thought I could do this, but I can't. I need to get off.'

'Is this a medical emergency, Mr Neville? What is it that I need to know?'

'It's my breathing. I can't control it. I think I'm going to collapse.'

'Is this something that's just happened or is this a long-term condition?'

Mr Neville looks down, embarrassed. 'I've had claustrophobia for ten years. I thought I could cope with this cruise but I can't. I have to get off.'

'Are you on any medication?' He shakes his head. His breathing is ragged now. I can't tell if he's going to burst into tears or run away.

'Can you give me a moment?' he asks. We sit in silence as he calms himself down. Then he apologises to me. 'Doctor,

I'm so sorry. I promised myself I wouldn't get that bad again. I've learned how to hold this together, I just need to remember how.' He stands up, then sits down again. 'I am going to cope. I'm not going to let this beat me. It won't ruin my cruise. I owe it to my wife to get through this. We've not had a holiday in six years because I haven't been able to get a train, let alone fly. She needed a break so I got myself ready for this. I worked up to getting this far. For her sake I won't lose it now.'

He smiles a weak smile and I warm to him. 'You know there is medication I can give you to help you with this,' I say. 'It's nothing heavy, so there's no chance of you getting addicted to it. But it will calm you down through any bad moments.'

'It won't be enough, doctor. I'll kill myself if I have to stay on this ship. I need to go home.' He's looking distraught again.

'Mr Neville I'm new to this ship myself but I've already found plenty of places where you'll have enough room to cope. We can find you places that are quiet. We can help you deal with this.'

He shakes his head again. 'It's not the daytime that's the problem. It's the nights. We don't have any windows in our cabin. There's no air. It's tiny and I can't stay in it. I made it through last night but I'm at my wits' end already. I sat out on deck for about four hours shivering. I think that was from the fear, not the cold. My wife's been crying and she has angina so I can't have her getting upset. I need to ask if we can move into a different cabin. I won't survive this cruise if we stay where we are. If we can get a big cabin with a window I'm going to be fine. I just need to be able to see something beyond four metal walls.'

I look right into Mr Neville's eyes as he stops talking. Everything's changed in the last couple of seconds. All of a sudden I've got a horrible feeling I'm being had. I tell him I'm not authorised to make a decision about his cabin but that I can help him find other ways to deal with his panic attacks. It seems as if that's not enough.

'Doctor, I'm telling you we need a new cabin. I'll throw myself off the back of the boat if I don't get one. I'll jump into the water. My wife will hold you responsible – personally and corporately responsible. I'm a sick man and you're a doctor. You've taken an oath and you're obligated to help me. You have to do what I ask.' He's half shouting and half crying now and I'm hit by a sudden wave of doubt. I have got this right, haven't I?

'Mr Neville I'll happily make some calls on your behalf,' I say. 'But you will have to give me some more information about your state of health first.' He stays close to tears as he answers all my questions. His hands seem to be shaking as he leaves the room. And I'm still not entirely sure what I think about him.

'I've got our Hot Man on the line for you,' Eileen says passing over the phone five minutes later.

I explain about Mr Neville and hear the Hotel Manager snort with laughter. 'A man with chronic claustrophobia books one of our smallest, windowless internal cabins. One of our cheapest cabins, of course.' The man's soft Scandinavian accent is alive with mischief. 'Now if you truly believe he is a danger to himself or to others then you'll have to write up some sort of report and call for the appropriate action. But let me just run a few checks first. This gentleman said this is his first holiday in, what, six years?'

'That's what he said.'

I can hear the manager tapping away at a computer. 'He and his wife were our guests eighteen months ago. They took a two-week Baltic cruise. They had an internal cabin on that occasion, though I don't have any record to say if they requested or were granted an upgrade. Two years earlier they joined us in the Caribbean. On that occasion our friend somehow managed to fly to Barbados and survive fourteen nights at sea. Is this your first cruise with us, doctor?'

'Yes it is.'

'Well this won't be the last time you'll hear a story like this. To give them some credit, passengers are getting more ingenious about upgrades all the time. Using claustrophobia to get out of an internal cabin is one of the oldest tricks in the book, doctor. I suggest you call your patient in and tell him you're very disappointed in him. Tell him to come back when he's had a more interesting idea. Then, perhaps, we can do business.'

'Would Edward have fallen for that?' I ask Eileen when I've passed on the news.

'You didn't fall for anything. There's nothing to be embarrassed about and Edward will be very impressed with the way you handled the situation. He'd have treated the patient in exactly the same way.'

'Well, can you make sure Mr Neville is sent to me if he comes back down here? I'd like another little chat with him. Presumably I'm not allowed to give him a quick nudge if I spot him standing by the railing on the upper deck one day?'

'No you're not. But if you want revenge then just give him

a full, gloved up internal examination if he ever comes in complaining of a sore throat.'

I smile at her. 'Good tip. First rule of medicine: never annoy your doctor because he always gets his own back in the end. I like your style. Thank you.'

Eileen heads out to tidy up the waiting area while I pop into the first passenger room see Mrs Coates. She could have left hours ago but has apparently been enjoying the company in the Medical Centre. She's had a full English breakfast delivered as well as a change of clothes and has sat with Eileen, Kiri and, mostly, Dakila. She's chatting away to him when I walk in and she appears to have just got to the end of a funny story. I take a look at her bandages and give a nod of approval.

'Congratulations. I think you are well enough to see your bill,' I say. She grimaces.

'I do hope I don't have to pay extra for these awful jokes.'

'Amazingly enough they're all included in the price. Now, I gather you were seen by Doctor Marlborough first thing this morning?'

'I certainly was. What a fascinating man. He told me all the bar stools on board have weights in the bottom to stop them tipping over in bad weather. He feels they should carry Government health warnings. It seems my little tumble could have happened to anyone. I was an innocent victim of circumstance.'

'Mrs Coates, I can't quite imagine you as a victim of anything.' We chat for a bit longer before she puts up her hand to stop me mid-sentence.

'Do forgive me for interrupting but I've remembered something. I've got a medical joke for you.'

'Doctor Marlborough warned me about this. Do your worst, Mrs Coates.'

'It comes courtesy of my ten-year-old nephew, Sean,' she says. 'How do you cure water on the brain?'

'Mrs Coates you can tell your nephew I'm well ahead of him. Every doctor knows it's a tap on the head. Now, I've got some paperwork to do so I'll say goodbye to you for now. Can I perhaps expect to see you in the bar this evening if I pop in for a quick visit?'

Another mischievous look flashes across Mrs Coates' face. 'Oh no, doctor,' she says. 'Hasn't he told you? Doctor Marlborough is expecting you at the Gala Reception for those of us doing the full world cruise. It starts at eight and you're to be the guest of honour. I'm bringing my camera. I do hope you've prepared your speech.'

'I can assure you she was joking,' Eileen says for perhaps the tenth time. We've had a quiet evening clinic and she's in my cabin helping me with my bow tie. 'The Captain will be the only person making a speech. He will welcome the passengers, talk briefly about the voyage, introduce some of his senior officers then raise a toast. All you have to do is smile and mingle. It will be a lovely evening.'

'So why aren't you coming?'

'I haven't been invited. But there are more than enough formal evenings to go around so I'll probably be at the next one. Now, stand up straight.' She surveys me from a few paces back. 'Perfect. Edward always looks very dashing in his formal rig. I'm glad to say that you do too.' I glance in the mirror as she leads me out into the corridor. Our formal uniform is a white jacket, white starched trousers, a white belt, white shoes and a white bow tie. I wouldn't quite use the word dashing. I look like a 1970s ice cream salesman on Italian TV.

Two friendly faces smile out of a sea of strangers as I walk into the reception. Edward is in the middle of the room chatting with Mrs Coates. She raises her one good arm in greeting and I head over towards them. As I approach, one black-clad waiter offers me a very slim glass of champagne, while another holds forth a vast silver tray of canapés.

'Not quite the blue rinses and pink gins you were expecting,' Mrs Coates says triumphantly when I make it through to her. 'Never let it be said that the old-timers don't know how to party.'

I look around and have to agree that she's right. There's a real buzz about the room. A band is playing in the corner and a few couples are already dancing. Everyone is dressed up to the nines – one lady is wearing a dress that appears to be made entirely of feathers – and looks ready to make a night of it.

'Your eye looks a little better, dear boy,' Edward booms over the hum of conversations. 'I told dear Mrs Coates about the events of last evening.'

'I'm certainly a lot happier now I know why the poor man in the room next to me spent the night moaning like a rat in a trap. I'd been imagining all sorts of terrible things. Some of them were so exciting that I may still tell them to my friends when I get home. A little exaggeration adds spice to life, don't you find?' She asks after Mrs Philip and is chatting away happily when the Master of Ceremonies calls for silence.

The captain steps forward to speak. He welcomes us and fires everyone up with a run through of the facilities at our disposal and the countries we're due to visit. He introduces the Chief Engineer, the Cruise Director, the Hotel Manager and 'our magnificent Ship's Doctor, Edward Marlborough'. Each man takes a round of applause as they step forward into the spotlight.

'A whole lot of silliness,' Edward says when it's all over. It's clear that he adores it.

Our little trio breaks up and we mingle for the rest of the reception. I chat to several incredibly well-travelled groups of guests, including one seventy-two-year-old lady who hopes to kiss a stingray in the Caribbean, while her husband wants to try his first zip-wire ride in Costa Rica.

'It will be my seventy-ninth birthday the day we arrive in Costa Rica and I plan to make it one to remember,' he declares. 'Our grandchildren are all travelling the world and we've decided to do the same, though in comfort. This is the gap year we never had.'

Even more impressive, though, is Mrs Coates. Less than twenty-four hours earlier she was nursing a badly fractured wrist. Since then she's been tanked up with painkillers and forced to walk around with her arm in a cast. But as I look across the room she's happily holding court on one of her beloved bar stools. I catch her eye and say goodnight when I decide it's time to slip away. She mouths the word 'lightweight' back at me.

'I think this may indeed be the perfect time to leave,' says Edward suddenly. He's appeared at my side and, as we head back towards our cabins, I notice he's dragging his right leg behind him slightly. 'I try not to let anyone in the surgery see how bad it can get. I tell the ladies at the galas that it's an old war wound. In truth, of course, it's a combination of arthritis and a tired hip that should have been replaced several years ago. Some days it barely troubles me at all. Tonight, perhaps, that second foxtrot was something of a mistake.'

I smile at him and we slow down a little more. The wide, richly carpeted corridor seems to stretch out to infinity in front of us. 'There is a lot more walking on board than I'd expected. Just as well, given the amount of food we get to eat,' I say.

'You should have been on board before we got proper stabilisers. On the old ocean crossings it felt as if you climbed up and down a mountain ten times between bed and breakfast. Uphill for ten paces until the ship hit the crest of a wave. Then brace and it was downhill until the next swell began. We certainly didn't need any fancy gyms to keep in shape back then.' He stops suddenly and leans next to a piece of shockingly bold modern art. 'It will be auctioned later in the voyage. The auctioneer makes more money than anyone else on board. Defies belief, really,' he says when he catches me looking at the piece.

'I'm not quite sure where I'd put it.'

'Down a coal hole would be my suggestion but then I'm not an art collector.' He stands up straight again and looks right at me. 'I assume that you know I'm retiring this year?' I'm startled by his directness and stumble over how to reply. Fortunately he doesn't need a response 'Of course you know. No-one has secrets in this job. That will be the only thing I don't miss.'

'Well I know that everyone in the Centre will be upset to see you go. Eileen has barely stopped singing your praises since I got on board.'

'Eileen is a very wonderful lady – and she sings your praises as well.' We start to walk again, though at an even slower pace. 'Do you know, I would give absolutely anything to be young again, Doctor MacFarlane,' Edward says as a very glamorous couple flit by us. 'I would give anything to be starting out my career, not ending it. I wish all the adventures and the excitements and even the naughty bits were still ahead. I envy you more than I can say. Will you assure me you won't waste your youth and your time on this ship? Tell me you will grasp every moment of this cruise and live your life to the full?'

I promise to do my best and Edward shakes my hand very tightly at his stateroom door. 'I've become unaccountably maudlin and I do apologise,' he says. 'The guests always blame everything on the air-conditioning so I shall do the same. I wish you a quiet night, doctor. And welcome, yet again, to our floating madhouse.'

# CHAPTER SIX

Edward's good mood has returned the following morning. He roars out a greeting and gives a cheery wave from his desk as I arrive at the Medical Centre at seven thirty. Eileen brings me a coffee and introduces me to our steward, a short Filipino man called Romeo. He's put a vase of fresh flowers on the reception table and is spreading out a series of printouts of the day's newspapers. 'We have *The Times*, the *Independent*, the *New York Times* and the *Wall Street Journal*,' he says proudly. 'I make sure we get new magazines for you at most ports as well, sir. This is the best-kept Medical Centre in the fleet. If there's ever anything else you need you make sure you ask me.'

'Romeo is an absolute treasure,' Eileen says, making sure he can hear as he polishes the already gleaming coffee table. 'Now, we've got a few minutes before surgery begins. Tell me how you got on last night.'

I'm describing Edward's prowess on the dance floor when Kiri and Dakila arrive. Ten minutes later our doors are open and morning surgery begins. My first patient is a Latvian chambermaid who's in agony after slamming her fingers in a bathroom door. She's got some nasty bruising and will lose a couple of nails but there's nothing broken. I give her some painkillers and suggest she takes the rest of the day off. She looks at me as if I'm out of my mind.

'It will be four months before she gets a day off,' Eileen tells me later. 'Cruise ships are all about extremes. If you're in the orchestra you might work only three hours a day. If you're a chambermaid like that poor love you'll work five times as long and many times as hard.'

My next patient is a chef who's got a nasty wound on his hand. If I can't sign him off work, I can at least have him moved to other duties till it's healed. Next up I try to fine tune the medication for a hypertensive accounts manager who might get more benefit from an anger management class.

Every so often I hear Edward's laughter ring out as he shares a joke with one of the passengers. His clinic certainly sounds more enjoyable than mine. The only light relief I get is with a very bashful musician who has caught something very sensitive in the zip of his jeans. He doesn't need stitches, thankfully, and I try to be as tactful as possible when I give him some advice: to accept his middle-age spread and stop forcing himself into the same size jeans he was wearing fifteen years ago.

The two hours fly by and afterwards I jump at the chance to join the others for an early lunch. Edward suggests the Officers' Dining Room but he gets outvoted as the others want me to see how the lower half live first. We head to one of the two crew mess rooms instead and I have to say I quite like it. Everyone is criss-crossing each other and carrying trays from one food station to another. We've got about a dozen different types of food to choose from and in the seating area we've got the usual United Nations of workers from every different department. No-one pays much attention to anyone else. It's crowded, chaotic but strangely comfortable. If this is going to be my life for the next four months then I think I've pretty much landed on my feet.

'Well, we're two days, three emergency calls, three clinics and one gala reception in. What do you think of it all so far?' Kiri asks as we settle around a table.

I tell them the truth. I'm loving it.

'So you're going to give up on your crazy plan to work in some A&E department in the autumn?'

Eileen raises her hand. 'I blabbed,' she says, 'I'm afraid it's clinically impossible to keep a secret once we've left Southampton.'

I'm about to say something when Dakila interrupts me. 'You've spent nearly three years working for a medical repatriation company near Heathrow but you've got about a billion air miles so you decided to stop. You're going to apply for an A&E job when the new rotations come up in April and you're hoping to start in October. You've given up your flat in London and you're hoping to save some money by being away from England for the next four months. You've been with your girlfriend, Cassie, for eighteen months. She used to be a flight attendant but is now training to be a doctor in Cambridge. I didn't get all of this from Eileen, by the way. Kiri and I have gathered intelligence from a variety of sources including Edward and Mrs Coates. So, have we missed anything?' he asks with a smile.

'My favourite colour? Or the name of my first pet?'

'I don't know, but I bet someone in the IT department will be able to find out for us in less than ten minutes.'

I sit back and pretend to look offended. 'I feel as if I've been mugged. It's worse than when Paco hit me in the face.'

Kiri sees through me. 'This is just the way it is on board,

baby doc. You have to make decisions about people quickly in this job. Even on a worldie we don't have time to make normal friendships. It might be ages before we end up on the same ship again. So we might as well cut to the chase and find out what we've got in common straight away. It's like a social short-cut.'

'It's like stalking.'

'Well you've signed up for fifteen more weeks of it so there's no point in moaning. Anyway, you've been avoiding the question. Why would you give all this up to chase targets in some crummy A&E department?'

I smile for a few moments and finish off my lunch. Then I realise everyone's looking at me. That wasn't a joke or a rhetorical question. They really are waiting to find out what I plan to do at the end of the cruise.

'I just want to settle down,' I offer. 'I was on a plane every third day in my old job. It was great fun but it was freelance and I thought I should get on a proper career path with a pension and everything. Being a doctor on a cruise ship was the one last thing I wanted to do before rejoining the real world.'

Eileen claps her hands together and beams her most motherly smile. 'I know someone else who said that when he did his first cruise. He wanted to do one big, round the world voyage before moving into private practice and making his fortune.' I look around the table at four smiling faces. I've got a horrible feeling I know where this is going.

'It was me. That was more than thirty years ago,' Edward confirms with pride.

Eileen reaches over and puts her hand on my arm. 'Don't look so scared, Ben. We don't stay here because we have to. We stay because this is the best job in medicine. Come back down to the Medical Centre this afternoon. Three o'clock everybody?' The others all nod. 'Join us at three,' she says. 'We'll let you in on another little secret.'

The whole team is there when I arrive. Edward and Eileen are squeezed on to one sofa in the waiting room, Dakila is on another and Kiri is clearing the magazines and flowers off the top of the coffee table.

'I've ordered us tea and scones. Romeo should be here with them shortly,' Eileen says as I sit down. Dakila passes me a pen and a pad of paper.

'You'll be needing these,' he says.

'Ladies and gentlemen, I do declare this congress to be in session,' Edward announces once our cream tea has been served. 'Now, Doctor MacFarlane, this is your first such meeting. It is a tradition I began many years ago. It may be that no other Medical Centre observes it with such formality or such gusto. More fool them, I say.'

'Here, here,' says Eileen.

'Itinerary, please,' Edward says. Kiri hands two freshly printed pages of A4 to each of us. It's a list of the ports we're visiting as well as the dates and approximate arrival and departure times. 'Now, first things first. Opening bids for Madeira.'

No-one speaks.

'Oh come along, people. It's a marvellously pretty island. Charming little capital, "pearl of the Atlantic" and all that. The weather might clear and the views will be quite spectacular.'

I'm scanning the tour notes and quite like the look of some weird basket ride down a hill that's on offer as 'an island essential'. But I don't want to be first to volunteer in case I look too workshy.

Fortunately Kiri ends up speaking for me. 'I think Ben should take it. It's his first cruise. He'll want to stretch his legs on solid ground. We'll be doing him a favour by giving him Madeira.'

'Doctor, I must warn you that Kiri's motives may not be entirely pure,' Edward tells me before I have a chance to speak. 'You must use your own judgement. Does our dear Australian friend truly want you to enjoy the bracing air of Madeira? Or does she want you to use up all your shore leave early so she is free to enjoy the delights of Barbados and Bonaire?'

Eileen put her hand on my arm as I try to work out what it all means. 'I think Doctor Marlborough is teasing you,' she explains. 'We normally need to have at least one doctor and two nurses on board in every port, so strictly speaking you're not in competition for shore leave with Kiri. But as I'm the senior nurse there may well be occasions when you're in competition with me. And I'm telling you now that I've made an appointment to see a herbalist in Costa Rica, I am determined to have lunch at *Chez Panisse* when we get to San Francisco and I intend to have a new wardrobe made up for me in Hong Kong. Oh, and there's a new restaurant in Sydney I want to visit as well.'

Dakila pulls himself upright. 'Eileen, I've got two new nieces to see in Hong Kong. Plus, I missed Costa Rica last time when that guy got blood poisoning after falling over in the street. I'll fight you for both of those.'

Kiri pipes in. 'Well I missed Phuket when the girl in the orchestra got bitten by a spider and nearly had a respiratory arrest. When we get to Thailand I warn you now, I'm playing dirty as well.'

'Our meetings don't normally descend into chaos and recrimination quite so soon,' Edward tells me cheerfully. 'Especially not before we've even looked at the shore events or the excursion list.'

'The Captain likes to have as many officers as possible at the shore events. We can also get paid extra if we go on some of the passenger trips and act as mini-hosts and roving medics. There are new ones on offer every year and some of them are quite wonderful. But not as wonderful as the organic green garlic and ricotta soufflé at *Chez Panisse* so don't think for one minute I'm giving it up,' says Eileen pointedly.

Kiri thumps a new pile of papers on the coffee table. 'Here's the tour list. Let the battles begin,' she says.

The room is quiet for a moment as we leaf through the offerings. I get a bit of a surprise, to be honest. I'd thought it might all be ancient battle sites and backstage tours of opera houses. In fact there's everything from canoe trips and volcano climbs to dune-bashing and shooting parties.

'I think I want to do every one of them,' I admit. 'I've always wanted to swim with dolphins and I've never knowingly turned down the chance to do a bit of wine tasting. This is finally starting to feel like a holiday.'

Pens scratch away on our master file of excursions as we divide up the spoils. Then we move back to the main ports of call and check we're not double-booking anyone or leaving the ship unmanned. I put in an early bid for Honolulu but Edward snatches it away from me with a smile. For the most urbane and well-mannered man I've ever met, he's no slouch when it comes to getting his own way.

'Next time, dear boy, next time,' he booms as he ticks off all his other first choice ports around the world as well. Eileen doesn't do too badly either. She looks set to see her tailor in

Hong Kong and raves about the ginger, coconut, tamarind and lime in the food she hopes to eat on a day out in Bangkok. Kiri and Dakila both get the breaks they want in Phuket and Mumbai though they remain locked in battle over Singapore. On top of all my shore leave days I opt to help out on guest trips in Barbados and Costa Rica. It all sounds so much better than I'd expected.

Time passes as we gradually work our way around the globe.

'Who's up for Dubai?' Kiri asks as she turns the page on the excursion list.

Edward visibly flinches. 'I think I shall pretend that particular city is not on our itinerary. I shall stay at work with my clinic door closed. Hopefully I will have so many patients that I will barely know the ship has stopped moving.'

'Edward bought a flat there three years ago as an investment,' Eileen whispers.

'And we don't talk about it, my dear. So much for my second pension. I should have just put the money on a horse at Kempton Park.'

'Do you dive, Ben?' Eileen asks as we move on down the list.

'Yes. I love it, but I haven't had the chance in years.'

'Well you'll want to get off in Sharm el Sheikh. It's got the most amazing reef-diving. You go and enjoy yourself there – leaving me free to do the pyramids the day after. I've not seen the new Museum of Egyptian Antiquities yet and last time I was there most of Tutankhamen was out on tour.'

We're still working out who else will get shore leave in Egypt and who will run the Cairo excursions when Eileen looks at the clock and stands up. 'I think we will need to wind this up for now. We'll leave Athens and Venice for another day as well. It's time to open the doors.'

My first patient of the afternoon can't seem to stop smiling. She practically bounds into my room and for a moment I think she's too excited to sit down.

'I think I might be pregnant,' she says when she finally does. 'I did a test in my cabin but I want to know if you can confirm it with something more professional.'

I take a quick look at her file. Her name is Jasmina French. She's thirty nine, married, one of the performers in the theatre and is on board until Sydney.

'Most pregnancy tests are pretty much the same. But we can do another one if you want us to,' I say.

She very clearly does, so I fetch her a specimen pot and lead her towards the nearest lavatory. A few minutes later she's back. I take the sample into our laboratory area and check it out. It's another positive result – and if Jasmina was excited before she's ecstatic now.

'I'm going to have a baby! I'm finally, finally going to have a baby!' she says.

I offer my congratulations – then start to warn Jasmina that it's still very early days. We've worked out that she's probably only two weeks gone. She won't even be ready for her first scan by the time we get to Sydney.

'If I were you I'd keep this quiet and just carry on as normal until then,' I begin. She holds up her hand to stop me.

'I'll try but I'm not sure I'll be strong enough. I know it's ridiculous and I know I need to be careful but I can't keep this inside. This is the best news I've ever had. This is what I've been waiting for all my life.' She leans forward and talks me through her story. She's been married for fifteen years and has been trying for a baby for almost all of them. She and her husband have had every test going. They've tried every strategy and quack cure they can find. All their friends have started families and Jasmina has long since stopped going to christenings or kids' birthday parties because she finds them too painful. She stopped working on ships two years ago because she decided that the food or the air-conditioning or something else was stopping her from conceiving. She's only back on board now to save up for a last-chance course of IVF in the summer.

'They always say it's when you stop trying that it happens,' she says. 'I need to go and call my husband. He's going to be over the moon. You've made us very, very happy, doctor.' I can tell she's itching to leave as I run through the usual list of do's and don'ts for expectant mums. 'Bless you for trying but there is absolutely nothing about pregnancy that I don't already know,' she says when I get to the end of them. 'There's not a book about it that I've not read. I am aware of how precarious my situation is. I know the odds are probably stacked against me, even now. But I know in my soul that this is all going to work out all right.'

She gets up to leave, then stops and turns in the doorway. 'Can you do one more thing for me?'

'I'll try to.'

'Can you just say "congratulations"?'

I do and her smile, if it's possible, gets even wider. 'You have no idea how long I've wanted to hear someone say that. Come see me in the show any night that you're free. I'm only in the chorus but I'll be easy to spot. I'll be glowing.'

The rest of my afternoon list goes smoothly – though I'd sooner forget the man from the boiler room with the extraordinarily stubborn ear wax. I finish updating the crew illness log when we close the Centre for the night.

Eileen heads off to eat in her cabin while Kiri and I grab trays in the crew mess. All four of us are going to see Jasmina's show and after wolfing down our meals Kiri calls the theatre manger to check our seats are still on hold. We'll have to give them up if any passengers are waiting. But if we get them they're among the best in the house.

'Do we really have to stay in our uniforms?' I ask when we get the all clear. 'I feel like I should be on the stage, not just sitting in the audience. How long does it take to get used to these outfits?'

'About a decade,' says Dakila helpfully. 'Anyway, you're welcome to get on stage in the Crew Bar later. You can join all my fellow Filipinos at the karaoke machine.'

'Will it have "Rhinestone Cowboy"?'

'Almost certainly.'

'Then I might just take you up on it.'

The theatre is incredible. It's got all the dark velvet and gilt wood you'd expect in something from Edwardian London. But scratch the surface and it's twenty-first century all the way. The aisles are so wide a sumo wrestler could get up to go to the loo in the middle of the first act without anyone else needing to stand up. Meanwhile the raking is so steep that a basketball player in a hat could probably sit in front of you without obstructing the view. The air-conditioning is great and there are mini-tables with built-in wine coolers next to each seat. We even get waitress service before the curtain rises.

'It's a bit different to the Students' Union where I did

amateur dramatics at Med School,' I whisper at Eileen. She's in the seat next to me but it's so far away I'm not sure if she can hear.

We're there for a Broadway review – couple of people from TV talent shows sing the big songs, there are some amazing dancers and an endless series of costume and scene changes. In the background most of the time is Jasmina. I know that it's the spotlights. But she really does look as if she's glowing.

She sees us during the curtain calls and mouths an invite to come backstage.

'You probably know that Ben arranged a pregnancy test for me this afternoon. I'm going to have a baby!' she says once we're all squeezed into a big communal dressing room. So much for trying to keep the news under wraps until Sydney.

'Congratulations!' says Eileen giving her a quick hug.

'I'm guessing you're not going to want to celebrate with champagne? A sparkling water instead, perhaps?' asks Kiri, looking at Jasmina's nonexistent bump.

'A sparkling water would be wonderful. Let me just round up some of the others.'

In the end the group is too big for us to go to a passenger bar – there are strict rules on how many seats we can take up at any one time – so we head down to the staff mess. It's packed but one of Jasmina's friends, a sleek American dancer called Mary-Grace, manages to get a very unwilling group of Greek men to move so we can all sit together.

'One day she's going to get herself killed doing that sort of thing. You can be stabbed for less on a Caribbean ship,' Jasmina says.

Mary-Grace shrugs, smiles and stands up to toast her friend's pregnancy. Jasmina looks gloriously happy but says she's going for an early night when we get ready for another round of drinks. 'I'm going to play this safe,' she says. 'See you all tomorrow.' Eileen leaves with her while Dakila excuses himself to join some friends on another table. Kiri then heads off to see if Kieran is able to get away from the casino. A new wave of people immediately swarms into the empty seats.

'These are some of our "shoppies". They work in the galleria,' Mary-Grace says. Everyone knows each other and they all seem thrilled to discover I'm a newbie.

'Tell him what the sushi chef told us last night,' says a man called Lukas who works in the cashmere store.

'This is something you might as well know,' admits Mary-Grace. 'Basically, you don't need to panic if one of the high rollers gets brought into the Medical Centre on a stretcher after eating poisonous sushi.'

'Why not?'

'Because they're not going to die.' Lukas continues the story. Apparently the world's keenest sushi lovers like nothing better than playing a bit of Russian roulette with the blowfish. The chefs dissect out the gall bladder to remove the toxins – but leave a tiny bit of the bile duct intact so the diners feel the buzz of poison on their lips as they swallow. 'Too little poison and you don't get the tingle. Too much and you die. Apparently the rich passengers love that kind of thing,' he says.

'So how do I know that no-one's going to die?'

'Because our chef takes a bit of a short cut. He gets rid of all the dangerous stuff and just dabs a bit of mouth ulcer cream on what's left. Ready made tingle with far less risk of sudden death and a law suit.'

'It's a win-win situation. The passengers think they're dying when in fact they're just clearing up some cold sores,' says Mary-Grace. One of the other shoppies then interrupts to tell me about one of the scams they've got to fleece extra cash out of customers. Five minutes later Mary-Grace introduces me to a tall, stunningly beautiful woman called Tamara. 'She used to be a gent,' Lukas whispers.

'No way,' I say. I'm looking at her hands and her Adam's apple for telltale signs of gender reassignment.

'A Guest Entertainer, idiot. She was a solo artist, now she works backstage,' Lukas says before I make a total fool of myself.

'This place seems to get more bizarre all the time,' I tell him when we head to the bar to get some more drinks.

'That's because we're all trying to freak you out. Us old-timers love trying to terrify the cruise virgins,' he says. 'Wait till we get back to the table. I'll get one of the girls to tell you where all the cockroaches live.'

I try not to look at the ceiling panels in my cabin when I finally make it back for the night. I'd always assumed that there may well be rats on the lower decks. It hadn't occurred to me that there could be other horrors scampering around above us as well.

The cold air wakes me up when I step out on my balcony to look at the moon. When I get back inside I log on to my computer. We're heading west so we get an extra hour's sleep each night and I want to make the most of it. I email Cassie to say hello then type 'The story so far' in the subject field of another message and write out a long round-robin progress report for my family and other friends. Cassie has replied by the time I've finished so I try my first ship to shore phone call and it's brilliant to hear her voice. In theory we're used to being apart – she was a flight attendant and I was travelling the world doing repatriations when we first met. But we got used to seeing a lot more of each other when she started Medical School in the autumn – and anyway there's a huge difference between a few nights and four months apart.

'We're doing the right thing,' she says, reading my mind as we talk. 'I need to focus on my exams and you need to get another good job on your CV. The summer will be here in no time. It's all going to be worth it in the end.' I know she's right and I'm feeling good about the world when we say goodbye and I settle down for the night. The engine noise and the slight roll of the ship are as soporific as ever. As usual I fall asleep fast but tonight I don't stay that way for long. My phone rings just after 1am.

Less than five minutes later I'm dressed and storming out of my room with my medical bag under my arm. Apparently the purser has taken an emergency call from a cabin on the upper deck. Something has happened to Mrs Philip.

# CHAPTER SEVEN

A worried-looking middle-aged man, who introduces himself as Lars Jonsson, is standing beside a stateroom door as I approach.

'The lady is inside, with my wife,' he says, stepping forward to meet me. 'We were out on the deck trying to see some stars when we heard the sound of someone crying. She was sobbing, like a little child, all curled up on the edge of one of the chairs. She was freezing cold so we brought her in here and called for help.'

The couple have turned their heating up full blast and the man's wife has wrapped Mrs Philip up in blankets. She's sitting next to her on a sofa and is trying to comfort her.

'Mrs Philip, it's Ben MacFarlane, the doctor. I hope you remember me from the other night? Mrs Philip I don't like to see you like this again. Can I just check you over so I know you're OK?'

'We can wait next door to give you your privacy. If you need anything just let us know,' Mrs Jonsson says giving the old lady's hand a final squeeze.

I sit next to Mrs Philip and open my medical bag. I pull out a disposable thermometer and pop it under her tongue. I lift up her hand – still freezing cold and limp – and check her pulse. It's weak and a little bit slow but at least it's regular. I put a blood pressure cuff round her upper arm and start to inflate it. Again the readings are low, but they're nothing to worry about. When enough time has passed I check the thermometer. Mrs Philip's hands might be cold but her core temperature is fine. At least we're not facing hypothermia.

I get ready to wash my hands and, as if reading my mind, Mrs Jonsson calls out: 'There's a guest cloakroom through there.' It seems 'through there' means through a dining area that can seat eight and alongside a balcony you could practically play volleyball on. And I thought I had a good cabin.

'Mrs Philip, can I give you some good news?' I say when I'm back on the sofa. 'The nurses and I finished all the tests on you yesterday and there was absolutely nothing unexpected or worrying in any of them. I don't think there's anything physically wrong with you any more. You're over the bladder infection and you're well on the road to recovery. So can I ask why you were making things worse by being outside so late at night?'

'I was trying to hide from everyone,' she says eventually. 'I had nowhere else to go. I've no friends on this ship. None at all.'

'Excuse me for listening in, but you've got us.' Mrs Jonsson walks into the room with a determined look on her face. 'My husband and I are your friends.'

'So are all five of us in the Medical Centre. And do you remember the other lady who was there? The one who had injured her wrist? She's travelling on her own and could probably use some company too. It's just not true that you're on your own, Mrs Philip.' I suddenly have an idea and look up at the Jonssons before turning back to the patient. 'Mrs

Philip I think my senior doctor suggested that you join us for dinner one day soon. Well I think we should do that later on today. Mr and Mrs Jonsson, would you like to join us?'

'It's Lars and Una,' she says. 'We'd love to.'

The couple are also happy to host Mrs Philip for the rest of the night. It seems that they have a guest bedroom as well as a guest lavatory. They also have an immaculate Burmese butler who appears a matter of seconds after Lars presses a call button. He prepares the spare room. With profuse apologies for troubling everyone Mrs Philip disappears into it.

'Thank you so much for looking after her,' I say as I repack my medical bag and get ready to leave. 'We took a liking to this lady when we met her the other night. She's going through a rough time but if we can build her confidence I think we can make a real difference for her.'

Lars smiles and stands up very tall. 'Consider it done, doctor,' he says. 'My wife and I like a challenge on holiday. Tonight we have found one.'

The morning and evening surgeries are busy but both shoot by. No-one seems to mind that I've volunteered them for a dinner date and we all put on our semi-formal uniforms to meet Mrs Philip and the Jonssons just after eight. I'm one of the first people there and when I arrive I can see Lars leading Mrs Philip to the table. Una drops back so say hello.

'How's the patient?' I ask.

'She's quite lovely. She slept through till ten, which she says she has never done before. She had a bit of breakfast, a bit of lunch and she has slowly come alive. She can't stop apologising for the fuss she thinks she caused. We can see why you like her. Did you know that she spent thirty-five years as the personal secretary for a family of racehorse owners in Newmarket?'

The others arrive as we talk. Eileen has picked one of the ship's smallest and quietest restaurants. It's a perfect choice. Soft lights throw even softer shadows across the floor and the tables are spread so far apart we're not distracted by the sounds of other conversations. 'I do appreciate you all doing this for me and I want to apologise again for being such a foolish old woman – twice,' is how Mrs Philip opens the conversation.

Dakila stands up. 'If you say sorry one more time then we will all leave,' he says dramatically. 'And I bet you don't have any idea how to get back to your stateroom from here. So you really don't want that to happen.'

Mrs Philip, bless her, smiles broadly as Dakila sits back down. She taps him on the hand, in much the same way Eileen tends to do. 'Do you know one thing that life has taught me?' she asks him. 'It is that the kindest men tend to be the handsome ones. That is very true in your case, my dear.'

'Oh Mrs Philip, must you have said that? You do know we'll never hear the end of it now,' says Kiri putting her head in her hands.

Once we've ordered our food we talk about the ship and the voyage. Una turns out to be right – Mrs Philip has slowly come alive. She's got a dry sense of humour and there's a slightly wicked look in her eye as she explains why she's here.

'I have one son and he very grudgingly visits me once a month for exactly an hour,' she says. 'In the late autumn I said I might one day like to travel. The next day he booked me on this four-month, round-the-world cruise. I wouldn't be at all surprised if he's not selling my house as we speak,' she concludes. 'If so, I just hope the subsidence is as much of a shock to him as it was to me.'

She asks us about our lives, our families and our past voyages as we eat. Dakila is still on a high from being called handsome and passes around the photos of his wife and daughters. Kiri talks about Kieran, I pass over a photo of Cassie, and Edward details the latest achievements of his three grown-up children and various grandchildren. Eileen turns out to have two sons. One of them is married and works for a firm of solicitors in South London while the other is refusing to settle down at all. He qualified as a ski instructor last year but is now living on a Kibbutz in Israel. Eileen says she has long since given up guessing what he might do next or where.

The Jonssons trump us all with a spectacularly complex family history involving three previous marriages and seven assorted stepchildren, two of whom are currently the talk of their native Norway.

'One of them had an affair with a chat show host while another has decided to paint the most awfully controversial nude pictures and exhibit them all over Oslo. People ask us why we cruise. Our family is why we cruise,' says Lars ruefully.

Conversation flows easily all night and there's an almost childlike look of excitement in Mrs Philip's eyes as the Jonssons ask her if she'll join them on a sightseeing tour the next day.

'Apparently we're going to take a taxi around the island and then come back on board to see a musical,' she whispers when she pops over to thank us yet again for the meal.

'I think our work here is done,' says Kiri as we head over

to the Officers' Bar for the rest of the night. 'That woman's seventy six, she's been on board less than a week and she's already got a better social life than me.'

I wanted to watch us arrive in Madeira but we're due in just after the start of morning surgery and we don't have any windows in the Medical Centre.

'Don't worry, we've got thirty-four more stops to go, and that's before we have any emergency diversions,' Dakila tells me as I put my camera back in my pocket.

Edward has been called to a consultation in one of the senior officers' staterooms so I've taken over his list. Eileen assures me that it will be relatively quiet.

'Most of the passengers will want to get off and see the island so a doctor's appointment will be the last thing on their minds. This afternoon will be a different matter. We get more accidents in the first port of call than almost anywhere else. The first time people get off the boat it's as if they've totally forgotten that curbs or cars or any other hazards exist. They certainly don't seem to expect them in a little place like this. By the time we get to Hong Kong or Mumbai the worldies will be able to cross the busiest streets or negotiate the worst pavements in the world. At that point it will be the crew who fill up the clinics after getting in fights or taking too many drugs on shore leave. Everything on cruise ships comes in waves – excuse the pun.'

When the clinic doors close at ten I clear my backlog of paperwork, then wish everyone well for the afternoon clinic. Mrs Coates has a three o'clock appointment to have her wrist scanned and I've agreed to accompany her to the hospital.

She's wearing a green and red silk blouse when I collect her in her stateroom just after lunch.

'Madeira is a Portuguese colony and these are the colours of the Portuguese flag. I like to believe that I can dress for any occasion, even an unexpected hospital visit in the mid-Atlantic,' she says as we walk to the nearest disembarkation point. We've booked a taxi and it's waiting for us on the dockside.

The hospital is near the middle of Funchal, the capital, and a nurse whisks us into a surprisingly large office where our consultant is waiting.

'Hello, *Bom dia!* We were expecting you, my name is Doctor Pedro Teles, you must be Belinda Coates and this, I assume, is a sporting injury,' he says, helping Mrs Coates on to the examination couch and gently removing her sling. She's clearly loving the attention and the banter as he unravels the layers of crepe bandage and cotton wool. 'So how exactly did this happen? I'm guessing that you, what, fell off the climbing wall or had an accident on a surf board?' he asks with effortless charm.

'What a wonderful theory and I certainly won't try to dissuade you of it,' Mrs Coates says, winking back and flirting outrageously.

'Well, we just need to take some more X-rays to check the alignment of the bones. Maria here will take you round to the radiology suite.' A nurse in crisp whites leads Mrs Coates out of the room and Dr Teles starts to interrogate me about life as a ship's doctor. It seems I'm not the only one considering a career break at sea.

When Mrs Coates is back Dr Teles examines the images on a large computer screen on the wall.

'Perfect alignment. Congratulations,' he says, moving over

and looking at Mrs Coates' arm one more time. 'Well, the swelling has gone down so we can now put you in a full cast. Maria will help you. As soon as the plaster is dry, you are free to enjoy the delights of our beautiful island. The ship's doctor did a very good job,' he concludes, directing his final words at me.

'I expected nothing less,' Mrs Coates tells him. 'Doctor MacFarlane is a quite marvellous man. Would you like to hear one of his jokes?'

I pop out into the hospital's reception area while Mrs Coates is having the new cast put on. I call the ship to see how afternoon surgery is going.

'It's busy, but it's nothing we can't handle. You go off and enjoy the rest of the afternoon with your fancy woman,' Kiri tells me.

As it turns out I do. Mrs Coates gets our cab driver to tour around some of local sights so I get an idea of what the island is like. Then we head to the terrace of Reid's Hotel where she has arranged to meet some other passengers. Most are fellow worldies and include the stingray and zip-wire couple from the gala reception.

'You want to watch this young man,' Mrs Coates says as she tells them about the hospital visit. 'It appears he badly misdiagnosed my wrist as having been caused in a bar room accident. I've since had it confirmed as a sporting injury.'

'I was confused by the whole evening dress, high heeled shoes, brought-in-from-the-bar-at-midnight thing,' I say. 'I should have realised we had a future Olympian in our midst.'

We're supposed to be having just an afternoon tea but Mr

Zip Wire has ordered some very expensive wine to go with it. His wife fills everyone's glasses to their brims. I get told off for looking at my watch all the time because I'm worried about missing the boat.

'Relax, it's a late sail and you're with professionals,' he tells me. 'We've never been left behind yet.'

His wife refills my glass. 'We won't be on dry land again for six days so we need to make the most of it. Especially now we know the weather forecast. Did you hear the captain's announcement this morning?'

'He just said it was going to be "a little bit boisterous", didn't he?'

'That's cruise-ship code.'

'For what?'

'For bloody awful.'

# Part Two

# The Mid-Atlantic

# CHAPTER EIGHT

I'm so excited that the real ocean crossing has begun that I wrap up warm and have breakfast on my balcony the following morning. Albert seems thrilled at the decision.

'You are a three-stripe officer, sir. You should not be lining up in crew mess for toast and eggs in the morning,' he says. 'I can bring you breakfast in your room every day.'

I try to wolf down my food before it gets cold. The sky is heavy with clouds and the ocean is an endless plain of greys, rich dark blues and even blacks. It seems to move as one, like a vast, rolling mass that finds energy from within. It seems crazy that we've chosen to be in the middle of it. If you can fly this route in six hours, isn't it madness to risk disaster by sailing it in six days? From above, this huge liner will be nothing more than a tiny white dot pushing out towards the heart of a vast, powerful ocean. I can't quite get my head around the fact that there's nothing to see in any direction. Nor will there be for nearly a week. This is my fifth morning on board. But it feels as if the real journey has only just begun.

Romeo is arranging some fresh flowers when I get to the clinic and the day's papers are already fanned out on our coffee table.

'So how did yesterday afternoon go?' I ask Eileen when I poke my head around her door to say hello.

She looks at a sheet of paper on her desk. 'Sleepy little Madeira brought us three sprained ankles, a badly grazed forearm, two cut foreheads, a broken toe and an awful lot of very badly bruised behinds.'

'Try saying that last one when you've had a few,' Kiri calls out from her desk next door.

Eileen pretends not to have heard. 'That's not too bad, to be honest. We've got a few of them coming back this morning for follow-up checks but the real issue today is set to be the weather.'

'A little boisterous, I gather.'

'Exactly. We'll carve through it without much of a problem but that won't stop people from worrying. There have been a few calls already and I think we'll get a lot more as the day wears on. It only takes one person to say they feel green for ten more to persuade themselves they feel the same. The first day of a big crossing is busy even if the water is as calm as a millpond. Once the rains come and the skies get dark we get even more people who want treatment, just in case. Edward will see all the passengers but as usual he'll pass some over to you if he's overwhelmed. If any crew members are feeling a bit shaky then they'll be coming in to see you as well.'

'What if I'm feeling a bit shaky?'

'You're not allowed to. Didn't you read your contract?'

None of my early patients are having trouble with the stormy seas. My first is a very chatty Bulgarian crew member. He's convinced he's got a brain tumour but in fact has nothing more than a head cold. He needs reassurance and a long explanation of why he doesn't need antibiotics, let alone surgery. I need five minutes to finish off his notes and log the case as a possible, but unlikely, source of a new contagion. Next up I see one of the linen-keepers who is getting some hefty migraines. I've got two more crew members waiting when Eileen pops in to say they both need to be bounced back in the queue as a passenger has come in and guests always take priority. He's one of the people who had an accident on one of yesterday's excursions. He looks perfectly well when he walks in. Then he takes off his baseball cap and gives me a big smile.

'Good heavens, Mr Drew. I'm not sure what to focus on first.' He's not got a lot of hair and has a long, ugly gash running right across the back of his head. He's also lost a tooth right at the front of his mouth. 'Did you do these two simultaneously?' I ask. I can't envisage an incident that could harm him from both angles at the same time. But if you've ever worked in A&E you know that nothing's impossible.

'I had a run of bad luck,' he says in a soft, West Country accent. 'I hadn't realised I was sitting under one of the television sets on the tour bus. It did the damage when I stood up to get my bag at the end of the trip. That young Australian lady stitched me back together but said I should come back today to check it's healing properly.'

'And the tooth?'

'A giant bar of Toblerone from the Duty Free shop. I only bought it because it was the largest one I'd ever seen. I thought the grandkids might like a picture of me trying to eat it. But when I tried to break off a chunk it took half my front tooth with it. That was just before dinner last night. I'm not sure how the waitresses managed to serve soup in these seas but I'm very pleased that they did.'

I lean in a bit as he holds his jaw still closer. It looks as if the tooth sliced almost exactly in half. Slight lines of shadow in the same position on his other front teeth suggest he's had weaknesses there all his life.

'Does it hurt?' I ask.

'Not at all. I've always had strange teeth. This has happened before and I never feel a thing. Every time they just rebuild the thing with enamel and remind me not to eat apples without cutting them up first.'

'Now you need to add chocolate bars to the danger list. Bad luck.' I lean back against my desk as the ship gives a very slight roll. It's barely noticeable but it's definitely there. 'Well, if it doesn't hurt and you don't mind looking like you've been in a fight, then I suggest you put up with it till we find a dentist in Barbados. We're expecting some rough seas in the next few hours and I doubt you want me trying my hand at root canal work when we hit them. Now, let me take a look at your head wound while I've still got my sea legs.'

The first of the rains hit when Dakila and I meet up for lunch in one of the passenger restaurants. 'I think we're in for quite a show,' he says, picking a table next to a floor-to-ceiling window. He's right. Ten minutes later it's like lunching in a car wash – and it's clearly putting a lot of people off their food.

'It's all in the mind,' Dakila says as we watch the first few passengers leave their tables early. The water in the glasses on our table is as still as ever. No-one's cutlery is falling to the floor. But it's hard to avoid the thought that it should be – especially when the first flashes of lightening start to cut through the clouds.

'It's terribly exciting, isn't it?' one passenger says as she steps towards the window to watch the spectacle. Not everyone shares her enthusiasm. The room is half empty by the time Dakila and I finish our meal.

'Maybe we should head downstairs and check everything is OK,' he says. 'Passengers never leave a restaurant without good reason. They're probably queuing up for their jabs as we speak.'

When we arrive the first person we see is Edward – and he seems to be in a spectacularly good mood. Bad seas or maritime crises clearly bring out the best in him. 'Ginger and ganja – that's what we ought to prescribe,' he's telling a disapproving Eileen as we walk through the doors. 'Ginger and ganja for the First Class passengers. Sea water and ketchup for Second Class. Fried pork and garlic for the rest.'

'Fried pork and garlic?'

'The stuff of maritime legend. A time-honoured cure for seasickness. As, incidentally, are both morphine and cocaine.'

'Well, in the absence of full clinical trials I suggest we stick to our usual pills and injections,' says Eileen tartly. She turns to me. 'Doctor MacFarlane, perhaps we could talk you through a few more of our emergency response protocols before everyone gets completely carried away?'

Edward interrupts before she can begin. 'Whether it is seasickness, food poisoning or the measles, our job is to protect the vast majority of the passengers and crew,' he declares. 'We have limitless power to stop illness from spreading. If someone has a stomach bug I have no hesitation in confining them to their cabin for two days. Four if I can't stand the sight of them.'

Eileen tries to speak but Edward is having none of it. 'I think the young doctor needs to be warned about the fakes,' he booms.

'Fakes?'

'Seasickness is a very convenient illness. You'll notice that the people who suffer the most are the ones who were in the bar knocking back mojitos at 2am the previous night. You'll also see that these people never have hangovers. They come to us with sore heads in the morning because they're prone to "migraines". They feel sick when they wake up because of the air-conditioning in their staterooms, not because of all the vintage port they consumed at midnight. Aren't I right, Eileen?'

She grudgingly admits that he is. 'Self-diagnosis for seasickness is a bit of a problem but most fit and healthy people can cope with the medication even if they don't really need it,' she says. 'You'll have to use your own discretion with every patient you see. But always remember that with paying passengers diplomacy is the better part of valour.' The phone rings at Eileen's desk and she turns to answer it.

'You'll also want to watch out for the Italian waiters,' booms Edward in his version of a stage whisper. 'If you are lucky then they will be your light relief on this stormy afternoon.' I'm about to ask him what he means when Eileen hangs up the phone and stops me.

'That's the first two passengers on their way down for some medication. I think clinic will have to start early,' she says. The phone rings again almost immediately and there's a knock on the Centre door as she picks it up. I'm not sure if I'm just getting carried away by all the excitement or if the floor really is moving a little as I walk across the waiting area to open it. Two worried-looking passengers are standing outside clutching plastic bags. Another is getting out of the lift and heading our way.

'Come in, come in and welcome all!' Edward booms from my left. 'Let the madness begin!'

The afternoon passes in a bit of a blur. There are moments when the phone seems to ring constantly and it's standing room only in the waiting area. Then the crowds thin and the five of us are left sitting around and feeling like lemons.

'You know the other thing we should prescribe?' Kiri says in one quiet patch as Edward starts extolling yet another of his ancient mariner seasickness cures. 'A couple of hours in the casino. Kieran says it's designed to be the most stable room on the ship. They don't want to compromise the roulette ball. Nor do they want any seasick passengers heading back to their cabins and interrupting a losing streak. If you're feeling queasy on board then Kieran reckons the casino is the only place to be.'

Eileen and Dakila have headed out to grab a bite to eat when the first injury is called in. Edward takes charge and treats a lady who lost her balance in the shopping galleria, stumbled and cut her forehead on a display table. Kiri and I have two sprained ankles to strap up and I see a Malaysian laundry-worker who bent down to pick up a bag of towels and stood up without realising that the door to one of the vast tumble driers had come open above him. The cut is not particularly deep and won't need stitches so I just glue the edges back together. It will heal itself in no time and, if the man looks pleased when I tell him he's able to go back to work, he's ecstatic when I say he doesn't need to come back for a follow-up appointment. The laundry is clearly one of those tough places where time off is barely tolerated, even in a medical emergency. The only people I don't see are Italian crewmembers. I'm starting to wonder if Edward was winding me up about them when the name Francesco Christofaro pops up on my computer screen. The file says he's a waiter in the best of our fine dining restaurants. I pop outside my room to call him in. Edward and Eileen are standing by the reception desk as I do so. He gives me a big comedy wink and a thumbs up sign. She looks at him the way a mother might look at a naughty child. I'm not sure who makes me smile the most as I lead Francisco into my room to see what all the fuss is about.

'Doctor, I am dying,' he declares, looking perfectly well. He's twenty eight, tall, slim and very deeply tanned. 'I have a problem inside my head. I cannot work and I cannot sleep or eat or drink. I am dying.' He throws himself down into the chair next to my desk and looks around the room with interest. 'Nice computer. You have the internet?' he asks.

'Yes I do. So, tell me more about how you're feeling.'

'We don't have the internet anywhere. Only in the managers' offices. It's not fair. We stand in line for hours, days, to use it in the crew rooms.'

'You feel as if you're dying, you say? You have a problem with your head?'

'Always I am waiting to use the internet.' He looks around the room again then points at the rechargeable ophthalmoscope mounted on the opposite wall. 'What is that for? I like that. What does it do?'

'Francesco I need to hear about why you're here. There are lots of other patients outside as you'll have seen. What is it that's troubling you?'

'I don't know this phrase, "troubling you".'

'What's the matter with you, Francesco? Why are you here?'

He lets out a long, extravagant sigh. 'I am dying. I know that I am. Maybe it will be slow. Maybe it will be fast. There is a problem in my head. There is nothing that you can do.'

'Is there anything that you'd like me to do? Can you tell me what it is that you're feeling?' He starts to talk and it is, of course, very mild seasickness. Francesco saw a passenger looking a bit pale just before breakfast this morning. He saw himself in a mirror in a lift and thought he looked the same. He convinced himself he could feel the ship rise and fall as he stood in the corridor. Now he thinks it will kill him.

'Francesco, would you like me to give you some seasickness pills to make you feel better? They'll help you though this.'

He slumps back in his chair, a picture of melodramatic despair and disgust. 'Seasickness pills? I need more than that. They will do nothing to help me.'

'We have an injection we can give as an alternative.'

Francesco perks up immediately. 'An injection? You think I need an injection?'

He looks so thrilled that I can't resist. 'You'll probably need a whole course of injections, Francesco. We'll have to watch over you very carefully. But if we start with one injection today then I think you'll start to see some improvements straight away.'

'A whole course of injections,' he says dreamily. 'I told you I was ill.'

The fun continues when I unveil the tiny, inch-long needle for the jab. Francisco could hardly be more terrified – or more excited. He's practically hyperventilating as I start to pull the needle out of its paper packet. He physically flinches and starts muttering a series of prayers just before I make the jab. Big, wet tears of relief and pride start to flow as soon as the deed has been done.

'Well done, Francesco, that's you all sorted,' I say. I'm about to ask him if he needs a plaster when I stop myself. Of course Francesco needs a plaster. By the way he's looking at the equipment in the corner of my room I think he's actually angling for a wheelchair. In the end he walks out of the Medical Centre his arm in a sling, his head held high and a look of proud martyrdom on his face.

'One very satisfied and very entertaining customer,' I tell Edward as we watch him leave.

'I told you the Italian waiters are good value,' he says with delight. 'You wait till one of them has a nose bleed. It's pandemonium.'

# CHAPTER NINE

Evening surgery overruns by about an hour, not least because Francesco has clearly told his colleagues how much fun he's had and sends several more down for the same treatment. Jasmina drops by as well. She's looking a bit pale and barely smiles when Kiri calls out to ask if she prefers morning sickness to seasickness.

'I've got myself in a bit of a state,' she says when my consulting room door is closed. 'My head's been all over the place. You know how happy I was at first. I was going to enjoy every minute of this pregnancy. But I don't think I can. Should I really carry on working? We do two shows a night. We have rehearsals for our next productions every afternoon. I signed up to do some private dance classes for passengers as well. It's too much, isn't it? I know I'm putting the baby at risk.'

I try to reassure her. We run through all the statistics. I remind her about the millions of women who work right through pregnancies, often in the toughest of jobs. I talk her through how well the body is designed to cope with all the challenges it faces. I suggest a chat with Eileen or any other mums on board. But basically I just want to come up with as many ways as possible to put her mind at rest.

'I know it's easier said than done, Jasmina, but you'll be so much better off if you can relax again.'

She promises to try. But her eyes are still full of worry when she leaves.

Eileen looks irritable rather than worried when my clinic is over and I finally pop by to say goodnight. She has a pile of paperwork in front of her and the reading light on her desk is casting deep shadows under her eyes. She shakes her head when I ask if I can help with anything.

'Just go off and have a good night's sleep,' she says. 'We're through the worst of the weather and I'll be finished with this soon. I'll only call you if there's an emergency.'

She turns out to be right about the weather. The clouds lift, the rains stop and the waters calm overnight. The waves are a brighter blue and there's even some weak sunshine on my balcony when I climb out of bed in the morning. Albert brings me breakfast and I eat it while flicking between the on-board Cruise TV and some news channels. The rest of the world feels a long way away as the headlines are being read out. I send Cassie a quick email and dig my gym kit out. I've not done any exercise for over a week and I'm hoping to check out the spa later in the day.

'Morning Eileen,' I say when I get to the Medical Centre. Then I do a bit of a double take. She's still sitting at her desk with her reading light on. She's still got a pile of papers in front of her. As she's in her usual uniform it feels as if the past ten hours never happened. 'You did leave last night, didn't you?' I ask. 'Please tell me you didn't sit there filling out insurance forms till dawn.'

'Of course I didn't,' she says sharply. I do another double take. It's the first time I've heard her snap at anyone. I certainly hoped she'd never do so at me.

'Is everything OK?'

'Everything's fine. We're just busy,' she says. But we're not. There's a good fifteen minutes until any patients are likely to arrive. Edward isn't in yet, Kiri has only just walked in behind me and Dakila is leaning back in his chair reading the day's newspaper front pages. Even Romeo looks relaxed. He's singing away quietly to himself as he packs up his cleaning cart and heads off to his next job.

Dressing a laceration on a very smelly crew member's shin soon puts Eileen's odd mood out of my mind.

'I walked into one of the metal boxes. It was silver. That is why I didn't see it,' he says in a thick Slavic accent. I nod as if this makes perfect sense and try not to breathe in until he's left.

After he's gone I see the usual mix of runny noses and runny tummies and try to keep on top of my paperwork. After clinic I then head down a companion way to the bowels of the ship. There's a windowless room below the water line where I give a half-hour health-and-safety lecture to a group of wiped-out room stewards. I try to put in a few jokes to keep them interested and they dutifully smile at each punchline. But overall they could barely be less interested if they tried.

At lunchtime Edward and I are both in our formal uniforms hosting tables at a 'meet and eat' for some of the ship's most loyal passengers. Mrs Coates waves from her seat at the Chief Engineer's table while two other familiar faces greet me when I find my way to my spot.

'This is Iris Knightly and this is her husband Ronald,' I tell the other guests when I do the introductions. 'But to me they will always be Mrs Stingray and Mr Zip Wire. Perhaps I should leave it to them to explain why.'

I give up on the gym when lunch in the ballroom drifts into afternoon tea in the Palm Court. If I didn't have an evening clinic I imagine I'd be joining everyone for pre-dinner cocktails in the Long Bar as well. In a piece of spectacularly bad timing Mrs Coates is joining the group just as I get up to leave. It means that for the second time in less than a week a seventy-eight-year-old lady with her arm in plaster gets to mouth the word 'lightweight' at me in a bar. That's not something I plan to mention in any of my emails home.

Eileen hasn't cheered up much by the time we get ready for evening clinic – but at least she tells me it's nothing to do with me.

'I think I've got the mid-cruise blues two months too early,' she says as I wait for my first patient. 'If you go to the Crew Bar later on you might just find me crying into my drink.'

I take that as an invitation so I head to the bar after dinner. Eileen's sitting in a corner with some of the chefs. She looks far happier than I'd expected and calls me over to join them.

'This is so much more fun than the stuffy old Officers' Bar. The boys here are being very naughty indeed,' she says. 'You'll never guess how they make the Dover sole last a lot longer than it should.'

The next hour or so flies by in a rush of stories and scams. Eileen laughs out loud at most of them. At the start of the trip she said she barely drinks, even when she's officially off duty. It's quite fun to see that she seems to have forgotten that tonight.

'Perhaps just the one more,' she says with a naughty smile as midnight strikes and one of the sous chefs heads back to the bar.

'You seem in a better mood,' I shout across the din.

'I'm not, I'm just hiding it better,' she replies.

'Well if I can help with anything just let me know.'

She's saying thank you when our new drinks are handed around. The sous-chef, a Frenchman called Nicolas, starts a wildly improbable story about one of the pastry chefs being caught in a compromising position with a crate of pineapples. I'm enjoying talking about something other than medicine when chanting begins in the karaoke room behind the bar.

'It must be penalties,' Nicolas says, looking up for the football on the TV screens above us. There isn't any. 'Oh dear,' Nicolas says. He looks across at Eileen and me as the chanting get louder. 'I think you two might be going back to work. It sounds to me as if there's going to be a fight.'

Nothing sobers you up like the sight of blood. And there's already a lot of it by the time Eileen and I push our way through the crowd to the back of the bar.

The battle was short but vicious. Drinks in the Crew Bar are all served in plastic cups but beer bottles make decent weapons. Table edges can do a lot of damage as well – as one of the men discovered when he got thrown against a table from across the room.

'It's a good job that the chairs are screwed to the ground,' Eileen says as two groups of people try to keep the fighters apart.

Security are in the bar within minutes and, after taking a

quick look at the combatants and the people who got caught in the crossfire, Eileen puts a call through to Edward.

'He'll meet us down at the Centre in five minutes,' she says. 'If he gets a choice he says he always prefers to treat the winner.'

As it turns out neither man can really claim that title. Both of them are in a bad way. Eileen and I narrowly beat Edward to the Centre and I take the one who needs attention first: the one whose face took the full force of the beer bottle. Someone handed him what looks like a T-shirt and he's holding it to his head as he's led into the Crew Ward. His clothes are soaked with beer and blood and he reeks of alcohol, cigarettes and late nights.

'OK, you're Oskar Hoxha, right? Let me take a look at what's happened to you. I'm going to pull some of this cloth away from your face. It's going to hurt. Are you ready?' I don't get much of a response. Oskar is too drunk, too angry and too wired to sit still. He's rocking violently on the edge of the bed. He swears constantly – or least I assume that's what he's doing. My Albanian isn't exactly extensive and this man's voice is so slurred that I doubt his own mother would be able to make out more than one word in four. 'OK, here goes, Oskar. Take a deep breath for me.'

I put one hand on the back of his neck and pull the shirt off his face with the other. He lets out a yell of pain and swings his right fist at my face.

'Not so fast mate,' I say as I grab it. The black eye I got from Paco has only just faded. I don't want to get another one quite so soon. 'That's the last time you do that, right? I'm here to help you, sir. I've got a feeling that you're going to need me.'

His wounds are extensive and deep. There's one main gash running from his mouth up to his cheekbone and there are several other smaller cuts on his face and forehead. The only good news is that the bottle seems to have missed his eyes. If we were on land I'd probably want him run through a CT scanner to check for head injuries. As that's not an option I just shine a light into each eye to check his pupil responses. They look OK and his other vital signs are fine so I get ready to move on.

I use gauze swabs to staunch the bleeding and clean up the dried blood. I shave part of his skull where the cuts go beyond the hairline. Then I check inside his mouth for other injuries. That doesn't turn out to be particularly pleasant. The poor sod seems to have an awful lot of black, rotten teeth but at least none of them appear to have become collateral damage of the night's events.

'OK, Oskar, we're ready for the big one now.' It's a wound that runs from his mouth to his cheekbone and it's not going to be easy. Any wound that crosses the line between the lips and the skin of the face is particularly tricky to stitch. However well you do it you're pretty much certain to leave a scar. Most of the time you're also going to spoil your patient's smile.

The voice of one of my Medical School professors rings out in my head as I pick a stitching pack off the tray Eileen has laid out for me. 'I can just about darn a hole in my socks but if I were patching up my finest dinner jacket I'd give the job to a proper tailor,' he would say. 'Only stitch simple wounds that won't show. If it's more complex and the world's going to see it then call in a plastic surgeon.'

'Sorry mate,' I say to Oskar in a whisper I'm pretty sure he can't understand. 'We don't have a plastic surgeon and I can't even darn socks. Do you feel lucky?'

I change my gloves and lay out a sterile stitching and suture pack. Then I draw up some local anaesthetic. It's got to go right into the edges of the wound and I'm ready for Oskar to hit the roof when the needle enters his flesh. He barely even moves. He's either a lot drunker than I thought or he's been through this so many times he knew what to expect.

'You're doing OK, mate. Now we've got the anaesthetic in I'm just going to check there's nothing in there we need to worry about,' I say, exploring the wound with a metal probe. There is one small piece of glass lodged deep in his cheek and I gradually ease it out with tweezers. 'That would have given you a nasty infection if it had stayed there but I don't expect you'll be thanking me,' I say.

He isn't. He groans every now and then but apart from that he totally ignores me. I get the needle and sutures out of their sterile packs and start to close the wound. I begin with one tiny stitch, then another, then another. I'm working deep in the wound, slowly drawing all the edges together. Every few moments I step back, not to admire my handiwork but to check everything is lining up the way it should do. Normally Oskar takes this as his cue to shake himself down like a dog climbing out of a river. Every few moments he also lets out a truly noxious belch.

'OK, that was a nasty one, Oskar. Let's try and hold them in and stay still from now on, right?'

I stitch away and the warmth of the room soon helps send Oskar to sleep. Between snores I spend a lot of time on the skin around his lip but I don't focus quite so much on the fleshier skin of his cheek. A couple of times I do wonder if any of it is worthwhile. He's already got more than his fair share of scars on his face and neck. One more won't make much difference. I also wonder how grateful he'll be for me spending all this time trying to save his smile. He doesn't strike me as the kind of person who uses it a lot.

When I'm finished I stand back and take in the full picture. It's not perfect but I doubt I could have done better on land. Oskar wakes up and his latest burp reminds me what I need to do next.

'OK, you know how this works, right? Blow in here, as hard as you can.' The breathalyser comes up with its very predictable result and I turn around to log it on the incident file for the security staff. At that point I realise my patient and I are no longer alone. Edward is standing in the doorway. He gives me a smile.

'All sorted, dear boy?' He pulls his green plastic apron over his head and pats down his hair. He's got some blood on his right sleeve and flecks of what looks like vomit on his shoulder. Somehow he still manages to look smart enough for the Captain's dinner table.

'All sorted.'

I give the nearest security man a nod. He wants to speak to Oskar the moment I'm done, but I doubt he's going to get much sense out of him.

'It was about a girl, the way it always is,' Edward says as we step into his room. 'She was new on in Southampton. My patient says he saw her first. Yours decided to cut in on him. The young lady's thoughts on the subject are, as yet, unknown.'

'How bad was your man?'

'A couple of broken ribs and a nasty gash on the back of his head from the table.' He gives me more details of the man's injuries, as well as those of some of the crew who tried to pull the two fighters apart. I look up as a second security officer goes into the Crew Ward to speak to Oskar.

'So what's going to happen now?' I ask Edward. This is the first time I've really seen our security staff in action. Apparently they're all ex-military and a lot of them are former Ghurkhas. They've also got a lot of power at their disposal. If they want you locked up then you're locked up. If they want you off the ship then it's goodbye.

'Oh, they'll be given the chance to blame everything on each other and I dare say they'll get the six o'clock knock when we get to Barbados.'

'The six o'clock knock?'

'They'll be escorted off the ship and left to find their own way home. In the good old days it happened at dawn. With these two it will happen as soon as we dock in Bridgetown.'

'Will they be locked up until then?'

'I'd imagine so, dear boy. They'll probably want to wreak some kind of revenge as soon as they realize their little adventure on the high seas is about to end. The captain doesn't want disaffected, soon-to-be-former employees running loose on the premises. They'll be confined to their cabins. Or if the boys in blue deem them to be particularly unpleasant characters they'll have their belts and bootlaces taken from them and they'll be held down below.'

The boys in blue – who are in fact wearing uniforms very like our own – lead our patients out of the Medical Centre. Eileen and Dakila are waiting on the sofa in the reception area. Edward thanks them for jobs well done and tells them to head back to their cabins for the night. 'War has been averted once again,' he says when security have led Oskar and his fellow combatant away and the Centre is quiet. 'It's about time we had a little nightcap. If you'll indulge me I'd love to have a chat.'

'To peace in our time,' says Edward, getting a bottle out of a drawer in his office and pouring me a drink. 'Now, would you like to hear about the first time I stitched up a crew member's face after an incident in a bar?'

I sit back without speaking. I've got a feeling it's a rhetorical question and that I'm going to enjoy hearing the answer. I'm right on both counts.

'It was 1962. Possibly '63. Or thereabouts. We were on the original Queen Mary. It was the finest of the fine. Southampton to New York was eight days of absolute luxury. In those days you had to be someone to cruise. Only the crew had tattoos back then. None of the officers, and certainly none of the guests. Anyway, one of our favourite passengers was the heiress to a great New York shopping empire. She was in her sixties but could have passed for thirty two. I doubt she had eaten a thing in twenty years. She had been so thin for so long that her skin was almost transparent. She had a stateroom for herself, one for her gowns and jewellery, one for her maid and one for her new, improbably young and very unsuitable husband.

'Her diamonds were quite extraordinary. How she could lift her hand to drink champagne with so few muscles and so much weight on her fingers I will never know. But drink she did. I think the only calories she consumed came courtesy of Moët and Chandon.' Edward gives one of his favourite 'those were the days' sighs. 'It was Tango Night in the First Class ballroom. We had a team of Latin dance-instructors, though every guest knew how to dance back then. By all accounts our aged heiress whirled around the floor all night. She dipped and pirouetted like a girl a quarter of her age. Then, at the end of one dance, she threw back her hand in dramatic, flamboyant fashion. Some say she struck a cocktail waitress in the face with her hand and slashed her cheek with the ring. Others say the ring slipped over a nonexistent knuckle and flew through the room before it hit the waitress and did the same damage. Either way there was a great deal of blood and confusion. The ring was recovered and the wound required stitches. The poor girl was then removed from duty till her wounds healed to protect the sensitivities of the guests.'

'That's a little different to tonight's little performance,' I venture.

'Well that isn't all. Two days later our heiress summoned the waitress to her stateroom. The young lady never said a word about the meeting, but her colleagues said she was smiling when she got back to her cabin. She stayed smiling for the next three days. She handed in her notice and left the ship in New York. No-one ever saw or heard from her again. But rumour has it she opened a cosmetics shop in lower Manhattan and ended up a very rich lady in her own right. That, dear boy, is how a bar brawl ought to be. Not a battle fought between two Neanderthal thugs who are too drunk to know they've even been hurt. Top up, my dear chap?'

I pass over my glass. I'd forgotten how much I hate brandy.

'Now there is one other subject I should raise with you,' Edward says when he's put the bottle away. 'Have you spoken to the marvellous Eileen this evening?'

I love the fact that nothing seems to get past him. 'We've not talked about anything in particular,' I say. 'Why?'

'She's a quite remarkable woman. Her husband passed away

many years ago. She sees too little of her grown-up children so she dedicates herself to us. Have you seen her cabin?'

'No.'

'You'll be amazed by it. Most people bring suitcases of clothes. Eileen brings home furnishings. Her room is unique. She has her own sheets on the bed, her own pictures on the walls. We are her family while we are at sea, Benjamin. And everyone knows that families can sometimes be a great disappointment.'

'Has one of us done something wrong? If it's me I hope she'll say so. What exactly has happened?'

Edward drains his glass and stands up. 'It most certainly isn't you, dear boy. Eileen likes and trusts you a great deal. She will tell you in her own good time. When she does I will rely on you to be kind.'

# CHAPTER TEN

A beautiful woman with the best figure and the longest eyelashes I have ever seen is my first patient the following morning.

'I'm a little bit embarrassed but I think I made a bit of a mistake last night,' she says when I ask how I can help.

'A mistake?'

'With a guy. I should be old enough and wise enough to take precautions but for some reason I didn't. Today I think I ought to do something about it. We can get the morning after pill on board, can't we? It will be too late by the time we get to Barbados.'

I check her blood pressure, ask her a few more questions, talk through the way the medication works, then get her the tablets she needs.

'There's nothing else you need to talk about – sexually transmitted infections, anything like that?'

Monique gives a strange smile. 'That's one thing I don't need to worry about. You'll find out why if you meet the man in question – he makes very sure he's clean.' I'm about to run through the usual speech about not judging things by appearance, then I stop. Monique is a thirty-four-year-old woman who clearly knows what she is doing.

'Come back and see us if you change your mind. Or just stop me if you see me walking around,' I say.

She smiles and thanks me as she gets up to leave. 'I work up on the reception in the health spa, by the way,' she says at the door. 'How come you haven't been up to see us yet?'

I tell her the truth. 'I've tried to get to the gym almost every day since I got on board. But something always gets in the way.'

'Well don't leave it too much longer. Did you hear about "Sweet Elegance" on our last cruise?'

'No.'

'They were one of the dance groups. They ate so much on their eight week residency they changed their own posters to read "Sweet Elephants" by the time they got off. Don't let that happen to you.'

I stick to the salad bar at lunchtime and vow that today will be the day I get to the gym.

It isn't.

I'm sending an email when my pager goes off. Eileen was doing paperwork in the surgery out-of-hours when a guest turned up. She got spotted, let him in for a quick chat and can't now get rid of him. I head down to help – and it takes me twenty-five minutes to persuade the man that the cancerous growth he thinks he's got on his hand is, in fact, a perfectly harmless liver spot. After that I've got a bit of personal business to do. Someone in the accounts department needs my bank details again, which I take as a sign that I must at least be getting paid.

Their offices seem a bit strange. They're full of desks,

computers, filing cabinets and clerical staff just like any other office. Everyone's wearing ordinary office clothes and works nine-to-five. But they do it all on a cruise ship that is constantly moving around the globe. I don't know why, but it all seems distinctly odd – though I'm sure they would probably say the same about all of us in the Medical Centre.

When I've finished in that part of the ship it's time for evening surgery. Afterwards we split up for dinner. Edward and Eileen are eating in the Officers' Dining Room, Kiri is eating with Kieran and his casino colleagues and I'm due to be joining Dakila and a few of his friends from the entertainment staff. Unfortunately I don't make it. It seems that way above us in one of the passenger restaurants a guest with a strawberry allergy has decided she likes the look of the strawberry gateau. I get the call two minutes after her head hits the carpet.

'Sir, please, I need to get past you. Can I get through please? I'm the doctor.' The curse of big restaurants is that there are an awful lot of people to crowd around if something goes wrong. Tonight a worryingly large group has amassed around my patient. I step on one man's toes and apologise fleetingly to a lady in a tight, strapless dress when I accidentally swing my medical bag at her head as I squeeze past.

'OK, can someone tell me what's going on?' About five people all start talking at once. Two are retired doctors who launch into very long-winded explanations. In truth, I didn't really need to ask. There's a well-dressed middle-aged lady lying on her side. Her lips have swollen up like some over-collagened Hollywood star. Her eyes are so puffed up she can barely see. Her arms are covered in a red, blotchy rash and her breath is shallow and wheezy. It's a textbook case of anaphylactic shock.

'She's my friend and we got her in the recovery position. She's breathing. Her name is Jennifer and we both used to be in St John Ambulance,' says a matronly lady, with a very worried face.

'You've done great, thank you,' I say, pushing her aside ever so slightly. 'Jennifer I'm going to help you now. I'm assuming you've had something like this before? Just lie back and I'll sort this out as fast as I can.' She peers at me out of the slits of her eyes with what looks like gratitude and carries on gasping for breath. I start off feeling for a pulse in her neck. It's present but weak. Now we need medication and oxygen.

'Can I get some room please?' I ask one of the maître d's who is hovering at the lady's feet, no doubt worrying what effect all this drama may have on his second sitting.

He ushers most of the people back to their tables as I reach into my bag for a preloaded syringe of adrenaline. Fortunately the patient's dress is slashed right up to her thigh and that's a great place for the jab. I swab a patch of skin with alcohol, get the needle in her leg muscle and depress the plunger. Job done I pull a mask over her face and connect it to the small portable oxygen cylinder in my bag. I'm tightening a tourniquet around her forearm and I'm about to insert a cannula in the back of her hand for the antihistamine when Dakila arrives with a rapid response trolley.

'Bang on cue,' I say. We do the lift and get our patient on board. I give the antihistamine while he switches the oxygen mask to the bigger cylinder on the trolley. 'OK, time to roll,'

I say. 'Are you feeling OK, Jennifer?' She nods, bravely. Tear stains have cut though her make-up and she looks desperately sad.

'Excuse me, doctor, but is she going to be all right?' A tall, distinguished man in a dinner jacket is at my side.

'We're taking her down to the Medical Centre now but I'm not anticipating any problems. And you are?'

'I'm her husband. My name is Harrison. Professor Harrison.'

'Well do please come down with us and I can explain everything as we walk.'

His hand is on my shoulder again. His right foot stops the trolley. 'Well, doctor, as long as you're sure she's going to be all right, I think I may just stay where I am. We're dining with friends, you know, and we've got a marvellous table. We'd only just begun dessert and there's an excellent harpist playing this evening. I'll try to pop down later, but I'm sure you'll let me know if there are any problems.' He moves his foot and we push his wife's stretcher out of the restaurant. We leave to the sound of a harp.

A frisson of excitement follows us as we run the trolley through the passenger corridors and down to the Medical Centre. There's a huge amount of entertainment on this ship already – but I can see why this ups the ante. It's live. It's real. We must look like an on-board episode of *ER*. A couple of passengers take photos. One swings a video camera in our direction. If we've got a connection this far out to sea then I've got a horrible feeling poor Jennifer might be on the internet before the night is out.

'OK, let's lift again.' Dakila and I get the patient off the trolley and on to the couch. He attaches a pulse oximeter, an automatic blood pressure cuff and ECG leads for her heart. The multicoloured displays on the monitors flick into life and it's clear that Jennifer's blood pressure is still stubbornly low.

'Can you set up a salbutamol nebuliser and run me through a bag of gelofusine?' I ask. If the *ER* fans from the corridor could hear us now I'm sure they'd love jargon-filled instructions like that.

'I'm already on it, boss,' Dakila says as he heads next door for the kit. I get a stethoscope to Jennifer's chest to listen to her lungs. It all sounds a bit wheezy but plenty of air seems to be moving around, which is a very good sign.

'You're going to be fine in just a little while,' I say. She tries to smile and mumbles something but her engorged lips leave it lost in translation.

Twenty minutes later she's clearly on the mend. Her blood pressure is picking up substantially, her pulse has slowed and her breathing is much easier. Her face and eyes are calmer and the dark blotches on her skin are starting to fade. I like treating anaphylaxis cases because the rapid improvements are always so rewarding.

'How are you feeling?' I ask, bringing six shiny, sugar-coated steroid tablets to her with a glass of water.

'I'm feeling much better, thank you so much,' she says. Then she puts up her hand at the pills. 'I can't possibly take them.'

'Look, it's just for a couple of days till you're over this,' I say. A lot of women are worried that steroids might make them pile on the pounds and I'm guessing Jennifer is the same, so I try and reassure her.

'It's not that, it's the colour. What flavour are they?'

I look down. The pills are all bright red. I can't stop myself from smiling. 'You know what, Jennifer? If a child asked me that question my automatic answer would be to say "strawberry flavour", so I can see your point. But I promise you they're not. It's just colouring. They are safe for you.'

'They still make me feel queasy,' she says as she swallows the tablets. We chat for a while and when she's clearly on the mend Dakila wheels her back to her stateroom. I file a report, finish of a bit of other paperwork and then lock up the Medical Centre. Her husband has yet to put in an appearance.

Monique is behind the desk when I finally get to the Health Centre the following afternoon.

'Welcome to our sanctuary in the sky,' she says. 'If the ship was a building then this would be something like the sixteenth floor. It's not a bad place to put a swimming pool, is it?'

It certainly isn't – and Monique asks a colleague to take over on the desk so she can show me around. We walk around the main cardio floor, which has three rows of trainers facing flat-screen TVs all playing news and sport rather than gangster videos that are always on at my old gym in London. There's a smaller weights area, two mid-sized studios for yoga, dance and all the other classes, sleek black locker rooms with stacks of fluffy white towels, a sauna, steam room and a set of treatment rooms leading off a zen-like, bamboo-filled corridor. The main pool is small but I love the idea of swimming in the fresh air while we're in the middle of the Atlantic.

'I can't believe it's taken me so long to get up here. One of the nurses showed me the crew gym on my second day and it was like something out of a prison film. I swear to God you'd not be surprised if Charles Bronson turned up and hacked someone to death in the free weights area. This place is brilliant. You'd pay a fortune to join it back at home,' I say as we head outside to what looks like the start of a running track.

I change the subject when I'm sure no-one can hear us. 'You took the medication? How are you feeling?' I ask.

She smiles. 'Medically speaking I'm as good as I can be. Yesterday was a bit rough but the cramps are settling now. Mentally I'm still feeling pretty foolish, to be honest. I should know better at my age. But there's something about the first and last few weeks of a new cruise that makes everyone go a little crazy. You'll find that out yourself once you've been doing this for a while.'

We walk a bit further then Monique stops. 'That's the man, by the way. That's Gavin,' she says. Ahead of us is a handsome man in his mid twenties. He's giving golf lesson and appears to be holding the waist of a well-groomed, fifty-something passenger just a little too closely. 'I still can't quite believe he went for me,' Monique says, almost to herself. I turn to her. There's no way I can let something like that go unchallenged.

'You're mad. Why wouldn't he go for you?'

Monique shakes her head and smiles. 'No, that's not what I meant. I don't know why he went for me because I'm crew. Well, I'm staff, to be precise. But either way I can't exactly give him anything.'

I think about that for a moment. 'I'm not sure I know what you mean.'

'Can you see his watch? It's a Patek Philippe that cost more than my car. That chain round his neck? It's from Tiffany. Even his sports socks are from Prada. You don't buy all those things on a personal trainer's salary. Have you got a safe in your cabin, doctor?'

'There's one in the wardrobe but I'm not using it.'

'Gavin is using his. If it's not full by the end of a cruise then he reckons he's slipping. See the woman he's up-close-and-personal with now? My friend Marcus does her hair every morning. He gets to see behind all the rich passengers' ears. This lady has had more facelifts than anyone else on board. That's what's got Gavin all excited. He's breathing in her perfume right now and all he can smell is money. You want to know what else we've found out? My other friend, Chanelle, works on the blackjack table in the Luxor Room. She works with the guy your nurse is going out with. Anyway, the woman's husband spends at least eight hours a day there. Yesterday he dropped a lot of cash so he could be served sandwiches at the table and keep on gambling right through dinner. Meanwhile the purser on the upper deck says his wife ate alone in their stateroom. First thing this morning she told Marcus she was bored. He recommended Gavin's golf lessons. She's booked a course of six.'

'You've got spies everywhere,' is all I can think of to say.

Monique smiles. 'They really needn't have bothered putting CCTV and webcams all over the ship. We're all watching each other twenty-four hours a day as it is.' She gives Gavin a discrete wave as his lesson ends. 'He'll be back as soon as he's walked her to the lift and I'll introduce you. He's a great guy. Just don't let him lead you astray. I don't know you very well but I get the feeling you're a decent bloke. I'll never forgive myself if I see you wearing a Rolex by the time we get back to the Med.'

I'm early for afternoon surgery and Eileen is on her own in the Medical Centre when I arrive. She's putting chocolate fudge brownies on a plate.

'I've paid the usual backhanders and have been allowed to spend a little time in the kitchen they use at the cookery school. I've decided to bake my way out of my bad mood. I'm making mochaccino ones tomorrow and I've got a recipe for almond and marshmallow swirls the day after that. I'll want to know which of them you all prefer,' she says.

I taste the first of them – and tell her they'll probably be hard to beat.

'So you're still feeling miserable?' I ask after a while. It's obvious that she's itching to talk.

'It's ridiculous but I can't snap out of it,' she says. 'It's also the tiniest and most trivial thing in the world. I'm embarrassed that it's affected me as much as it has.'

'Well tell me and I'll see if I can help.'

Eileen sighs. 'Kiri's resigned,' she says flatly. 'She and Kieran really are going to open up that bar together. But they're doing it in Australia not Dublin. She wants to break her contract when we get there. She's leaving in Sydney. She doesn't even want to finish the cruise.'

I'm not sure what to say for a moment. I really had expected something a bit more dramatic. 'Will the company let her go?' I ask in the end. I signed an awful lot of fierce papers about tours of duty when I joined. I didn't really read all of them, but I do remember getting the feeling that I was signing my life away.

'They won't make it easy but they can't really stop her. The last thing any ship needs is a nurse with a grudge. They'll find someone else in Sydney. Kiri will be with us for five more weeks then it's all over. We'll have lost her.'

Now I realise why this is such a big deal for Eileen. Edward had said we're her surrogate family. One of her favourites is fleeing the nest.

'I've really enjoyed the start of this trip,' she says softly. She's blinking a bit and my heart goes out to her. 'We've got to know each other really quickly and I felt as if we were a great group. I don't know why I allowed myself to think it could last forever. But Kiri's off, Edward's retiring and you're only doing this as a stopgap so you won't be staying either. This time next year it will just be me, the lonely old woman of the sea, trying to fit in with a new, ever-younger crowd and wondering where the years have gone.'

'You've got more friends on board than anyone else I've met. You'll never be lonely in this job. And anyway, I might surprise you by doing another tour myself.'

Eileen gives a weak smile. 'Well I hope you do. But I know that when you're young you need to follow your dreams. Kiri has reminded me of that. I'm happy for her. I'm thrilled for her, to be honest. But I'm furious as well. Does that make any sense?'

'It makes perfect sense. Is there any chance Kiri will change her mind?'

Eileen shakes her head. 'She's burned her bridges with the company now. Don't tell her I said this, but they wouldn't take her back if she was the last nurse in the world.'

We both look up as someone opens the clinic door. 'That might be her now,' Eileen says as she leaves my room. 'Don't tell her that I've told you what's going on. It's a cruise-ship secret rather than a real secret but I'd like to at least pretend that I've kept it.'

'Doctor, my husband has fallen over on the way to the bathroom and I can't get him back up.' It's just after eleven and the call has been patched through to my cabin. Most nights Eileen, Kiri or Dakila take it in turns to sift emergency calls before getting on to me. Tonight it's my turn. Kiri's gone to a birthday party with Kieran, Dakila's gone to see a TV magician in our main auditorium and I thought Eileen just deserved a break.

'Is he conscious? He's breathing OK?'

In the background I can hear a gruff male voice shout out: 'Tell the man I'm perfectly fine.'

'He's perfectly fine. He just can't get back up of the floor and I'm not strong enough to lift him.'

'I'll be with you in two minutes.' I've grab my medical bag and head out into the corridor.

'Thank you so much for coming doctor.' The patient's wife greets me at the door of a quite extraordinary room. It's twice, maybe even three times as large as mine. No wonder the man fell over on the way to the loo. He probably got exhausted halfway.

'Hello, sir, let me help you. You didn't injure yourself or hit your head when you fell?' He says no so I get him to his feet and we shuffle slowly across to the bathroom. It puts mine to shame as well. I stand outside while he does what he has to do. It's not the fastest process in the world.

'All done?' I ask when the door finally clicks open.

'A lot of fuss over nothing,' he growls as I support him back across the room to his bed. 'But thank you, all the same.' His wife presses a banknote in my hand as I leave and I pass it back. 'It's my pleasure. Call any time if you need any more help.'

My phone goes off again just before 1am. 'Is that the doctor who was here before?'

'Yes, is that Mrs Keswick?'

'Yes it is. Doctor I'm so sorry. But my husband has fallen over again.'

'This time I made it to the blasted lavatory but I couldn't make it back,' he tells me when I've manoeuvred him back to bed. I give him a smile. A man with prostate problems, poor mobility and one of the largest staterooms on the ship – I get the feeling this won't be the last night-time visit we pay to the Keswicks.

I try not to feel too hard done by at the size of my own cabin when I get back there. I've had a couple of new emails from Cassie and some friends so I take advantage of the latest extra hour we get crossing another time zone by replying.

'What time is it over there? Why aren't you in bed?' Camilla, one of my former colleagues, asks from her desk near Heathrow. My first reply goes into a lot of detail about our on-call system and the fact that with 2,000 passengers and 1,000 crew on board there's always someone needing help. Then I delete it and replace it with a much shorter message.

'Because I'm packing my swimming trunks and my sunscreen. In eight hours time I'm going to be on the beach in Barbados.'

# CHAPTER ELEVEN

Bridgetown is as noisy, colourful and crazy as I remember it. I spent four months working in a hospital on the island during my elective period at Medical School.

'You say you gonna come back and see us. But you doctors never do,' one of the nurses had grumbled at my leaving party. Six years on I'm hoping to find her and prove her wrong.

Dakila is spending the day with me and I'm looking forward to showing him around. But before the adventure can begin we've got a bit of work to do. We've agreed to help out the excursion team by guiding several hundred guests through the port terminal then on to the right buses for all the different island tours. I didn't think it would take very long, but I'd underestimated how keen cruise passengers are to shop. Whole swarms of passengers buy souvenirs within minutes of leaving the ship. They've got 'I love Barbados' shirts and hats before they've really cleared immigration. Many are so laden with bags they need us to open the luggage holds underneath the coaches. In the confusion several pile their packages in one coach then turn around and board a different one. Several more manage to lose their purchases in the short walk from stall to bus.

'It's always this chaotic. It's hard to believe that these are some of the richest and most successful people in the world,' Dakila says when the last tour group has finally departed.

We head slowly into town. 'I used to have breakfast in a little café that was just about here,' I say, standing outside an ice-blue shop that now seems to sell nothing but rum.

'Is breakfast what they call it nowadays?' Dakila asks.

We wander further into my old neighbourhood and I point out the supermarket where I bought my groceries – where my bill fell by half the day the vast lady on the till realised I was there for a while and could be charged 'local prices' rather than tourist ones. I then find the store that sold week-old British tabloids, the office where I lined up to ring home and the bar where I did, in fact, drink quite a lot of rum. Most of the time I'm pleased to say that Dakila seems genuinely interested.

'Maybe one day I will live somewhere rather than just pass through,' he says as we sip milk from a coconut in a café by the cricket ground. I ask him more about his family and get the usual mix of sadness and pride.

'When they are older my girls can live anywhere. Maybe one will work in your Harley Street, another at Cedar's Sinai, another in Paris or Rome. When I'm fifty I'll finally go home and settle down.'

He's describing his favourite places in the Philippines when we spot a familiar face across the street. It's Gavin, our golf instructor and roaming Casanova, who is with one of the shoppies – a good-looking Belgian girl called Chloe. They're carrying small rucksacks and look cool and relaxed in shorts and T-shirts. We're still in our whites after helping get all the guests off the ship and on to their buses. It makes us very easy to spot.

'Room for two more?' Gavin asks, pulling up two chairs. 'First rule of cruising is that you can never escape your colleagues on shore leave.'

'The shops aren't allowed to open when we're in port so I've got the whole day off,' Chloe says happily as they order a cold beer, a fruit punch and some jerk chicken. 'Gavin, meanwhile, has been dumped.'

'I have not been dumped. I have been put on hold. A certain someone is spending the day with her husband. Tomorrow it will be business as usual.' He's wearing a different watch, I notice. A leather strapped Breitling. Less showy for shore leave, perhaps. But still worth ten times more than any watch I've ever bought.

'So, what are your plans?' I ask.

'We're doing a hike in Bathsheba on the east coast. There's a route that the tour groups totally avoid and it's supposed to be breathtaking. It's wild and windswept out there. It's where the big waves roll in from the Atlantic. You're welcome to join us,' Chloe says, looking doubtfully at our uniforms and shiny white shoes.

'Don't rub it in. I'm still struggling with having to wear a uniform at all. I'm not sure I'm cut out to spend my life looking like an extra from *Top Gun*.'

Gavin puts his hand on my shoulder. 'Don't flatter yourself, pal. I'm thinking more the Village People,' he says.

Dividing up the bill and paying up takes a while – not least because the whole concept of having a bill and adding up cash is a bit of a shock after ten days at sea.

'You know the first tour I ever did was transatlantic to New York,' says Chloe. 'When we got there a friend and I went out for a real blow out dinner in Manhattan. We had wine, desert, coffee, the whole deal. Then we just left. I distinctly remember smiling at the maître d' and saying: "Thank you very much, it was delicious" as I walked by. But we'd totally forgotten that any money was supposed to change hands. They sent one of the waiters to run down the street after us. I was so embarrassed I went straight back to the ship and didn't leave again till we sailed. I've still never been to Bloomingdale's or climbed the Empire State Building.'

When the others have set out on their hike Dakila and I grab a ZR – one of the hundreds of packed minibuses that stop to pick-up and drop-off passengers wherever they need to go. As it bounces along past all the funny-looking, hairy fig trees towards my old hospital I start pointing out some of the other places I used to hang out. I'd loved working overseas. That was one reason why I'd not wanted to settle down and work in a traditional hospital straight after graduation. Today the heat and the smell of Barbados ensnare me again. There's the thrill of the unknown when you work abroad. You're coping with a new system and a new culture. You get an extra challenge and a new sense of achievement every day. I think about the A&E applications I'm planning to fill out later on in the cruise. I'm planning to put London as my first choice, Liverpool and Newcastle as second and third. There's a lot to like about each of those cities. But none of them will look or feel like this.

'Penny for your thoughts?' Dakila is looking at me.

'Oh, I'm just reminiscing. I'm trying to work out where I want to be in six months time. Part of me knows I should go home, but part of me can't help listening to Edward when he goes on about how good life is at sea.'

He gives me a rueful smile. 'Edward is a sly one. He looks like the perfect English gentleman – but he always gets his own way in the end. So my money is on you signing up for one more cruise. Then one more after that. Everyone says they're only doing this job for the experience. But everyone comes back for more. Cruising is like "Hotel California". We can check out any time we want – but we can never leave.' We're humming the song when we get to my old hospital.

'Check out the windows,' I tell Dakila. 'When I was here there was hardly any glass in them. It meant we had constant sea breezes in good weather and plenty of patients regained consciousness to find they had a lizard on the bed next to them. The nurses said they were a sign of good fortune and always tried to lure them back when they ran away.'

Nearly a decade on the windows look a bit more modern but the atmosphere is as relaxed as ever. A man on the enquiry desk greets me like an old friend when I say I used to work there – and there's almost a riot when we find my old nurse, Elizabeth.

'You came back to us! You came back to us! I always said you would keep your promise.' She dances around, hugging me, hugging Dakila, hugging all of her colleagues and then dragging us off to see the old staff rooms. To be honest, the more she talks the more I start to doubt whether she can really remember me at all. But she's clearly worked out that my arrival is good for at least half an hour off work, so I know she's genuinely pleased I've turned up. We drink tea ('All my English doctors drink tea!' Elizabeth says, beaming.) We shake dozens of hands and check out some of the new equipment. I meet a young, tired-looking American doctor from Phoenix, Arizona who is doing the same sort of short-term contract as I did. I seem to morph into Edward when I tell him to enjoy every minute because he'll be back in his old life before he knows it.

'Well, so much for nostalgia. Let's hit the beach,' I say when Elizabeth has finally been called back to work. Dakila and I step back out into the sunshine. We get a cab this time and head to the surfing beaches on the south coast. A reggae band is playing in a wooden hut and we have a couple of hours chilling out nearby. We've both got mobiles and pagers with us, but with three people back on board we're not expecting to get any calls.

'This is our first real break in ten days. Let your mind drift and pretend that Code Alpha calls and red norovirus alerts don't even exist,' Dakila advises.

We get back to port alongside the last of the tour buses. Most of the passengers have done full island tours or have been celebrity spotting on the ritzier west coast. Just ahead of us on the harbour side is Gavin, who seems to be limping slightly, and Chloe who is power walking ahead and chatting to some of the passengers.

'Did she tire you out?' I ask as we catch up with him. He starts to make another joke about the Village People but his heart doesn't seem to be in it. He also turns down the chance to join the rest of us on the crew deck to watch our departure.

'What's the matter with him?' I ask Chloe as we push through the crowds to find a spot by the railings.

'He's sulking because I beat him to the top.'

About twenty minutes later the ship is finally ready to sail.

'There's something special about leaving port, isn't there?' Dakila says as the hull begins to pull away from the harbour.

He's right. We don't seem to move more than an inch for ages. Then the gap between the ship and dry land suddenly becomes a chasm. Moments later we're free. The waters swirl around us as we find our new course. Tomorrow the adventure will continue somewhere else. This is one of the addictions of cruising. This is what Edward doesn't want me to give up.

They're holding a barbecue on the crew deck so Dakila and I grab some food and watch the sky get dark. It's well past eight when I look at my watch.

'Clinic's just finished. Shall we head down to see if they missed us,' I ask.

Dakila smiles. 'It's impossible to forget about that place isn't it? They've probably only had to treat a bit of sunburn and some sandfly bites but we still can't stay away.' He's trying to wind me up by humming "Hotel California" again when the lift gets to our floor. He stops as we step into the corridor. Eileen is standing, grim-faced, by the Medical Centre door. It's obvious that something serious has happened.

'We've just had an emergency call,' she says as we approach. 'Kiri's gone to collect her with two of the porters. It's Jasmina.'

# CHAPTER TWELVE

'She had severe abdominal pains in the late afternoon, then collapsed when she got back to her cabin after rehearsals. She's weak and she sounds scared,' Eileen says as I wash my hands at the nursing station.

'Can we turn the ship around if we have to?'

'We can, or we can evacuate her if it's serious. But I don't want it to be. Jasmina needs this baby. I want this to be a false alarm.'

'They're here.' Dakila shouts out. We all stand back. Jasmina's in a wheelchair and Kiri is holding her hand as she's pushed into the Centre.

'Jasmina, it's Ben. You collapsed? Can you tell me what happened?'

There are tears all over her face. 'I can't lose this baby, Ben,' she says. 'That can't be what's happening here. You can't let it.'

'Well we're all going to do our best for you. You're in good hands now.'

'Ben, she's lost a lot of blood.' Kiri is at my side and that's the one thing I didn't want to hear. It's the first sign that this is going to be serious. Kiri moves the monitors closer and reaches for Jasmina's arm so we can get readings of her blood pressure and pulse.

I turn to face her. 'Jasmina, tell me exactly what you felt and what happened.'

'It was two hours ago. I was reading my book. I was fine, absolutely fine,' she says. 'Then all of a sudden I started getting these sharp, cramping pains. I knew, the first moment, that it was the baby.' Her face is white and sweaty as she looks up at me. If that's been triggered by blood loss then it's the next sign she's in trouble.

'I'm going to examine you now. Tell me where it hurts the most,' I say, moving my hands gently over her abdomen. More tears squeeze out of the corners of her eyes as I do. As I expected she winces hardest when I press down in the right iliac fossa where the ovaries and fallopian tubes are. If it hurts there then this looks set to be an ectopic pregnancy. This time at least, Jasmina's dream of being a mum is over.

Kiri has begun monitoring Jasmina's vitals and I look up at the screens. The blood pressure reading is worrying low. I'm really concerned now. Complications to an ectopic pregnancy can mean we lose her as well as the baby. If the fallopian tube has ruptured and she's losing blood into her abdomen then death is a real risk.

'We're looking after you, Jasmina,' I say. 'I'm going to pop in a drip and give you some fluids. We can also use the drip to give you something to dull the pain and help you relax a little.'

She reaches out and grabs my hand. 'I don't want anything that might hurt the baby. I won't do anything that will make things worse. Please just get me to a hospital.'

'It's just going to be a bit of pethidine that will take an edge off the pain and won't affect the baby at all. That's why midwives use it.' She shivers as she gives her consent and we start to move. My eyes are always on the monitors and the picture isn't good. Her pulse is fast and if the pressure gets much lower she'll go into a form of medical shock. I slip the cannula into her forearm and connect the bag of fluid Kiri has primed and hooked on to a portable drip-stand.

'Jasmina we're in control of all of this. I'm just going to talk to the others.' I step outside. Edward is there. My subconscious records the fact that, for all our jokes about his work rate, Edward is always there when we really need him.

'How is she?' he asks.

I run through what I've seen. 'We can't do enough here. We need to get her to hospital. Can we turn the ship around and get back to Barbados?'

'You're certain she needs to be evacuated?'

'I'm certain.'

'Then I'll make the calls. We'll call for a tender and do a scoop and sail evacuation. She'll be on land in no time. I'll sort out all the official arrangements. You just go back there and take care of your patient.'

I head back inside. Jasmina's eyes are wide open now. They're big, green and very scared. 'Can someone call my husband? Can you tell him what's happening?' Kiri promises to do so and writes his number down.

I look at the screens.

Bugger.

The drip isn't making much of an impact on her blood pressure. I slide the valve open a little further to speed up the rate of flow and consider putting a second line into her other arm.

'Jasmina, I know this is the hardest thing to do, but if you can just try to stay calm you'll get through this so much better.'

She looks at me suddenly. The fear has gone from her

eyes. All of a sudden she's angry. 'You did this. You made it happen. This is all your fault,' she says. She's almost spitting the words and she shakes away my hand when I reach out to her. 'You told me to carry on working. You said it was OK to stay in the show. But you knew how much this meant to me. I've been waiting my whole life to have a baby. You knew that and you didn't look after me.'

'Jasmina we're not at the end of any road here. You can pull through this. If you've been pregnant once, you can be pregnant again. I put my hand on hers but she thrusts it away again.

'I'm not stupid. I know that it's over,' she says. She screws her eyes tightly closed, squeezing more tears out on to her face. She turns her head to face the wall and starts to sob silently.

Eileen moves over from the corner of the room. She takes Jasmina's hand and gently dabs at her tears. A couple of minutes later the storm has passed. Jasmina turns back towards me. She reaches out for my hand and she holds it tightly.

'I'm sorry,' she says very softly. 'It's my fault, no-one else's. I decided to go to the bar that first evening. I carried on dancing. I didn't even give up rehearsals for the second show. I shouldn't have said what I did to you. It's my fault and I'm sorry.'

I tell her she's got nothing to apologise for and she settles back on the bed. But while her mood is now calm, her situation is getting increasingly dire.

I head out to see Edward again. 'She's stable now but if she loses a lot more blood then it's going to get really serious really fast,' I tell him.

'Well we're ready for the worst. The captain has taken his

foot off the gas so a boat can come aside as soon as it's available. They've looked into a military option but in the end they think there's a coastguard vessel that can be scrambled for us. Once it's here it will get her into port fast. There will be an ambulance waiting at the quayside. The hospital is on alert and will be ready to receive her. Everything will be ready.'

Kiri is coming out of the nurses' station as I head back into the Crew Ward. 'Did you reach her husband?' I ask. She shakes her head.

'I got a machine and left a message asking him to call. They'll put him through to here if he does. One of the stewards is packing her things so everything can go with her to the hospital. Mary-Grace is coming down here as well. It's all just a matter of time now.'

Jasmina looks up as I approach her bed. 'Everything's under control,' I say. 'You'll be in hospital in no time at all. They'll do some proper scans and you may need an operation. But I know the hospital really well. I used to work there and I visited it this afternoon. They're good people and you'll get the best possible care. You will be OK'

'Can you come with me?' she asks, holding my hand so weakly I can barely feel it.

'Jasmina, I'll try,' I say. But I don't know how long the ship will hang around if I leave. I don't know how or where I'll be able to re-board if it moves on. So deep down I've got a horrible feeling Jasmina will have to face this nightmare on her own.

'We're ready to go. A tender is on its way.' Edward squeezes Jasmina's hand after coming in with the news. A pulse of energy and optimism runs through the room at his words.

We move Jasmina on to a trolley, wrap her in a blanket and strap her in securely. Kiri attaches a drip stand and transfers the bag of straw-coloured fluid across. It's nearly empty so she squeezes the remnants through and replaces it with a full one from the re-sus trolley. Then we start wheeling Jasmina through the bowels of the ship towards one of the loading bays. We use override buttons to commandeer the lifts we need.

'God bless you,' says a Filipino housekeeper who darts out of one to let us past. Mary-Grace is with us and holds her friend's hand whenever the corridors are wide enough to allow it.

'The whole crew is going to miss you. It's not going to be the same without you,' she says at one point.

'Nothing's going to be the same now,' says Jasmina flatly.

Two officers and three crew members are waiting for us at the disembarkation point. The exit, a doorway the size of a minivan, is opening out and down in front of us. Hot, humid air blasts in. So does spray from the waves.

'It's not as bad as it looks. The sea will be calm, I promise,' one of the officers says. 'The tender is coming from the starboard side. It's only minutes away.' He joins his colleagues and climbs down the steps on to the small, flat pontoon that has opened out at the base. It's already soaking wet as the wash from the ship hits it. The rubber covered steps look very steep. The polished wooden handrails look incredibly slippery. The whole thing looks utterly unsafe.

Edward steps forward to check Jasmina is secure on her stretcher. 'OK, my dear, we've done this a thousand times as you know. We'll check you're safe and sound then we'll move you down there,' he says. Her face is horribly pale in the evening light. There's a greyness in her cheeks now, an emptiness in her eyes. Just a few days earlier I had confirmed the one piece of news she had always wanted to hear. She had truly glowed. Now she looks dry, tired and beaten. I squeeze her hand a little tighter.

An orange and black coastguard boat full of men in baseball caps and fluorescent vests has come out of nowhere and is edging towards us. Jasmina, who can't even see it, starts to cry. Her tears remind me how much of a hurry we're in. I look out at the men throwing and catching the guy ropes. Every part of me is willing them on. I'm desperate to see the ropes pulled tight. I want the boat to be alongside. We need this to be done now.

'Ben, we're ready.' Edward makes the call. The two crew members lift the stretcher and start to manoeuvre it to the top of the steps. I hold the fluid bag at Jasmina's side. We take each step carefully in turn trying, but not always succeeding, to keep Jasmina's body level. I'm sweating before we're even halfway down to the platform. When we're there I can't believe how much it seems to be moving. My ears are full of the shouted instructions from the lifeboat staff, our own officers and crew as we stabilise ourselves there. And if I'm overwhelmed then I can't imagine how Jasmina must be feeling.

'It's going to be OK. We're there; the boat is right here. We're going to pass you over to it now. You'll be in hospital in no time at all,' I tell her. Then we do the transfer.

There's nothing so terrible as the awful, slow-motion moments when a stretcher is being passed from ship to tender. The patient is so vulnerable, trussed up, unable to move and utterly dependent on everyone else. We're all shouting but no-one can breathe. We all know that one sudden wave, one slip or one loose grip can spell disaster. It's obvious that we need to take it slowly. But we all want it over fast.

'Perfect transfer! Well done, gentlemen!' the officer next to me shouts as he passes the fluid bag to one of the coastguards. Jasmina is safely on the tender. The worst part is over. Kiri climbs down the steps and hands over a waterproof file containing Jasmina's case notes and the other paperwork we've rushed through for the company's agents on land.

'I don't want to be on my own,' Jasmina says as she locks eyes on me one last time.

'I can't come with you, Jasmina, I'm so sorry.'

'We're ready to leave, sir.' The man at the boat's controls shouts out the words as the ropes are pulled back in. There's a roar of engine noise, a cloud of exhaust fumes and then Jasmina is gone.

'Good luck – we'll be thinking about you!' Kiri shouts as the boat slips away from our side. Our rocky little platform seems even less safe now there's nothing in front of us. We hold on tight as we climb up the stairs and step back into the body of the ship. The hydraulics pull the vast door closed and it self-seals behind us. 'Job done,' one of the officers says as we walk away.

'A good job,' Edward confirms.

But I've still got a few doubts.

'Should one of us have gone with her? I'd have done it happily,' I say as we head back through the maze of corridors to the Medical Centre.

He shakes his head and very briefly puts his arm around my shoulders. 'You're more use here,' he says. 'We can only go with patients if they need constant care and no-one on the lifeboat can administer it. All Jasmina needed was the transfer. She'll be at the harbour in minutes. Everyone did the right thing today and you mustn't think that she will be abandoned. The theatre people are on her side. They'll keep in touch and they'll keep her family up-to-date so they can arrange anything she wants to do next. We do look after our own in this business. But at the end of the day the ship has to sail.' He smiles and says hello to a group of passengers before leading Kiri and I into the lift down to the Centre. 'Now I can positively guarantee that Eileen will have put fresh coffee on,' he says. 'We should celebrate what we've done. I want everyone smiling again within the hour. Always remember I'm your senior officer. If you're not in a better mood I'll call security. You'll all be put in the brig till we get to Panama.'

We've got a full day at sea before arriving in Bonaire. Some of the least likely passengers are getting ready to go kayaking in the mangrove swamps and I'm very glad I'm not going to be their tour medic. I ring the hospital in Barbados after morning clinic and get the latest on Jasmina's condition. The nurse confirms everything we had thought and feared. She's lost the baby, of course. The ultrasound has confirmed a ruptured ectopic pregnancy. They had to remove one of her fallopian tubes but they have saved her life. She'll have to stay in hospital for at least two weeks before being allowed to fly home. Apparently her husband hasn't been able to make it out to be with her. I just hope she's got a lizard on her bed.

Up in the gym I put on my headphones and try to focus on better things.

Eileen's certainly been in a better mood. 'I'm taking Kiri to my cooking classes. I want to make the most of her company while I still have it,' she told me that morning.

Dakila, out of nowhere, has signed up to an acting class. 'When did you ever see a Filipino leading man?' he asked. 'I could be the first. I'll make so much money I'll come back on board one day as a passenger and demand everything I want whenever I want it. I'm going to model myself on that American man Edward saw yesterday. I'll refuse to eat any fruit and I'll just come down and demand a daily vitamin injection instead.'

My afternoons are set to be a bit less interesting. I've enrolled on an e-learning course to get credits for my continuing medical education and I'm determined to do at least an hour a day. If I ever want to become a consultant or a GP I've got a lot more exams ahead so I might as well make a start on those as well. I'm also planning to take another look at all the main recruitment websites in case any early job opportunities come up back in Britain. But it's not easy to focus as I look out through the gym windows and watch us edge our way through the Panama Canal. The countryside is mesmerising and often looks close enough to touch. We're due in Costa Rica tomorrow and I've signed up to accompany a passenger trip to see one of the cloud forests. I get to go for free as long as I wear my uniform, carry my medical bag and step forward if anything goes wrong. I'm not sure that's a perk I'm likely to be offered on the NHS.

Gavin creeps up on me at the end of my workout. He's obviously caught some sun lately but he still doesn't look his usual self.

'You know, I've never seen a doctor on board before. How would I go about getting an appointment?' he says evasively.

'You don't. Just turn up this afternoon between five and

seven or tomorrow between eight and ten. Is there something you're worried about?'

'Not here. But I might see you later.'

He turns out to be one of my last patients of the night. He steps unwillingly through the door and throws himself down into the chair next to my desk.

'Nice to see you again. So what is it I can do for you?' I ask.

He screws up his face like a sulky teenager and refuses to say anything. 'Do you want me to read your mind?' I ask. The face screwing and the sulking go on for a while. If he ever gives up the fitness job he'd be perfect as an Italian waiter. I'm starting to wonder if this is all some sort of wind-up when he speaks.

'I think I've got gout. Feel free to laugh as much as you want.'

'I might just do that. I've not forgotten that crack you made about the Village People back in Barbados. So why do you think you've got gout?'

He runs through a pretty comprehensive list of symptoms. Swelling, extreme pain in the joint of his big toe, agony if it's touched by as little as a sheet. 'I've checked it all out online. I'd have been less embarrassed going to the internet café to look at porn than I was looking at that medical site. But I know that it's gout. I've read up all the symptoms. I also know that it doesn't just hit fat old men. But why the hell has it hit me?'

'Let me take a look at your feet.'

Gavin kicks off both his deck shoes and I can see why he looked a bit unsteady when he walked into the room. The big toe on his right foot is perfectly normal. The one on his left is a rich and angry red. It's swollen and looks fit to burst.

'Is it OK if I touch it?'

'Is it OK if I hit you?'

I ignore him and put my fingers on the joint. It's hot to touch, just as I expected. 'You want some good news, Gavin? Gout is really easy to misdiagnose. You might not have it, even if all the external symptoms seem to be there. Do you know if anyone else in your family has ever had it?'

'There's no way anyone in my family would admit to something like this.'

'Well if you've looked online you'll know that it's a tricky little disease to pin down. You can get something like this once and then never get it again. If you get several attacks we can get a definitive diagnosis and then you can treat it with drugs. But to get that diagnosis we need to get a needle between the bones to collect some fluids then examine it under a microscope. I'm guessing you don't want me to do that just yet?'

'You're guessing right.'

When he's told me a bit more about when the pain began, I talk him through the anti-inflammatory drugs I can give him but warn him that they'll take a while to kick in.

'In the meantime, we can get you a wheelchair to take you back to your cabin,' I begin, knowing full well what his reaction will be.

'Yeah, right, and destroy my reputation forever. This watch collection doesn't pay for itself, Ben.' He looks serious, all of a sudden. 'Look, I cannot be seen to have something like gout. This is a sports injury, right? That's what I'm going to tell people and I need you to back me up. If it's going to be more convincing I'll happily pay to have my foot put in a cast.' We agree to think about that another time.

'Edward's got a very attractive collection of walking sticks,' I begin.

'You'll have one of them cracked over the back of your neck if you carry on.'

'Well, how about crutches?'

After a bit of thought Gavin perks up at that one. 'So will you tell people I've had a sports injury?' he asks as he swings himself out into the corridor.

'Only if you'll give me a Rolex.'

He says he'll think about it.

The following day Mr Zip Wire achieves his ambition on our shore excursion in Costa Rica – and I don't think I'll ever forget the sight of this seventy-nine-year-old man giving the thumbs up before whizzing across the sky at what looks like a hundred miles an hour.

I won't forget the noise he made either. He whoops and cheers from beginning to end of his high-wire ride – and he keeps on chuckling with laughter for the rest of the afternoon.

'I've smiled so much today my face hurts,' he tells me on the coach when we've finished our brief nature tour and are heading back to the ship. As usual his enthusiasm is infectious and I happily join him and his wife for dinner where he regales the other guests at the table with ever more exaggerated tales of his exploits. I'm still in a great mood the following morning as we edge up the coast of Central America. I blow my self-imposed weekly phone budget on an hour long call to Cassie and I'm grinning from ear to ear as I arrive for morning clinic. Unfortunately my first patient of the day brings me right back down to earth.

His name is Matty Benson and his skin is a horrible, lifeless yellow. So are what should be the whites of his eyes. 'Hello, you work in the engineering department, don't you? How can I help you?' I ask as he sits down in my surgery. But I've already guessed. The skin tone and eye colour are only two of the clues. Another is the outline of his wildly swollen belly. The last is his general air of confusion. He looks around at one point as if he's forgotten where he is or why. This is the man Paco will become if he starts drinking again. It's a man who should have had treatment years ago.

'There's something different when I go to the toilet,' he begins, awkwardly. He's got a faint south London accent and a tattoo of a half-naked woman running down his right arm. I wonder how long he's been suffering before coming to see me. I wonder if he knows how bad this could be.

'Is it in your stools? Is it their colour? Their texture?'

'They're black,' he says. That's what I'd expected him to say. It's another piece of bad news.

'Could I look at your stomach, Mr Benson?' I ask. A blush of embarrassment flashes over his face. When he finally takes off his shirt I can see why. It's one of the secret ironies of alcohol that men who drink too much and think it's manly can see their testosterone levels slump. They can lose the hair on their chest and even develop breasts. Mr Benson has done both. He has no hair under his arms either. When I look closer I see his skin isn't just yellow. Telltale spots called spider naevi are scattered over his arms and torso. These tiny red dots have thread-like legs making them look like faint, gruesome tattoos.

I carry on the investigation by feeling under his jawbone. As expected his salivary glands are swollen. I ask about his diet, sleep patterns, mobility and energy levels. With each answer he worries me more.

'Would you lie back for me Mr Benson? I'd like to examine

your stomach more closely.' This is the real test. It's so swollen that the skin feels hard to the touch. I reach under his left ribs. His spleen has blown up like an airbag. I place two fingers on the skin and tap on them with the fingers of my other hand. I repeat this as I move my hands around his sides and up to the top of his stomach. I remember what my old Medical-School professors said: 'It's like a percussion orchestra. Your job is to listen and learn from the sounds you hear.'

As expected I hear hollow echoes when I tap the top of Mr Benson's stomach. Lower, towards the sides, the sound gets heavier and duller.

'Would you lie on your left side for me?' I let him settle and begin the percussion again. The hollow sound has gravitated to the top, the dull sound now comes from his side. It's a sign known as shifting dullness and indicates that there is an awful lot of fluid trapped in his abdomen. This too is bad news.

'Sorry, pal, but I'm going to have to examine your back passage,' I say, pulling on gloves. When that's done I've got one final check to make, though I think I already know what the result will be.

'Mr Benson, could you sit up again and hold both hands out in front of you? A bit like you need to stop the traffic. Hold your hands still as if you're telling people to stop.' Mr Benson struggles to do it. His hands are still for a moment. Then they start to jerk and flap.

'I'm sorry,' he mumbles as he screws up his face and tries to hold steady. His arms are still only for a moment before the flapping begins again. There's a look of shame on his face now. 'I'm very sorry,' he repeats.

I put my hand on his shoulder. 'There's nothing to apologise for. Just sit back and try to relax. I'll take your blood pressure in a moment and then we're all done.' When I've got the readings I click open his file on my computer and he sinks back, beaten, on to the bed.

'If you want to put your shirt back on I'm just going to go and speak to one of my colleagues,' I say when I've tapped in the key details of the case. I'm as good as certain that he has cirrhosis caused by a lifetime of drinking. I'd say his liver is so scarred that his blood can no longer flow freely through it and has found other, more dangerous paths to follow. This explains the man's black stools and low blood pressure. I take one final look at him as I leave the room. His hands are trembling violently as he tries to fasten the last of his buttons. Some of that is caused by all his years of drinking. But an awful lot of it is fear.

'Edward, I've got someone next door who's in a pretty bad way.' I've squeezed in between two of Edward's patients and start to run through what I've learned of Mr Benson.

'How old is he?' Edward asks.

'He's fifty two but you wouldn't know it to look at him.' I finish describing Mr Benson's symptoms and look at my boss. 'His blood pressure isn't dangerously low, but it's certainly worrying. I'm going to check his haematocrit but my guess is he's lost quite a bit of blood already. If he turned up at A&E like this they'd get him into endoscopy straight away in case he's got a variceal bleed. If we were on land I'd want him scoped and checked out immediately. I'd make him a priority.'

Edward stands up. 'Would you consider it an impertinence if I took a look myself?'

'Not at all.'

'Then lead on.'

Mr Benson is still trembling but tries to smile when I introduce Edward to him. 'Can you call me Matty? No-one calls me Mr Benson,' he says. 'You're making me feel like I'm in court.'

'I've always had a secret yearning to be a judge so I'm very pleased to hear I have that effect on people,' Edward says. 'But Matty it is. Now, I want you to know that Doctor MacFarlane and I are going to do everything we can to look after you. There's no need to worry unduly about any of this.'

Matty's blood pressure has barely changed and after his examination Edward calls me back into his room to discuss it.

'It's impossible to know if he's bleeding at the moment but my feeling is that he's not,' Edward says. 'We're less than twenty-four hours out of San Francisco. I say we give him some IV fluids and drain the ascites in his abdomen to make him more comfortable. We can start him on some terlipressin and keep him under close observation.'

'You don't think we should evacuate him?'

'He's not in immediate danger. We can manage him so his condition eases rather than deteriorates from here. He'll make it to San Francisco where he'll get the best care in the world.'

Edward takes over the rest of my clinic while I brief the others on Matty's condition. There's a pallor under his yellow skin as I lead him from my consulting room into the Crew Ward.

'I know I should have owned up to this a long time ago,' he says quietly.

I won't patronise him by lying. 'To be honest, Matty, I can't believe you've kept going as long as you have. Most people would be knocked out by now. Your body's stronger than you know. That's good news.'

'Because I'm going to need it, right? Because I'm a lot sicker than I think. That's what you're too afraid to tell me, isn't it?'

'You're not well and you're going to need a lot of help

when we get you to hospital on shore. But it's not too late. Here's what I'm going to do straight away.' I tell him about the fluid that has been building up in his belly. 'It's called ascites and it collects in the cavity around the guts. I can get a tube in there and we can drain it off. That'll relieve a huge amount of pressure. When I was a medical student I had a guy in my care who gave us nearly twenty litres in four hours. He looked like he was going to give birth to triplets when we first saw him. When we'd sorted out the ascites he pretty much had a six-pack.'

'It's a long time since I had a six-pack. Unless you're talking about cans of Special Brew,' Matty says, putting his hands on his stomach and wincing with pain. 'Last night I thought my whole body was going to explode. That's when I knew I needed help.' He says hello to Eileen and Kiri and makes a weak joke about his man-boobs when they help him out of his shirt. I ask him about alcohol and he says he can barely remember a time when he didn't drink. 'That's why I did my first cruise,' he says. 'There's no other job where you can drink so much so easily.'

'Or where you can hide it for so long,' chides Eileen. 'Though even in this badly-lit sardine can I'm surprised that none of your friends spotted the fact that you had gone as yellow as a banana.'

'Most people stopped coming anywhere near me as far back as Barbados,' he admits ruefully.

'Well next time that's your cue to come and see us. But I don't want there to be a next time,' I say. 'Now, are you ready to be burst like a balloon?'

Two flushed, bashful-looking passengers arrive as we get Matty ready for his treatment. The ship held a big Burns' Night dinner earlier on and several hundred passengers have moved on to a *ceilidh*. These are its first casualties.

'I was "stripping the willow" without a care in the world,' explains my first patient. 'Then this very exuberant lady in full highland dress whacked me in the eye with her arm. I'm not sure she noticed. She certainly didn't miss a beat.'

The area around his eye is already swelling and I have to tell him he'll have a shiner for at least a week.

His wife sighs. 'He'll tell everyone that I did it,' she says with a smile. 'He'll milk this one for all it's worth. He'll be unbearable until we get to Hawaii at least.'

Fortunately the eye itself looks unharmed. I examine the eyeball and put some eye-drops in to check for corneal abrasions. All looks well.

'We can give you a cold compress or you're more than welcome to go back upstairs and rejoin the party as you are,' I say. He says he'd prefer to let his war wound show and, holding out his arm for his wife, heads back to the dance floor.

The next lady has sprained her ankle but is convinced she's broken it.

'Can I please have an X-ray?' she asks. 'I'm more than happy to pay.'

The results show I'm right and there are no broken bones. I prescribe a lot of RICE – Rest, Ice, Compression and Elevation. I offer to get someone to wheel her back to her stateroom but she too wants to return to the party. It must be quite a night.

'Do we need to be on alert all night for more disasters?' I ask as she tells me how it's going. 'I had no idea that special events like this could be so hazardous to everyone's health.'

My patient smiles. 'I've been doing winter cruises for as long as I can remember and I've never seen as many dangerous dancers. There's one absolute terror of a lady who looks quite adorable when she first comes up to a table looking for a new dance partner. Five minutes later she's berating some poor man for putting a single foot wrong. Then there's some dear old boy who's got the natural rhythm of an ice sculpture. Everyone else takes two steps left, he takes two steps right. He's been doing it all night. He'll break someone's toes by midnight. I just hope they're not mine.'

I raise my eyebrows as Kiri wheels the lady to the door. 'I thought you had agreed to stay on the sidelines with your foot on a chair? I don't want to wake up tomorrow and have someone tell me that you spent the rest of the night on the dance floor with a walking stick.'

'Then I sincerely hope no-one tells you anything of the sort,' she says with a twinkle.

Matty has seen about eight litres of fluid drain out of him by the time I see him next. His stomach isn't flat but it's a whole lot better than it was. He's slept a little, or at least pretended to, and we're giving him some intravenous albumen and some antibiotics to fend off any potential infections in what's left of the ascites. We're also giving him an intravenous drug to lower the pressure within his liver, plus some mild sedatives in case he follows in Paco's footsteps and gets alcohol withdrawal symptoms.

'So how are you feeling, mate?' I check his pulse and I'm about to test his blood pressure again.

'I feel better. I'm still a bit freaked out by it all. I can't watch medical stuff on TV and I've never been in hospital in my life. But at least I'm doing something about it. Last night I thought I was going to die. Today I'm sorted, right?'

'You're on your way to being sorted. They'll have to take a proper look at you on land to see how much further you need to go. In the meantime I need to take those tubes out to stop them getting infected. If you're as squeamish as you say then this is a very good time to look away.'

I put some antiseptic on the tiny exit wounds and tell Matty it's safe to open his eyes. When he does I get the usual shock at how custard yellow they are. We've won a minor battle by easing the pressure in his belly. But there's still a war going on inside his body. It's impossible to know which way it's going to go. I get Kiri to sit in the ward and watch over him as I rejoin Edward in his surgery. Eileen is already there. 'He's stable,' I say. 'I think we're in control.'

It's fifteen minutes later when it all goes wrong. Kiri shouts out for help and Edward, Eileen and I fly across the hall to the Crew Ward. The smell hits us as we enter the room. Inside Matty is vomiting bright-red blood into the kidney dish Kiri is holding out for him. She's got him sitting on a bedpan that's rapidly filling up with black tarry stools made up mainly of partly digested blood called melena. They stink to high heaven.

'Bugger, bugger, bugger.' I'm not sure if it's worse to swear in front of a patient or in front of my colleagues. But I can't keep the words to myself. I'd told Matty we would save him. Now we're all being put to the test.

Eileen hands out plastic aprons, gloves and eye protection

as I check the electronic monitor. Matty's blood pressure is dropping and his pulse is rising. Edward pulls over the re-sus trolley while I drop the head of the bed. We both set to work getting a wide bore cannula into each of Matty's arms. It's easier said than done. His peripheral veins are starting to shut down to preserve his central circulation. To my right I can see Dakila putting a tourniquet on Matty's leg in case we need to get access there. Kiri meanwhile is busy running up more IV fluid so it's there to be connected as soon as we get the lines in. These are good people, and we make a great team. I hope it's enough.

'I've got it,' Edward says as he gets the cannula into one arm, just as I succeed on the other. We squeeze the plastic bottles to get the fluids in faster.

'Can we call for blood donors?' I ask Edward.

'It will take several hours to arrange,' he says. What he leaves unsaid is the fact that Matty may not have that long to live. He's really suffering now. His awful vomit comes in waves. As soon as his stomach fills with blood he rejects it in spectacular fashion. Dakila has grabbed the suction machine to try and clear Matty's mouth. He's wiping Matty's face clean with his free hand and trying to reassure him that all will be well. Though Matty isn't aware of it – he's drifting in and out of consciousness.

'Matty hold on for us,' I say. 'We're going to get you through this.'

Kiri runs out to put an emergency call through to the Bridge but we all know that it's too late even for an airlift. If this happened in a hospital car park it would be too late. No-one would be able to tie off the bleeding veins fast enough to save him. We do what we can and watch as his blood pressure drifts ever lower. His pulse disappears in less than ten minutes. The ECG still shows an electrical trace but Matty's heart has no more blood to pump. After a few more moments Edward reaches up and switches off the monitor. Then he gently closes Matty's eyelids.

We declare him dead at exactly fifteen minutes past midnight. All five of us stand around his bed in silence. After a few moments Eileen reaches out and briefly touches each of us in turn.

'It's the first death of the cruise,' she says softly. 'Let's clean up, then take a break. I'll put the coffee on next door if anyone wants a chat.' None of us does.

When Kiri and Dakila have left for the night I sit in to watch Edward and Eileen prepare the final stage of Matty's journey. Apparently the company will speak to his family in the UK and, once the medical formalities are completed, they can decide if they want his body flown home, buried overseas or left on board till we complete the voyage. In the meantime we tag the body and when we've checked there are no passengers in the immediate vicinity the three of us wheel him down to the morgue. We all shiver slightly as the thick metal door closes on him.

'It's the cold air,' Edward says gruffly. 'Now let's go upstairs, get some sleep and think of happier times. I do believe that's what dear Mr Benson – I mean Matty – would have wanted.'

# Part Three

# The Pacific Ocean

# CHAPTER THIRTEEN

I've got Dakila to thank for waking up to the latest information on haemorrhoid cures. He told me to tune my radio alarm clock to a local station every time we approach a new port.

'There are English-speaking stations everywhere and they give you a flavour of where you are. It reminds you that there's more to life than this floating sardine can,' is his theory. It's actually quite a good one. I woke up to a lot of cool jazz from a station in Bonaire. I loved hearing the heavily accented traffic reports from Panama City. Now, as we head towards San Francisco, I get to learn about all sorts of feminine hygiene and other personal care products that are unaccountably placed alongside the weather reports on breakfast radio.

I skip my usual workout in the gym so I can join Kiri and Dakila on the deck before morning clinic. I'm not sure that anything can beat sailing under the Golden Gate Bridge just after dawn. It's a wet, grey morning when we approach. It's also freezing cold. But what an extraordinary doorway to a new city. What a way to make an entrance.

Edward and Eileen have got the two shore leave slots. She's off to grab some dim sum, then have lunch at the restaurant she's been raving about since Southampton. He's planning to do an architecture tour then go to a talk about the post-Impressionists at the de Young Museum. Like most people, San Francisco is one of my favourite American cities but I'm happy to just see it from afar on this trip – because staying on board means I get a lot more time off when we get to New Zealand and Australia.

'Do you remember the last time we were here? Kiri asks Dakila as we approach the port terminal. 'With the guy who had the heart murmur?'

'You mean the crazy medi-vac?'

'Exactly.' She turns to me. Their ship had spent two days in LA and an American passenger had complained about very mild chest pains. 'It was probably indigestion, to be honest, but we booked him into a hospital for a check up in San Francisco just in case. But the message must have got confused because when we arrived in harbour it was as if the President himself was in respiratory arrest. They had something like four ambulances on the quayside. Seven or eight paramedics practically stormed the ship like some kind of medical SWAT team. The poor patient did nearly have a heart attack when he saw them. Our senior nurse on that cruise nearly got trampled underfoot as they powered the guy out of the Centre and off the boat. They were all barking instructions into their walkie talkies and holding people back so they had a clear run to the quayside. Then when they got him into the ambulance they fired up the blue lights and siren and disappeared at about a hundred miles an hour.'

'They even had motorcycle outriders. Four of them,' Dakila adds.

'It was like Hollywood. The insurance claim must have

been astronomical. And all the guy really needed was a five-dollar pack of indigestion tablets.'

There's no such drama today and, after watching the first of the passengers flood down the gangway, the three of us head down to the Medical Centre. We're expecting a busy day. A lot of the crew can only get time off to see us when we're in port and many of the ship's normal functions are on hold. Eileen has also warned me that San Francisco normally brings more than its fair share of passenger problems.

'It's the first really big city we go to and the hills and the traffic take people by surprise,' she said at breakfast. 'Call me if you really need me. But try not to between twelve and two. That's when I intend to be in gastronomic heaven at *Chez Panisse*.'

Funnily enough it's at exactly twelve o'clock when I get the first call from our guest relations department.

'Doctor MacFarlane? We're just bringing a guest back on board who's got a very badly damaged knee. Can you get down to the Medical Centre now to see him?'

A bashful-looking gentleman in his early sixties is being wheeled down the corridor as I arrive. A well-dressed lady is at his side.

'You're Kenneth Mortimer?' I ask the patient. 'It looks as if you've had a bit of a bad day.'

'It's because he doesn't listen,' the lady says before he has a chance to speak. 'I'm his wife, June. And trust me, he doesn't listen.'

'So you had an accident?'

'The young man on the cable car could hardly have made

it clearer: "Stay sitting down. Hold on tight. Don't move until I give everyone the all clear." If he said it once he said it a hundred times. But did my husband listen?'

I sneak a look at Mr Mortimer. 'I didn't listen,' he admits, with a grin.

'Well let's see how much damage you did.' We sit him down on the examination bed. His brown corduroy trousers are muddy, blood-stained and ripped around both knees.

'These were brand new at Christmas,' his wife informs me. 'They were full price as well. We didn't even wait for the January sales. I told him to take care of them.'

'You didn't listen, did you?' I ask with a smile.

'This young man has the mark of you, my dear. He will go far – and would you like to know why?' Mrs Mortimer asks her husband.

'Because he listens?' he ventures, giving me a wink.

'Exactly. Now, try not to cry like a baby if he needs to give you an injection.'

Mr Mortimer takes the damaged trousers off and his gently tutting wife empties the pockets then folds them up neatly.

'They're barely good enough for gardening now. A shocking waste of money. Quite criminal,' she says. But she sits alongside her husband and puts her hand on top of his as I start to clean up his wounds. Every time he winces in pain she gives him a reassuring squeeze. I wonder if Cassie and I will be like this in thirty years time. We could certainly do a whole lot worse.

'Well the good news is that this isn't as bad as it looks. They're grazes rather than cuts and even the nasty ones should heal quickly now we've got the grit out and cleaned them up.' I spray some iodine on them to kill any bacteria, top it off with some plastic skin, then wrap both knees in sterile gauze dressings. 'Try to keep these dry and if you pop down tomorrow I'll get one of the nurses to change them for you. Now, you are up to date with your tetanus, aren't you?'

He is and Mrs Mortimer gives a visible sigh of relief when she knows everything is going to be OK.

'I'm going to find him a new pair of trousers,' she tells me before heading back to their stateroom. 'People have paid good money for this cruise. They don't expect to see my husband's knobbly knees just after lunch.'

'Peace at last. I'll give you twenty pounds if you lock the door,' Mr Mortimer says when his wife has gone. But his face lights up and the banter begins again the moment she returns. When one of the porters wheels him out of the Centre and up to their room she's complaining that his accident stopped her from seeing San Francisco's shops and he's accusing her of trying to bankrupt him. I doubt that we've got a happier couple on the whole ship.

'Eileen said it would be busy and Eileen never lies. There's someone else being sent down right now,' Kiri says as I finish off Mr Mortimer's paperwork. 'It's a lady who's just re-boarded after an asthma attack. Apparently she came down with it on Alcatraz.'

Two women walk into the clinic a couple of minutes later. The first of them looks dressed for the golf course in tan shorts and a green and yellow sweater.

'I'm Annabel,' she says, rushing ahead. 'I was standing next to the lady when she collapsed. I'm afraid it's my fault we didn't go to hospital on land. I thought it would be fearfully expensive and the lady might not be out in time to rejoin the ship. I offered to help her get a taxi and bring her back here. The older doctor saw me a week ago. He worked miracles with my recurrent . . . well, it really isn't relevant what it was. But he was marvellous so I brought us straight here.'

'I'm sure you've done the right thing. If you could just let me see the patient.'

Annabel finally steps aside. Behind her is a short, sleek lady in black trousers, a shiny black T-shirt and huge Prada sunglasses.

'Terrible fuss,' she rasps as I guide her into a chair. 'Name's Rosemary.'

I tell her to relax and that we can talk more when her breathing has eased. But she seems determined to tell her story as I set up a nebuliser and get the other kit I need together.

'Worst attack – I've ever – had. Genuinely thought – going to die. Prison corridor – utterly embarrassing.' She's forcing the words out in short, staccato bursts. She's still struggling to breathe. But I've got a feeling that this isn't so very far removed from her usual speech pattern. She's clearly a confident woman who doesn't like being at a disadvantage. She reminds me a little of Mrs Coates.

When the nebuliser is running I reach for a syringe.

'I want to know how much oxygen you've got in your blood. I'm just going to take a sample from the pulse in your wrist. It might hurt a little but if you could try and hold your hand as still as possible I'll get it done much quicker,' I tell her. I'm aiming for an artery, which is a little harder than a vein, but I get one straight away and watch as the blood pushes into the syringe under pressure from the heart.

Kiri takes the sample to our lab where she runs it through the blood gas analyser while I press hard over the puncture site. I cover it with a big plaster and I'm swapping the nebuliser for an ordinary oxygen mask when Kiri comes back holding a slip of paper that looks a bit like a till receipt. It's the blood test results.

'Not bad,' I say, looking at them. 'I think you're going to live.'

'Well thank goodness for that,' she says, able to speak a lot more clearly now that her breathing has eased. 'I've often wondered what my obituary might say. I never thought "died in a foreign jail aged sixty three" would be its final line.'

We sort out a new inhaler and do a chest X-ray just in case there's an infection, or worse, a collapsed lung. It all comes up clean but I ask Rosemary if she's happy to stay in the Centre for a few hours just in case. Her new mother hen, Annabel, proves equally willing to stick around, but in the end Kiri persuades her that the drama is over and it's time to go.

While Rosemary reads magazines in the passenger ward, I spend the afternoon in my office catching up with some online journals. I also flick through a few medical recruitment websites from back home. One job jumps out straight away – an A&E post in a hospital in Stratford, East London. I'm not sure I've got everything they're looking for, but as they're accepting applications online I decide to send one in anyway. Half an hour later I carry on the search. All the next jobs I spot seem to be based overseas. The best is a new hospital in the Gulf that's offering a villa with a pool as well as an eye-wateringly large tax-free salary. I scan the details quickly then log off. I'm supposed to be settling down, not starting off on another overseas adventure. Stratford is what I want, I tell myself. Then I try to forget all about it.

Dakila takes Rosemary back to her stateroom in the late afternoon. He's back to help at evening clinic where we get a fair few other bangs and scrapes to deal with as well as a couple of crew injuries. Then the three of us wrap up warm to watch the San Francisco skyline light up from the crew deck. Eileen finds us arguing whether the view beats Hong Kong, New York or Sydney. It's clear she couldn't care less. She wants to talk about her lunch.

'It was sublime,' she says before we've really asked. 'Elegant, simple, healthy, classy. Afterwards I went to a farmer's market further up the bay. Oh, I could happily retire to somewhere like this. The colours of the fruits, the wonderful vegetables, all the different types of oats and muesli. People love their food over there and they're prepared to pay for it. I don't know why I didn't just abandon ship. Everything I eat for the next ninety days will come from a giant cold store on the cargo deck, out of a catering pack the size of a car. I must be absolutely out of my mind.'

Kiri gives her a hug as the crew begin to release our tethers. The engine noise is building up and black water is swirling around below us. All of a sudden I feel an immense rush of anticipation. Arriving in San Francisco had been amazing. But the real excitement only hits me now that we're leaving. I've just realised that this is the start of my fourth full week and my second full ocean. We're about to cross the Pacific.

'Let's hope Edward made it back from his exhibition in time. It's a long way to Honolulu,' Dakila says when we get back to the Centre after helping out with the latest evacuation drills. Eileen has called a quick meeting because

San Francisco is the start of a new sector. Several dozen new passengers and crew joined us in California and will be here until at least Singapore. Eileen has updated medical lists from guest relations and crew welfare to show if there is anyone we need to watch over or worry about along the way.

'Bless her little cotton socks but we've got one lovely lady who felt the need to notify us about her in-growing toenail on the medical disclosure form,' Eileen begins. 'Apart from her, we seem to have far too many people who may be in genuine medical difficulty. They appear to have bought into the old line that a cruise will do them good. Hence there are the usual respiratory problems and several new passengers with oxygen concentrators. Another epileptic came on board in San Francisco as well as two more insulin-dependent diabetics. When you add new and old passengers together it means we've now got a gentleman who's recovering from heart surgery and a lady who's just completed a course of chemotherapy for breast cancer. We've got a man with two new hips and a woman with a new kidney. We've got an awful lot of people on blood-thinning medication plus, of course, all the other conditions that haven't been declared or will only show themselves once we're at sea.'

'To hidden nasties,' Dakila toasts.

'To the start of our fourth week together,' says Edward, striding into the Medical Centre at the perfect time. He's already in his formal rig and seems even more ebullient than normal. 'If any of you philistines can stomach some truly challenging culture on a future cruise then I humbly offer you the post-Impressionists at the de Young,' he booms. 'Your restaurant was everything you hoped it would be, my dear?' he asks Eileen.

'It was all that and more. If I die at sea please take my ashes back there and scatter them around the table by the window.'

'Federal law may prevent us, but we will certainly make the effort. Even though I have a sneaking feeling that you will outlive us all. Even dear Kiri, unless she starts using a bit more sunscreen.' He pats her hand absentmindedly then turns to me. 'Doctor MacFarlane. Any crises while I was at one with the muses?'

'None we couldn't handle.' I run through the list and feel myself smile at his approval. He's like a Victorian father at these meetings.

'Dakila. Charmed any more of our lovely lady passengers? Put any of the gentlemen hosts out of a job yet?' Dakila's smile tells me how pleased he is to be included in Edward's team talk as well.

'Not as far as I know, sir. But they'll have to watch out when I learn how to waltz.'

'Marvellous. Quite marvellous. And what a splendid team we make. I fear I shall miss you all terribly when this adventure ends. Though not quite enough to stay with you for this evening's clinic. Doctor MacFarlane, if I could be so bold as to ask you to look after any dear passengers who need our aid? Eileen, if I could prevail upon you to call me only in an emergency?' We all nod and he beams around the room. 'Quite marvellous. I shall see you all tomorrow.'

The evening list goes by relatively smoothly and Eileen calls me over when my final patient leaves.

'Ben, we've had a call from a guest who'd like someone to visit her suite. It's certainly not life or death so we'd normally ask her to come down here but I thought you might like to take a look. It's one of the split level suites right at the aft of the ship. They're worth seeing and this couple have taken two of them so family and friends can join them every few weeks. Those suites don't have a balcony, by the way. They don't even have a terrace. They have a wraparound veranda. Each of them has about four different rooms on two levels, a baby grand piano and all sorts of other nonsense.'

'Wow. I'd love to have a nose around. What's the matter with the guest?'

'It's something to do with her feet. I told her we'd happily send a nurse but she said she'd prefer to see a doctor. That's a rich woman's code for saying she *expects* to see a doctor. As she and her husband are paying £1,000 a night to be here I suppose it's the least we can do. Her name is Louisa but when she rang she introduced herself as Mrs Benjamin Compton, so be on your best behaviour. It'll be a social minefield up there.'

I head up and towards the back of the ship to check it all out. I seem to remember that my deck has six stateroom doors along this final stretch of corridor. Here there are just two. Size clearly matters.

One of the blond, Eastern European concierges opens the door for me and leads me down a hallway to the living area. It's like the presidential suite of hotel rooms you see on TV. One whole wall of the room is made of glass and there are unobstructed views out over the ship's wake.

'It's very nice, isn't it?' says my patient, who must be able to read my mind and is far less formal than I'd feared. 'I'd happily give you a tour but I can't really stand.' She's a handsome woman in her mid-fifties. She's wearing a vibrantly-coloured silk kimono and is almost swallowed up by a vast, upholstered armchair. Her feet are stretched out on a matching footstool. They're red, swollen and have little blisters all over them. As I get closer I notice something else. They reek.

'Do you have pedicures?' I ask. That smell has to be *pseudomonas aeruginosa* – a bacterial infection that can easily creep through small cuts into the tissues of the foot.

'I am positively addicted to pedicures,' she says proudly. 'I have one at every destination and every day on board. But I do believe there may have been a problem with the one I had in Chinatown.'

I shake my head a bit. 'I'd say this infection has been brewing for a bit longer than that. It looks like something you've got from a foot spa somewhere. I'll need to take a few swabs so we can isolate the bacteria and check they're not resistant to any of our treatments. As soon as that's done one of us can bring you the right antibiotics. In the meantime, though—'

'Don't say it,' she interrupts, pretending to block her ears.

'In the meantime, no more pedicures.'

I head back down to start work on the swabs. Kiri is the first person I see in the Medical Centre.

'So, how did it go? Did you manage to get yourself legally adopted?' she asks. 'Kieran and I still need a bit more cash for our bar. If you've got money, I'll take back all those things I've been saying about you behind your back.'

I look across at her. There's no-one else around and I decide I can't keep quiet about her resignation any longer.

'So it's true that you're thinking of leaving?' I ask, trying to sound as vague as possible.

She smiles. 'About bloody time too. Didn't Eileen say it was a cruise secret, not a real secret? I've been waiting for you to ask about this for days. I was starting to think you didn't care. Well, yes, I am leaving. It turns out Kieran's not that bothered about going back to Ireland and I've realised I miss the good old Australian sunshine. We're going to find a place in Byron Bay. We've decided it's now or never.'

'So much for Dakila's theory that none of us can ever leave.'

She smiles. 'I feel a bit bad for poor old Dakila. I think he really might be stuck in this job till he retires.'

'Eileen is going to miss you too.'

Kiri smiles again. 'Not half as much as I'm going to miss her. Telling her I'd resigned was harder than telling my mum when I signed up for my first worldie. I'm relying on you now to keep her company for the next, I don't know, twenty years.'

I say I'll do my best. 'What does Edward think about you going?'

'He's been adorable. Part of him wants to support Eileen but another part wants to tell me to follow my heart. As he's such an old softie he's leaning towards the latter. The company's being a bit difficult about letting me break my contract and he's being a real help calming them down. I think I'll lose out on my share of our bonus pool and I won't get a great reference, but if the bar takes off none of that will matter.'

'Meanwhile we'll have a new Kiri in Australia.

'Honey, there will never be a new Kiri. Apparently that's a sticking point with the company, to be honest. They're still looking for someone to take over. You don't know anyone, do you?'

I'm about to say no when I stop myself. I actually know the perfect person. She's an old colleague from my repatriation days. She's the cruise-ship nurse who helped persuade me to do this job in the first place. She's just spent two months doing expedition cruises in the Antarctic and I was hoping to catch up with her in Australia. Her name is Rebecca.

# CHAPTER FOURTEEN

Evening clinic ended half an hour ago and Dakila and I are waiting by the reception desk. Eileen is standing in front of us holding a stopwatch and a clipboard.

'OK. We have a suspected heart attack in the engine room. The patient is a member of the crew but we know nothing of his medical history. Your time starts – now!'

I head to the medical store and collect my medical bag. Dakila grabs the re-sus trolley, effectively a chest of drawers with wheels that contains all the equipment required to manage a cardiac arrest. As usual the portable defibrillator is sitting proudly on top.

'I'll meet you there,' I yell over my shoulder as he stabs furiously at the lift call button. I head for a companionway and start jumping down the stairs as fast as I dare. Out on the lower corridor I slam through several sets of doors and leap over all the lips and doorjambs in my way. Somehow Dakila must have got lucky with the lift and he's caught up with me as we key in the security codes to get through the last set of heavy metal doors. We push through into the site of the emergency. Then we freeze.

'Oh, you have got to be joking,' I say. In front of me, with a huge smile on his face, is quite possibly the largest person I've seen on the ship. As we took on an awful lot of new American passengers in San Francisco, that's saying something. Only the other day Kiri and I had been talking about how few fat people there are among the crew. There is an exception to every rule. This twenty-stone man is it – and in a few moments Dakila and I will have to help lift him.

'I thought you'd be pleased,' booms Edward, appearing, Hitchcock-style, from behind another door. He too is holding a stopwatch. 'You made it here within the time limits. Now let's find out what's wrong with the patient.'

I kneel at the man's side and try and ignore Edward's smirks. 'OK, I'm checking to see whether he's breathing,' I begin.

'He's not breathing,' Edward informs me.

'I'm feeling for a pulse.'

'It's weak and irregular.'

'Then I'm going to examine his airway and insert a pharyngeal tube.'

'I shall assume you have got that in place. What are you going to do next?'

We run the exercise through to its conclusion.

'The patient is stabilised. I think, dear chaps, that it is time to move him,' Edwards says. He's clearly finding it very hard not to laugh.

'OK, get the stretcher out,' I tell Dakila as Edward clicks the stopwatch and calls through to Eileen upstairs. I marshal the two fellow crew members who are waiting with Mr Big and look just as annoyed as we do at the task ahead. When the scoop stretcher is on the ground we all half roll and half lift the patient on to it. He clearly sees himself as something of a method actor, refusing to give us any help whatsoever.

'OK, lift!' We get the scoop stretcher on to the trolley's low point then jack its legs up so it's at the proper height.

'OK, the clock's ticking guys. Let's move!' Sweat is soaking through the back of my shirt as I step backwards through the doorway and help pull the trolley out into the vast lino-lined corridor. I'm guessing that the laundry is the only place on board that is as hot as the engine room, but most of the people who work there weigh less than nine stone. Next time I do an emergency drill I want the patient to come from there.

Eileen, timer in hand, is waiting for us in the Medical Centre when we finally stagger down the corridor.

'Oh dear, someone doesn't like you,' she says as she sees the size of our patient. We manoeuvre him into the Crew Ward and roll him on to a high dependency bed. It feels as if we've been carrying him for about an hour.

'Forty five seconds within the outer limit. Well done boys. You've done me proud,' Eileen says. She's baked a cake in her cookery class and has wrapped up a slice each for the volunteers. Our fake patient has eaten his before he's even left the room.

'So am I going to like this Rebecca person?' Eileen asks as the three of us share out the rest of the cake.

'I think you'll love her,' I say. 'She's a great nurse and she's also good fun. I did a couple of repatriations with her in my old job. She gave that up because she preferred working as part of a team. That's why she likes cruise ships.'

'Have you spoken to her yet?'

'I emailed her last night. I don't know when she'll be able to pick it up but I'll let you know as soon as she replies.

'I just hope she won't break our hearts by falling in love with an Irishman and jumping ship to start some hare-brained business,' is Eileen's verdict.

We move on to talk about our next ports in New Zealand. Dakila is taking shore leave to visit family and as usual Eileen has a few restaurants she's hoping to try. I'm trying to think where I might have eaten when I was last on the islands when I remember something. It's Valentine's Night and we're supposed to getting ready for a party.

A new theatre company is joining the ship in Sydney and Mary-Grace has invited us to a costume party for the old cast and crew. At the start of the cruise Kiri told me: 'If you think it's only students who hold fancy dress or toga parties then think again. They're still huge on the crew decks of cruise ships. It's the easiest way for the engine room boys to see some female flesh.' Since then we've had invites to at least one big party a week. But something tells us that the show people will throw the most elaborate bash of all.

The party is a masked ball and the theme is 'Love's Young Dream'. Red roses appeared, as if by magic, across the whole ship overnight in honour of St Valentine. Plenty of people at the party seem to have nicked them and pinned them to their costumes. Getting the right outfit is probably easier for the theatre crowd who have easy access to a professional costume, hair and make-up department. But that hasn't put the rest of us off. Eileen, bless her, has given it her best shot and has come dressed in a form of Elizabethan costume as, she ruefully admits, a somewhat middle-aged Juliet. Dakila was able to get some help from the people on his acting course and has a full Casanova outfit, complete with a tall, powdered wig. Kiri and Kieran have made a joint effort and are two of the many Cupid and Venus couples on display. I'm on call so I can't wear anything too outlandish in case I have to go to a £125k suite or get called up to the bridge. Only Edward turned the invitation down, citing 'the dignity of office'. He's put on his formal rig to accompany Mrs Coates, Mrs Philip and some of the other single ladies to a recital in the Piano Bar. The poor man had only to come out of his surgery this afternoon for Kiri or Dakila to start humming *Love is in the Air* and sniggering like children.

Mary-Grace comes over, drink in hand. 'Welcome to a world of absolute debauchery. Most of what happens tonight is only legal because we are in international waters. I do hope you approve.' She introduces us to a group of dancers and stage hands then explains the other reason for the masked ball theme: to help hide the fact that a select number of passengers are partying with us. The ship's *Upstairs, Downstairs* rules had been made crystal clear to me when I'd been given the job back in London. The vast majority of the crew will be fired on the spot if they are found on any passenger deck. That's why so many launder sheets for rooms they will never see, or wash dishes for restaurants they can only imagine. For their part, passengers can be booted off if they are caught on the wrong side of a 'Crew Only' door. The idea is to protect everyone from danger, as well as from jealousy and guilt. On this cruise, though, our passenger list includes a pair of theatre owners from New York and some film company bosses from California. For Mary-Grace and her friends this is one of their last chances to impress. It seems that actors, like doctors, are never entirely off duty.

'Come on Ben, let's get you dancing.' Kiri drags me on to the stage. Gavin, who has clearly shaken off his gout, is already there and he makes his usual Village People moves when he sees me. The music is good and the hours fly by. Eileen and Dakila leave just before midnight but I reckon I'm up to stay as long as the party lasts. If that means going straight to my morning clinic, then so be it. For the first time since I boarded I'll take advantage of our fabled seven-hour lunch break and sleep it all off then.

A group of shoppies are trying to persuade me to do shots when a woman grabs my arm.

'You're the doctor, right?' she shouts over the noise. I nod and start to stand up. 'Someone's collapsed,' she says. 'I think he's dying.'

The man on the floor can barely be more than twenty years old. He's been pulled on to his side, he's unresponsive and his breathing is worryingly shallow. I kneel down next to him and shout out questions at the crowd.

'What happened to him? Did anyone see it?' No-one says anything but everyone looks guilty. 'OK, you two,' I say, pointing at two guys in tiny devils outfits. 'Help me lift him. We need to get him somewhere there's more space. And does anyone know my nurse, an Australian girl called Kiri? She's here somewhere with a guy called Kieran. She's dressed like a Greek goddess.'

'Ben, I'm here.'

'Thank God. I'm going to need a hand with this one.'

The music is still blaring but the crowd on the dance floor parts as my two red-suited assistants and I carry the patient out into a corridor. It's the first time I've been grateful that the lights in the crew areas are so harsh. I need to get a decent look at the guy's eyes. If they're pinpoint sharp then, along with his bad breathing, this looks like a heroin overdose – and bad as it sounds that's something I can treat right away.

'Do you know what he took? I'm not playing policeman. I just need to know to save him,' I ask the guys one more time.

'He had some smack. We all did,' one of them mumbles.

'Idiots,' I mumble back as they edge away and then make a run for it. I hope my friends would be braver if I was ever in trouble.

'I'll run up and bring the kit down here,' Kiri says as we watch the men go. 'We won't be able to move him on our own.'

I keep my hands on the patient's chin, protecting his airway while I wait for her to get back. She's fast. She's got a med bag, a face mask and a portable oxygen canister. She gets the mask on and starts the air flowing while I attach a tourniquet and get a cannula in his arm.

'Naloxone?' she asks. It's an immediate-acting heroin antidote. The last time I used it was when I answered an 'is there a medical doctor on board?' call on a flight from Jamaica. A fellow passenger had swallowed condoms full of the drug. She lost consciousness when one or more of them started to leak.

'That's the one,' I say to Kiri as she prepares the syringe. 'Now I doubt this guy will be very happy with us so let's be ready.' It's one of the ironies of medicine that so many heroin users lash out when you save their lives like this. You're congratulating yourself that they didn't die. They want to kill you for taking away their high.

This guy, whose name we still don't know, regains consciousness almost immediately as the medication reaches his brain. He sits up and gives me a very wary, very calculating look. I can almost see him working out what's happened – and what the implications might be. If he's angry that we've 'wasted' his hit then he's even more worried about what we're going to do about it.

'I feel OK,' he says quietly in a soft French accent. 'You're a doctor, right? Can I get up?' He does, even though we'd prefer him to stay on the ground a bit longer.

'You're still OK?' I ask.

'Yes I am,' he says. He's got his hand on the cannula on his arm and he's frowning slightly.

'That's where we injected you,' I say. He nods. Then he rips the cannula out, throws it at Kiri and runs down the corridor, through a no-entry door and out of sight.

'Jesus, that could have got me in the eye,' Kiri says reaching out to steady herself.

'What a tosser. Are you OK?' I ask, rushing after the guy but not finding any trace.

She's fine and when she's caught her breath we re-pack the medical bag and trudge back to the Medical Centre to lock it away. We log the incident on the system, call security and give the officer a description of the guys involved when he comes up to take a report.

'I'm going to really miss this place,' Kiri says when he's gone. 'I'll probably have a lot worse thrown at me when I'm running a bar but I doubt I'll get an ex-SAS man to track down the culprit.'

Neither of us feels like going back to the party when we've finished up in the Centre so we head up to a passenger deck to look at the sky. It's warm, sultry and wonderful.

'I bet you'll miss this as well,' I say as we lie back on some sun loungers and drink in the night air.

She smiles across at me. 'Two months ago it was me trying to persuade you that this was the best job in the world. Now you're doing it to me. It's yet more proof that everyone who works on cruise ships goes crazy in the end.'

# CHAPTER FIFTEEN

'Peace at last,' Edward says to me with a wink as Eileen, Kiri and Dakila all walk out of the Medical Centre for the day.

'I heard that,' Eileen shouts back.

We docked in Wellington during morning clinic and for the first time since we left Southampton all three nurses are heading off on shore leave at the same time. Edward has been winding them up for days with his talk about leaving the true professionals in charge. Now that they've gone he heads back into his consulting room and rings for Romeo.

'My dear young man, could I prevail upon you to bring two white coffees and perhaps a small selection of iced buns?' he asks. I give Romeo a sympathetic look when he arrives with the goods a few minutes later. No wonder the poor man's English is a bit eccentric at times. With Edward as a role model he can hardly fail to sound like a character from a Jane Austen novel.

'So we're losing dear Kiri and gaining a former colleague of yours,' Edward says as we tuck into our mid-morning feast. Rebecca had emailed me on a break from her latest expedition voyage and said she'd do anything to get back on board a proper cruise ship.

'My current doctor is from Russia. He speaks no English

and knows no medicine,' she had written. 'The X-ray machine is older than I am and I don't think we've got a single drug in the dispensary that's within its use-by date. Don't even get me started on the passengers. "Fit to travel" my arse. The only thing that matters to the tour firm is that they're fit enough to write a big cheque for the trip. One of them conveniently forgot to note her prosthetic foot on the medical form. We've had arguments every day over whether we can get her on the safety boats and out to the ice. I'll put my application in for your job today.' Within a week the company had approved her and she's due to join the night we leave Sydney. I'm thrilled about it. Cassie, who's always been a bit wary of Rebecca, seemed less so in her emails, and had clearly softened up when we spoke on the phone first thing this morning.

'I think Rebecca will fit in really well. But Kiri's a hard act to follow,' I say to Edward.

'At least dear Eileen has got over her disappointment at the news.'

'She's taking Kiri to lunch at that new place she's been talking about since San Francisco. It's nice how well they're getting on. I hope they stay in touch.'

Edward shakes his head. 'I fear that very few people ever do. That's the hidden curse of this life. We've got everything in common while we're at sea – but nothing to say to each other once we're back on *terra firma*.' He looks up, suddenly. 'My dear chap I appear to have become maudlin again, how very irritating. Especially as I've been charged with something of a mission today. Listen in, dear boy. It's time to talk about your future.'

Edward puts a clear plastic file on top of his desk. 'I've been taking a look at the latest requirements for the position of a senior ship's physician. That's the job I shall be leaving when

I retire in the summer. To paraphrase Oscar Wilde, when a doctor retires he creates a vacancy.'

'You think I should apply for your job?'

'It won't be that simple, of course. There are no straight swaps and there are many other young – and not so young – doctors who will want to step up the ladder. But mine will not be the only vacancy this year. There are plenty of ships and there are always opportunities for senior doctors who have proved their worth.' He opens the file. 'Now, in the cold light of day your career may not be long or extensive enough to ensure you will automatically be considered for a promotion. The requirements, as I have researched them, are getting more exacting all the time.'

I stay silent. I'm not entirely sure where Edward is going with this. Has he forgotten I'm going back to an A&E post in the summer?

'Look at this photograph,' he says, handing me a framed picture from the corner of his desk. 'That's Maureen and the children in the pool on the original Queen Mary. It must be twenty years ago, possibly a little more. When the children were young Maureen brought them on board all my ships. We spent every school holiday together and we had the most marvellous time. We swam every day, the boys were fussed over by the chambermaids when they were babies and then flirted with the waitresses as they grew older. And while my tours of duty lasted four months I had the usual two-month break between each of them. That's two full months, twice a year, to be at home. I'd look at the lives of some of my old Medical School chums. They never travelled further than their surgeries but they all worked ridiculous hours. I knew my children far better than they knew theirs. People say you can't do this job with a family. They're very wrong.

'There's been something else you should know about my old Medical School chums,' he says after a slight pause. 'Most of them have been wonderfully successful. They've worked in top hospitals, Harley Street, universities. They're all eminently respectable. Some are leaders in their fields. When I see them I learn that they've got glorious houses, several cars, a villa or two in Spain or Portugal. It's wonderful stuff and I'd never criticise a single one of them, not for a moment.'

There's another silence. Edward does his usual thing of brushing imaginary dust from his sleeve. Then he takes a sheet of paper out of his plastic file and seems to change the subject. 'I've just been asked to provide a reference for you, young man,' he says.

I take in a sharp breath. The Stratford job. I'd almost forgotten it. I must have made it through to the next round.

'I will complete it in the most glowing terms, of course,' Edward says before I get a chance to speak. 'As I told you before I'm happy to respond to as many of these as required. With each one I will wish you all the luck in the world. But can I tell you one final thing about my career and my life?

'Of course.'

'It's very simple. At least once a year, Ben, I've been fortunate enough to stand and look at Sydney Opera House at midnight. At least once a year I've walked through the markets of Kowloon. I've smelt the surf on rocky Pacific coastlines. I've sat and drunk wine in Venetian squares. I've felt the wind on my face as I've sailed into magnificent harbours. I've seen waterfalls, temples, mountain ranges and extraordinary cities. I've been paid handsomely for all of this and over the years I've shared much of it with a family I love. And now, young man, I'm going to ask you to leave me in peace. I've got to write a reference so you can spend twelve hours a day in the very exotic locale of ...' he looks down at the sheet of paper, '... East London.'

I grab a bit of lunch then head to the gym to try and clear my mind. Monique is nowhere to be seen and the running machines are all free. I tap my programme details into the one with the best view of Wellington and start to run. It feels bizarre to be exercising on board instead of being out in the glorious New Zealand sunshine. When my forty minutes are up I head on to the deck to watch the comings and goings on the port. It's not quite as manic as the main 'turnaround' ports where vast containers of rubbish are taken off and equally large containers of new food and provisions are taken on. But there's still a lot to see a dozen or so decks below me on the harbour.

One group of guys is on ropes cleaning, repairing or repainting a section of the hull – something that happens every day we're in port. Official vans dart to the immigration and customs buildings and back. Lots of people with clipboards seem to be pacing around talking into mobile phones and walkie talkies. It's too early for the tour buses to be bringing the passengers back but a few people who've done their own thing occasionally head back to the gangway to clear security and re-enter our world.

I head back inside to shower and change. I've not ironed a shirt in six weeks, I realise as I pull on my uniform. I've not had to commute. I've not cooked a meal, washed a dish or cleaned a toilet. Is Edward right that this is an enormous privilege? Or is it a way of running away from reality? The time difference means I can't ring Cassie or my family for advice. For the first time since I got on board in Southampton I feel isolated and alone. I can't even find Albert to chat to when I get back to my cabin.

I step out on to my little balcony. The sun is stronger now and it feels fantastic. I've got two wooden chairs and a little wooden drinks table. This is not a bad place to be. And, as I look out over the harbour again, I get the feeling that things might be about to get exciting again. I'm far too high up to be able to make out much detail but there seems to be some kind of commotion going on outside.

The white uniform of one of our officers is flashing in the sunshine. A thin, blond woman in shorts is alongside him, leaning down to talk to a girl who's just sat down on the concrete floor. A little boy is tugging at the officer's arm and pointing at the ship. As the woman helps the girl back on to her feet two uniformed officers run down the gangway towards them. Two of the local agents from the port office join the group as they all move towards the ship. That's when my pager goes off.

The blond woman is the first to get out of the lift at the Medical Centre.

'My daughter's broken her shoulder. Please. She needs help,' she shouts. She's got a Scandinavian accent and there are tears running down her cheeks as she leads the others towards me.

The teenage girl is right behind her mum. She's got someone's cotton shirt wrapped around her shoulders so I can't see how bad her injury might be. But her eyes and her manner tell me what kind of girl she is. The work I did in A&E at Med School taught me that injured teenagers come in two basic types. Half love the thrill of being the centre of attention and turn minor dramas into their own personal crises. The rest are so desperate to fade into the background that they would head home with a rock in their eye just to avoid a fuss. This girl is firmly in the second category.

'I'm Peter Monaghan, Kristina's father,' says the man in clipped English tones. He's wearing a three-stripe officer's uniform. 'My family are with us until Hong Kong. We were in the Te Papa when Kristina fell down some steps. She twisted round and landed badly, very badly in fact. I decided we were cutting it too fine to get to the local casualty department so we headed straight back to the ship. This is Kristina's birthday, by the way. Her fifteenth birthday.'

We're in the first passenger room now and I turn to my patient. 'Kristina can you sit on here for me? Can you tell me what happened and then let me take a look?'

She describes the fall in a dull whisper. Then her little brother interrupts. 'She hit the ground so hard you could hear something crack. I thought she might die,' he says gleefully.

'She was never going to die, that's a ridiculous thing to say,' the boy's dad says as he pushes the youngster out of the door. 'I think perhaps the two of us should get out of your way. Kristina, I'll be next door if you need me.'

When they've gone I offer Kristina's mum a chair, then take my first clear look at my patient. With the cotton shirt gone it's pretty obvious what's happened. She hasn't broken her shoulder, she's dislocated it. From behind it's clear that her right humerus is hanging a centimetre or two below where it should be. In the process it has dragged the deltoid muscle down over the edge of her shoulder blade, leaving a sharp angle rather than the normal smooth contour of the shoulder. Kristina flinches a few times but doesn't complain once as I examine the joints. She really is quite a character. When you dislocate your shoulder a whole army of nerve ends scream out in anger. Your whole shoulder will be in agony and there is no easy way to hold the arm to get release. This happened half an hour ago and Kristina's endured a taxi ride and a whole lot of unwanted attention. So far it's just been her mum who's cried – and I've got a feeling that's embarrassed Kristina all the more.

I talk her through what I've seen, then ask her dad to come back in so I can explain what needs to happen next.

'I'll do some X-rays in a moment but it's looking like a simple dislocation,' I tell them in the corner of the room. 'Now, for a child, we'd normally want to treat that under a general anaesthetic, but as you said there's no time to get her off to hospital and back before we sail.'

'So you want to do it without the anaesthetic?' her mum asks, eyes full of tears again.

'We can do it under sedation. That will take the edge off the pain. As a side effect Kristina probably won't remember much about it afterwards, which could be an added advantage. We'll ease the bones back in place very carefully. It will hurt but the pain will only be momentary. Dislocated shoulders are extraordinary things. You do start to feel better the moment they're sorted.'

'So what do you need from us?' Dad asks.

'Your permission to go ahead.'

He looks at his wife and they both look at Kristina. 'I was listening. I want it done as soon as possible,' she says. Mum and dad both nod and we get ready to go.

Kristina starts to shiver as I take the X-rays. The pain and the shock are all coming together now and I really do want to move fast.

'Look, there's good news,' I say when the images flash up on our screen. 'There are no breaks or fractures. The bones in your shoulder and your arm are fine. You're not going to need an operation or have your arm in plaster or anything.'

'But the bone's got to be put back in place, right?' she asks. The first tears are starting to fall down her face. Her voice is little more than a whisper. 'I've seen that on TV and my boyfriend plays rugby. He says it happened in a game once. He says the boy was in so much pain he threw up and he wet himself. I'd die if I did that. I'd just die.'

I try to tell her it will be a lot easier to do the job here than on some muddy rugby pitch. I tell her that the sedation will dull the pain, make it all fly by and means she will barely remember it tomorrow. But she's not really listening. She only snaps back to attention when I say I'm going to give her parents a progress report.

'Please don't tell them I cried,' she whispers urgently. 'And don't tell them I've got a boyfriend.'

Her little brother's eyes nearly pop out of his head when I confirm what I'm going to do next.

'That is so cool. Can I watch?' he begs, thrilled. His dad silences him with a look.

'Do you want me to hold your hand?' Kristina's mum asks when she's kissed her daughter's hair one more time.

'Mum, I'll be fine. Just as long as it's quick.'

Edward has just arrived and I put my head around his door when I've settled Kristina in my room.

'As all three of our nurses are off having fun I'm going to need your help,' I say when I've explained the situation.

His eyes light up. 'How very exciting! I've not done one of these for years. Lead on Macduff!'

Back in my room I give Kristina a shot of painkiller, push my chair aside and make some room on the surgery floor.

'Hopefully you'll never have another birthday as bad as this one,' I say as I put an oxygen mask over her face and clip a pulse oximeter on her finger. We give her the first of the sedatives and her eyelids are starting to flicker within seconds. Edward loops a towel under her armpit and braces himself against the furniture. He looks more like an ancient mariner than ever and if I wasn't so worried about Kristina I'd probably say so. 'OK, Kristina, we're ready to go. The pain won't stop straight away but it will get better the moment we've done it. Just imagine you're a million miles away.'

She's only semi-conscious but she still manages to give a quick nod. I count to five under my breath. Then I start the job. I hold on to her right forearm, pulling her arm out and upwards. I want to guide the ball at the top of her humerus back into to the socket of her shoulder blade. Edward's job is to hold Kristina still on the ground as I move the arm and it's not easy. I can see him gritting his teeth and using all his strength to provide counter-traction and stop her moving. Tiny beads of sweat are appearing on his forehead. Meanwhile I'm praying under my breath that I'm getting it all right first time. Moving an arm that is already in agony is bad enough. Having to do it twice is a nightmare.

'Yes! That sounds right!' There's a surprisingly loud, and immensely satisfying, clunk as I get the bone in the right position. It clicks right back into place and stays there. Kristina screams at the sound then starts to swear repeatedly. Another side effect of sedation is that patients lose their inhibitions. Every doctor has a favourite story about utterly respectable, pillars of the community who turn the air blue in moments like this.

'Kristina that's the worst of it finished. You did brilliantly and I think it's over. I think it's sorted and you didn't even throw up,' I say, trying to talk over her words to save her embarrassment. Her parents may not know she's got a boyfriend, but they must now know she's got an extensive repertoire of bad language. After one final, particularly imaginative expletive she sinks back on the ground and sleeps. She'll probably be out for at least the next twenty minutes.

'The young today. Who says they lack eloquence?' says Edward with a big smile. Kristina's shoulder looks and feels good when we examine it, so we put a pillow under her head and a blanket on her while she rests. Her mum comes in to sit with her until she fully wakes up. When she does I tie her arm up in a sling and we head across the hallway for a final X-ray.

'You're going to be just fine,' I say. Kristina doesn't look so sure. She's still groggy but she's clearly got something on her mind.

'The rooms aren't soundproof, are they?' she asks just before we head back to the waiting area to discharge her.

'Bad luck,' I say, shaking my head. She gives me a worried smile.

Her parents thank me profusely, listen to my instructions about Kristina's painkillers and say they'll bring her back down in the morning to check everything is OK.

Kristina whispers a very quiet thank you of her own as the family prepares to leave. She's turned back into the embarrassed teenager who wants to be anywhere but the centre of attention. Not so her little brother. She tries to get him to leave ahead of her but he's still fizzing with excitement and isn't having any of it.

'That all sounded brilliant,' he tells me joyfully before he finally skips through the Medical Centre doors. 'And my sister is *so* busted!'

Edward calls an early morning meeting as we cross the Tasman Sea and approach the coast of Australia. Tomorrow morning we'll be in Sydney. It should be a time of celebration: the halfway point of the trip and the first place we're staying for two full days. The passengers certainly feel it. There's a real sense of excitement in the air as I walk down to the Medical Centre. I spot Mrs Stingray and Mr Zip Wire in the galleria and discover they're planning to do the Harbour Bridge climb.

'On a unicycle?' I ask, trying to be funny.

'That's a very good idea, my boy. If we can rent one we'll give it a go,' he says with a worryingly straight face.

Downstairs Romeo lays out a tray of coffee and croissants and Edward calls us to order.

'First of all, I want to congratulate everyone for having made it thus far. By my reckoning we've now worked forty-five consecutive days and I know a lot of them have involved some very late nights and very long hours. On my own behalf, and on behalf of the captain, I'd like to thank you all for the work you have done. I thought at the start of this voyage that we would make a good team and it turns out I was right.

'Now, Sydney will also be a very sad port of call. It will be the place we lose one of our own. Kiri, I had thought you might follow in my footsteps for thirty years. Instead you are following your heart. We wish you well, I invite you to join us all for dinner tonight, and I would like you to take this as a memento of our time together.'

Eileen stands up to pass over two parcels. 'As we've all been in the same shops every day since Southampton we didn't think there was anything exciting we could buy you on board. Dakila found you this first one in Wellington. I do hope you like it.'

Kiri opens it up. We bought her a silver cocktail shaker for the bar and had it engraved with the message: 'There's a top bunk with your name on it if you change your mind.' The second package is a box of furniture polish, a duster, some toilet cleaner and a dishcloth.

'Well, we thought you wouldn't have dear Romeo to clean up after you any more so we got you supplies,' Eileen says.

Kiri stands up and tries to decide if she's going to laugh or cry. 'I'm too upset to make a speech,' she says in the end. 'But in eight years of cruises I don't think I've ever worked with a nicer group of people. I don't know if I'm doing the right thing, but I do know I'm leaving on a high.'

When she's finished hugging everyone Edward calls us back to order.

'While Kiri deals with the sniffles I'd like to get back to business. We're all getting some well-deserved time off in Sydney, but for Ben's benefit as a first timer I should point out that the workload when we leave port may get even harder.' He turns to me. 'Ben, how do you think our charming crew may behave when they are let loose on the streets of Sydney for an overnight visit? Do you see them in the city's galleries, museums or joining Eileen trying out some of its finest fusion cuisine?'

'Not really, no.'

'Then you'll know what to expect. The first alcohol-related injuries will roll in shortly before dinner and will continue through the night. We may stitch a fair few more faces before morning. If anyone takes too many drugs then they will probably be treated on land, though if they have brought a stash back on board a problem may manifest itself at any time in the next few days.

'Then, of course, come the guests.' Edward turns to me again. 'Sydney is a world-class city where everyone eats well, speaks English and drives on the left. I can see why you might ask what can possibly go wrong. Perhaps Eileen can recall a few incidents from our last trip down under?'

'We had a very embarrassed gentleman who fell over and broke his nose when something scared him at the zoo. There was that lady who got a box jellyfish sting on her legs. I seem to remember that someone on the beach told her to put vinegar on it, but the nearest shop was a gourmet food store that only sold balsamic. Her husband refused to pay the extra and they ended up having such a big row she had an asthma attack. Then there was the crew member who caught a particularly nasty sexually transmitted infection. It didn't affect us down here, but last time I was in Sydney we also had some no-shows when we sailed. One married man and one married woman failed to rejoin the ship. Interestingly enough they weren't married to each other. Australia is many things but it's never dull.'

'Well on that note I adjourn our latest team meeting,' says

Edward, looking at his watch. 'Kiri we will miss you a great deal, but both before and after your departure in Sydney I expect it to be business as usual. Let's start our final day's work before the madness begins.'

# CHAPTER SIXTEEN

'You know what, gouty, we're out of our minds.' Gavin and I are on the ferry to Manley Beach and it's just occurred to me how ridiculous this is. 'We spend our whole life on one ship and as soon as we get a day off we jump on to another one.'

'It's only a twenty-minute ride and, trust me, the girls at the other end will be worth it,' Gavin says with a grin. He's not wrong. Everything about Manley is wonderful. Every bit of the view is spectacular as we walk from the ferry terminal through the town to the beach. It's a blindingly hot, late-summer day in Australia and the heat and humidity are getting right through to my bones. Walking along the shore feels wonderful after so long on a ship. There are so many different smells in the air. All of a sudden I get a sense of life without limits. I could walk into a crowd and disappear. No-one would know who I am or where I'm from. No-one would come up to me at lunch to show me a graze on their elbow or ask me if they're taking the right osteoporosis pills. It seems an appealing prospect. I catch myself wondering how Kiri and Kieran are getting on and whether they might give me a job as a barman.

'So how was the big goodbye?' Gavin asks when we start talking about the pair of them.

'Very sad, really. Kiri and Eileen both cried. Edward, Dakila and I all tried to act tough. But everyone's going to miss her. I feel like I've known her for years, not just two months.'

'That's ship life, mate. You wait till we get to Southampton. The girls won't be the only ones to start blubbing.'

We spend the day hanging out on the sand and in a few bars and cafés nearby. Gavin's got the whole night off and is planning to party with some of the spa staff and the shoppies. I join them for an early drink in a bar in Kings Cross but I'm due back on board at seven as I'm on call until the morning.

'If any of you get in trouble, go to Aussie A&E because I want a quiet night,' I tell them. Sydney is booming as I head back towards the harbour. All the bars and restaurants seem full. It feels strange to see so many new people after the enclosed little gene pool of cruise life. And there she is. I turn a corner down in the Rocks and the ship is right there in front of me. It's not dark yet but she's already lit up like a floating Christmas tree. It's almost a cliché of glamorous ocean living. I can't quite believe that's where I live. How many other people get to sleep with a view of the Sydney Opera House out their windows? I pick up the pace as I get closer. I've surprised myself by how much I want to be back on board.

A busy evening clinic is ending as I get to the Medical Centre. Eileen's also done the mandatory drug count to check Kiri hasn't taken anything naughty with her – or somehow been covering up a bit of long-term pilfering. On other ships I've been told that dodgy medics have built up nice little sidelines by writing false prescriptions for diamorphine and selling vials of it below deck.

'Everything adds up so unfortunately I don't need to call Kiri back for questioning,' Eileen tells me. 'I have had an email from her though.'

I lean over her desk to read it. 'I miss you all already! I think I might have made a terrible mistake!! Can I come back if I ask nicely?'

'Bless her,' I say. 'Delete it.'

Eileen smacks me on the hand and pushes me off into my office. I can hear her on the phone as I check my medical bag is fully stocked for the night. She pokes her head around my door.

'I've just had a call,' she says. 'Can you spare ten minutes to do a favour for an old friend of mine? He's a bit of a character and he's got one of his migraines. I'd normally get him to come down here or see him myself but he sounds ever so sad and I think he'd appreciate the attention of someone new. He's a bit of a treasure. If you go now I'll lock up down here and we'll see you in the morning.'

Antoine de Freidlander tells me he has been a steward for forty four years. 'That's longer than I claim to have been alive so please keep that information to yourself,' he says in a flurry of words as he gasps for air and grips his head. He's a wildly camp man in his sixties who has unaccountably dyed what little hair he has a near florescent ginger colour. He tells me he is a martyr to his migraines – and his most recent attack came on first thing this morning as he was getting ready to hit Sydney in style.

'It's my favourite port on the voyage and now I've missed it completely. It's quite unbearable,' he says.

'So this migraine has been worse than normal?'

'My darling doctor, it is as if Rudolf Nureyev himself is dancing up a storm inside my skull. And would it were so,' he pronounces through waves of nausea. 'It's as if my brain were exploding. It's all darkness and gloom and everything I detest.' He pulls a satin eye-mask over his face and lies prone on his bunk. 'I've tried to pretend the rest of the world isn't there but it just won't let me alone,' he moans.

'How often do the migraines come on?'

'The bad ones come two or three times a year. They've done so ever since I was in my twenties, a mere decade ago.'

'What do you normally take for them?'

'I have a supply of this,' he says, passing over his prescription. 'I took them as usual but I'm afraid to say I vomited them up straight away. I tried again with the same result. It's all been very distressing.'

I calm him down and suggest an intramuscular injection to stop the nausea. 'When that kicks in you can take the tablets as normal,' I tell him. He nods his agreement so I do it, then write him a repeat prescription for his anti-migraine medication.

'You've been a hero,' he says as he pulls his face mask back on and gets ready to close the curtains on his bunk. 'Will you give my best to dearest Eileen? Do tell her I would barely survive this job without her pistachio cookies.'

I do a double take as I leave his cabin. 'I thought she only baked cookies for us.'

'That's ship life, my darling doctor,' he says, giving a regal wave from within his curtains. 'In this job you're never quite as important as you think.'

I don't get a single call all night. The guests must be coping just fine with an evening on solid ground. If the crew are in trouble then someone else must be patching them up. In the morning Eileen and I have a sunny breakfast on the crew deck. The temperature is rising and the view of Sydney is stunning.

'Best job in the world?' Eileen asks as we linger over our coffees.

'It's got to be a contender.'

Edward is on shore leave so I'm looking after the passengers in morning clinic. The first of them certainly looks in a bad way. She lifts a cotton skirt up over her knees as she sits very gingerly on the consulting room chair. I wince on her behalf. She's not just been bitten by some bug, she's been mauled.

'I'm a bit embarrassed about coming to see a doctor about insect bites but they are a bit extreme,' she says apologetically.

Extreme is the word. It's impossible to work out how many bites she has or how many bugs may have been having their way with her. The swellings have all piggy backed on top of each other to produce one giant red mound from her thighs to her toes. Her feet are so swollen she can barely wear shoes or walk.

'I'm hoping you got these on shore?' I ask. We've got a long list of illnesses and conditions that we have to notify the bridge about in case they put the ship, the other passengers or crew in danger. Infestations are right up there close to the top.

'I was on the beach yesterday morning and I think I started scratching when we were at lunch. It got worse last night when I was just itching like mad.'

That's what I was hoping to hear. Sandflies are nasty little creatures but they don't travel well so they're unlikely to have hitched a ride on to the ship. I examine her legs carefully. She says it's been an act of will not to scratch the bumps too hard and she's largely succeeded.

If the skin gets broken she's in danger of getting a secondary infection. So far she looks to be avoiding it and I tell her to keep up the fight. I prescribe antihistamines, get some calamine lotion to help stop the itching and ask her to keep the whole area scrupulously clean.

'If it gets worse come back any time. And come back in a couple of days anyway so I can check you've not got any infections.'

'So when will my legs look better?' she asks as Eileen brings in the medication and commiserates her on what's happened.

'It'll be at least a week, I'm afraid,' I say.

She sighs. 'There's the sixties party tomorrow night. I wanted to wear a miniskirt and go as Twiggy. I don't think that's going to look to good if my legs are still like this. I don't think I'll be able to wear high heels for a long time either. I could wrap myself in a sheet and go as a mummy, but it's not very sixties.'

Eileen goes unusually quiet as the patient says goodbye and walks out of the Medical Centre.

'What's the matter?' I ask.

'Shhh! I'm thinking. Oh my god. I've got it!' she says. She rushes out into the corridor. 'Mrs Sherman. I've had an idea! Long dress to cover your legs, no shoes to hurt your feet, a sixties singer with the perfect name, bearing in mind what's happened to you. Go as Sandy Shaw!'

A flurry of waiters and kitchen staff come down over the rest of the morning. Two of our main restaurants are closed for the day and this is probably the first chance the workers have had to see a doctor since Southampton.

Fortunately no-one's got any life threatening or infectious conditions, though how one of the sommeliers could hear the wine orders until I removed the heads of two long-lost cotton buds from the depths of his ears is beyond me.

When surgery hours are over Eileen asks me to help get the place ready for the next part of our voyage. Sydney's a re-stock port so we've got plenty of new drugs to log and lock away in the dispensary. Dakila's with me, checking through the emergency bags when we hear Eileen open the Medical Centre door.

'They told me there was some kind of doctor down here. I need you to get me a doctor right now.' A loud woman's voice with a hard-to-place mid-Atlantic or mid-Pacific accent drowns out the classical music Eileen always turns on when we're in the Centre on our own.

'Our surgery has just closed. Our hours are from eight until ten each morning. You will be able to see a doctor in the afternoon between five and seven. Unless it's an emergency, I'm afraid you will have to wait until then.'

Dakila raises his eyebrows as we listen in. I don't think either of us have every heard Eileen sound so clipped and unhelpful before. We're always flexible about who we see and when. We don't encourage it, but if someone comes down out-of-hours we always make the effort to see them. Eileen must have taken an instant disliking to this particular lady – and as far as I'm aware Eileen has never taken a disliking to anyone in her life.

'It is an emergency. I'm not just an ordinary passenger. I need to see a doctor right away.'

I edge closer towards the dispensary door to make sure I don't miss anything. I want to know what Eileen will say if the woman actually uses a phrase like 'Do you know who I am?' As it turns out the woman is happy to explain it.

'I'm Marianna Defoe. I'm the headline act in your theatre this evening. I'm a personal friend of the Cruise Director. I can assure you that the CD will expect me to be seen right away.'

'I think we need to show ourselves,' I whisper to Dakila. We pop out of my office like a two-headed jack-in-the-box

'Doctor MacFarlane. Nurse Bautista. I wasn't aware you were still in the surgery,' says Eileen, unconvincingly. I step forward to introduce myself and shake our diva's hand. Marianna is a small very well-preserved woman with very big hair and an awful lot of make-up. She's in her fifties and looks like a soap opera matriarch.

'I don't like the ship's air-conditioning system,' she tells me.

'Well, I'm afraid it's the only one we've got,' I begin.

'Something has to be done about it. I can't perform unless something is done.'

'What is your act, exactly? Do you work with a magician? I'm afraid your name doesn't ring a bell,' Eileen says, twisting the knife as much as she dares.

Marianna gives her a long, low look. 'I'm a singer. And I'm not entirely sure I like you. Any of you,' she says.

I lead her into my room before things get any more heated. Marianna is clearly terrified of performing but is too proud and prickly to admit it. She's just been to the theatre for a sound check and, reading between the lines, it seems she was freaked out by the size of it. She's desperate to railroad me into giving her a sick note so she can stay in her stateroom till Cairns. She flounces out when I refuse.

'So, do we all fancy going to see her sing tonight?' Dakila asks when she's made a regal exit.

'I'd rather clean the surgery floor with a toothbrush.' Eileen declares with uncharacteristic vigour. 'And if either of you go I'll warn you now that I'll be using one of yours.'

We're due to leave Sydney at eight o'clock and Rebecca arrives bang on schedule at three in the afternoon. All four of us are waiting in the Medical Centre to meet her. 'Welcome, welcome, I am Doctor Edward Marlborough, this is my senior nurse Eileen Cornish and our colleague Dakila Bautista. I believe you know Doctor MacFarlane.'

Rebecca shakes everyone's hands and reaches over to give me a quick hug. Unlike me on my first day she's already wearing her uniform. She looks good in it. She's twenty six and, since I last saw her, she's developed a great tan and has got sexy blond highlights in her hair. All of a sudden I think I've worked out why Cassie is sometimes a bit suspicious of her.

'Now, I gather you have plenty of experience in our world,' Edward continues.

Rebecca runs through the ships she has worked on and the routes she's covered in the past few years.

'But you gave that up to see the frozen south?'

'I thought that while I was on a break in Australia I might as well do a few expedition jobs on the side. I'm glad I did. But by the time your second passenger on blood-thinning medication cuts their hand on the ice you're pretty much ready to leave. It brings back too many memories of those poor baby seals being clubbed to death in the arctic. When Ben said there might be a job here I jumped at the chance. It was nice to be out of uniform and in amongst all the other passengers on the expeditions, but it was a bit stressful looking after everyone on my own or working with a single doctor who didn't really speak much English. I think all things considered I'm better suited to a bigger ship.'

I flash a glance at Eileen as Romeo arrives with coffee. I saw her bring a plate of her latest cookies into the Centre earlier on. She's not handed them round yet so I'm guessing Rebecca has a bit more to do to win her over.

'How has your voyage gone so far?' Rebecca asks.

Eileen runs through some of the incidents we've dealt with and lists some of the ongoing cases we've got on board. 'I do hope you're not expecting your workload to fall just because you're on a larger ship now,' she concludes, not particularly warmly. 'Our guests and crew can be very demanding. We work all the time. Ten minutes after Doctor MacFarlane joined us we had a man in the surgery practically killing himself during an attack of the DTs. I hope you will be ready for challenges like that.'

Rebecca looks at her. 'I love challenges. I've even started to like the unexpected – and funnily enough it does always happen when Ben's around. The first time we worked together we were promised a simple hand-holding trip in a fancy private plane. We ended up coming back from Morocco in a full-spec air ambulance that looked as if it had just come back from a war zone. The patient had a cardiac arrest at 35,000 feet and needed ventilating in extreme turbulence. I was beyond terrified at the time, but I've started to thrive on that sort of thing. If we had an emergency call right now I'd throw myself into it. That's why I'm here.'

'Young lady I like your spirit. I wholeheartedly approve of you,' beams Edward.

So, at last, does Eileen. 'Goodness me, I quite forgot I had cookies for all of us,' she says, rushing to get them.

When we've all chatted a bit more she and Dakila show Rebecca around the Centre while Edward gives me one of his big winks and a thumbs-up sign. We leave Sydney in four hours time and we've got about fifty days, twenty ports and half a dozen more oceans and seas to go before arriving back in Southampton. I'd thought everything might go downhill when we lost Kiri. Now it looks as if the next month and a half will be better than ever.

'So what do you think of everyone?' Rebecca and I are having a quick chat in the Crew Bar before Dakila joins us. Her first clinic had been packed – between us we all dealt with almost twenty guests and at least that many staff and crew. Afterwards Edward invited us all to dinner in the Officers' Mess and everyone got on like a house on fire. We even managed to divide up Kiri's shore-leave and excursion slots without falling out.

'I like them all,' she says. 'Edward's adorable and he totally sees you as his son and heir. Eileen's practically in love with him and Dakila is just hilarious. I think he should certainly carry on with his acting. His accents are amazing. He did you brilliantly when you went to the loo. Ben, this is exactly why I tried to get you on cruise ships before. You meet such good people and when the crap hits the fan you're all there to support each other. I can't believe this Kiri girl left. She must be out of her mind.'

I sit back in my chair and smile. 'You know you're really cheering me up. Maybe I'll stick around and do another tour of duty after all.'

'So you're not going back to the NHS and the lovely Cassie?'

'No, I mean yes, of course I am, I'm only joking. But it's tempting, you know what I mean?' Dakila arrives before I confuse myself any more. He's got an even bigger smile on his face than usual.

'What have you done?' I ask suspiciously.

'It's not me. It's our new friend. She's got some fans. Can't you tell?'

I look around the bar. It's the normal crush of jobs, nationalities and uniforms. Some people are watching the football or the Bollywood videos as normal. Others are playing the games machines or just enjoying their down time. But every now and then almost all the men sneak a long look at Rebecca.

'You need a protector. You can have this pasty Englishman, or you can have a warrior from the Philippines. Who will it be?'

'No offence Dakila but I've just survived a full season on a former Russian spy ship so I think I can look after myself. Big cruise ships are bizarre though. Three decks up it's all piano music and polite conversation. Down here it's more like a low security prison.' She looks around one more time then turns to face us. 'So tell me again why you come down here rather than go to the Officers Bar?'

We try to tell her we prefer the atmosphere but she isn't buying it. If I'm honest I wonder if I might agree with her. 'We'll go for an upmarket drink tomorrow night,' Dakila promises. 'But while we're down in the crew room we should at least take advantage of what's on offer. "Islands in the Stream" with me, Rebecca? Or shall we just sit back and listen to Ben murder "Delilah" as usual?'

I see a couple of my regulars in the first few clinics out of Sydney. There's a carpentry supervisor with high blood pressure who reckons he wants to change his medication but can't really explain why, so I leave things as they are. One of the accountants is still struggling with a bad shoulder and needs a lot of reassurance that it will, one day, start to feel better. I even see Antoine again. He's had another migraine but has made it to down to the Medical Centre this time to ask what else he can do to head them off. His hair, if possible, seems even more orange in our less than flattering lighting. Looking at that in the mirror every day can't help, I want to tell him. Instead I talk him through all the usual coping strategies, all of which he's heard before. He promises to try a bit of meditation, then says a surprisingly downbeat goodbye. I wonder, suddenly, how many friends he has on board. Loneliness triggers all sorts of mental and physical problems. For all his exaggerated levity I wouldn't be at all surprised if it's not why he's getting ill – and why he's started to ask for help.

Edward calls me into his office when morning clinic is over. Sydney was the start of another new sector and as usual we've been notified of a few more passengers who might need extra attention. We only check up on these guests if we have particular concerns or if we've got plenty of spare time. Today Edward says we have the latter and allocates the list to me.

'This part of my ongoing, unofficial plan to train you up as my successor,' he booms as he talks me through the task. 'It has absolutely nothing to do with the fact that I feel like a break and they're showing *North by Northwest* in the cinema at three.'

The first guest I call upon is in a small internal cabin. He had a stroke six months ago, he's in a wheelchair and has very limited strength in his right arm and leg. He's also one of the most cheerful men I've met in ages. I check his blood pressure, talk through his medications and listen as he tells me how happy he is to be on board at all. He then wheezes with laughter as he jokes about trying to open the nonexistent window in the room. I can't help thinking about my fake claustrophobic man as I leave. I think he was only on board for one sector. I wish I'd been there to say good riddance when he left.

Next on my list is a man whose kidneys packed up several years ago. He's now on continuous ambulatory peritoneal dialysis – CAPD for short. The process involves running several litres of fluid into his peritoneal cavity three or four times a day, then draining it out again four or five hours later. Our inventory shows the fluids he needs for the duration of the cruise have all been loaded as planned and his overall health, plus the equipment he's got for the dialysis, all look good. He's another guest with a great attitude to life. He's been on a transplant list for three years but has been suspended from it while he takes this trip.

'It would be just my bloody luck for the perfect kidney to come up while I'm swanning around Hong Kong. Still, everyone needs a holiday and you can't put the rest of your life on hold, can you doctor?'

I tell him I couldn't agree more. I'm still smiling broadly as I head off to see the last man on my list.

'I'm Mrs Baxter. Do come in.' A smartly dressed, grey-haired lady in her seventies opens the stateroom door and steps aside for me. She looks delightful, but very fragile. Her husband, in a shirt and tie with a thick checked jacket, is sitting by the closed window. He's got a blanket over his knees even though the room is incredibly warm.

'I'm Doctor MacFarlane, hello.' I stride across to shake his hand so he doesn't need to get up – or apologise for not doing so.

'Nice to meet you, sir,' he says.

'You're very young. That's nice,' his wife says in a slightly distracted tone.

'I don't always feel it,' I say. 'Now I'm just popping around to welcome a few guests who've just joined us. Our senior surgeon, Doctor Marlborough, and I work with three nurses and at least one of us is available twenty-four hours a day should you need us in an emergency. I'll happily leave you to enjoy your cruise now or I can answer any questions you might have.'

Mrs Baxter flashes a glance across at her husband. I get the feeling she's asking him some kind of question. After a slight pause she turns back to me. 'Doctor, could you tell us what information you've been given about us?'

I look at my notes. 'We've been told your ages, of course. We've been told that you're in generally good health, Mrs Baxter, and that you take tablets for your blood pressure. Mr Baxter we've been told you had part of your lung removed for a tumour three years ago. You're on a number of inhalers and have recently had a few problems with gallstones.'

The couple both nod their heads. Mrs Baxter looks across at her husband again. He clears his throat and tries to pull himself up a little more in his chair. 'All that is quite correct,' he says. 'But it's not the whole story.'

'My husband's lung cancer came back three months ago,' continues Mrs Baxter very flatly. 'The tumour has replaced what was left of his right lung. He also has a number of secondaries in his liver. The doctors were very thorough. They have explored every option but sadly the best they could offer was admission to a hospice. Their considered opinion was that my husband had little more than three months to live.'

'I'm very sorry to hear that, Mr Baxter.'

He bows his head in silent thanks. It's clear that this is as emotional as he wants it to be.

'We were afraid that the company would probably not allow us to take this journey if we declared all of this before we left Australia. It wasn't easy to keep everything under wraps. But at least the challenge gave us a focus for a while.'

'So this is a journey you've always wanted to do?'

'It is a great deal more than that. My husband fought in the Burma Campaign. He lost his brother in Malaya. He lost very many good, dear friends on the Burma Railway and others died in Changi Jail during the Japanese occupation. We moved to Australia shortly after the war and have been there ever since. He would now like to honour his comrades' memory by visiting their graves. We couldn't fly, doctor. My husband was too weak. This seemed the smoothest, least painful way to make the journey. Singapore is three weeks away. I can assure you we are going to be absolutely fine. But I wanted the doctors to be aware of our situation. I wanted you to be ready in case something goes wrong.'

She passes me a typewritten page of information on the medication her husband is taking and starts to apologise again for not submitting it to the company before departure. I put my hand on hers to stop her. Despite the heat it's cold to touch.

'Mrs Baxter, as far as I'm concerned you're our guests now

and we are where we are. I can't yet speak for my colleagues but I'm certain they will agree with me.'

'My husband needs to get to Singapore,' she says one more time as I take my leave.

'Then we'll make sure he gets there.'

I walk past the cinema on my way back from the Baxters' room. The afternoon's film programme appears to be over so I head to Edward's stateroom. I think I need to tell him what's happening as soon as possible.

'Dear boy, always a pleasure.' He ushers me in and I find myself smiling. The first thing I do when I get into my cabin is to take off some of my uniform and try and relax. I've come round unannounced, yet Edward is still immaculate in his full daytime rig. I wonder briefly what he's going to wear in retirement.

'Edward, I'm sorry to disturb you but I wanted to run something past you.' He slides his balcony door closed to ensure we can't be over-heard and I explain the Baxters' situation.

'Did you examine the gentleman at all? How did he appear to you?'

'He's clearly very sick and he must be in some degree of pain. But he was sitting relatively comfortably, dressed well, fully contributing to the conversation. I left it at that, to be honest.' I pass over the list of medications. Edward sucks in his breath slightly as he reads. Then he stands up straight.

'If Mr Baxter fought for the Allies in the Far East then we will help him complete his journey. I will speak to Eileen and I will mention it in passing to the Captain. I'll ask you to inform Dakila and Rebecca. Don't look so worried, Ben,' he says as I get up to leave. 'I've not seen the patient yet but I've already got more confidence than you in his ability to survive. Do you remember the photographs of the men coming out of Changi Prison? Can you imagine what it took to recover from that? Men who have lived through the darkest of nights do not give in when better days dawn. I've seen countless patients beat the odds when something really matters to them: a daughter's wedding, a son's graduation, a grandchild's first day at school. Now, here, a mark of respect to fallen comrades. Medicine is full of extraordinary stories. This Mr Baxter has vowed to travel to Singapore. Our job is to help him do just that.'

Rebecca had decided to spend her on-call afternoon in the Medical Centre so I head down to tell her about the Baxters. I don't get the chance. She's in the waiting area with the phone in her hand when I arrive. She slams it down and heads over to me.

'Ben, I was about to page you,' she whispers. 'I thought I'd be able to look after this on my own, but I can't. The guy arrived about five minutes ago and I've put him in one of the passenger wards. His name's Roger Boyt, he's thirty nine and he's here with his wife, Ellie. He's in trouble but he doesn't know it – probably because they're having a bit of a domestic.'

The first person I see as I approach the ward room is a very sunburned woman. The second is a tall, lobster-red man sitting in his underwear.

'I'm Doctor Ben MacFarlane. How can I help you both?' Mr Boyt, perched on the very edge of the examination couch, turns slightly to face me. Now I know why Rebecca thinks he's in trouble. If his front is badly burned, his back is practically incinerated. The skin is red raw and there are already pale, fluid-filled blisters developing across the whole surface. When I look down, it's the same over his legs. Even the soles of his feet are badly burned.

'This hurts like hell and I am very, very pissed off,' the patient says, slurring his words slightly and almost shivering in pain, as I walk in.

'I told him to use sunscreen. I always tell him that,' his wife tells me.

'And I told you to wake me up if I fell asleep.'

'I went inside and had a nap myself! It's not against the law. I'm on holiday and I fancied a sleep. I didn't think you'd be so stupid as to stay on the balcony all afternoon.'

'I bet she left me out there on purpose to get back at me. I bet she's loving this,' he says, turning back to me. 'Ruining my holiday is her idea of fun.'

I put my hand up to calm them both down. It's clear that the patient is in pain, embarrassed and angry – that's not a great combination and I need to take control fast.

'Mrs Boyt, I want you to step next door to give us some room. Mr Boyt, I need you to lie on the couch so I can get a closer look at your skin.' I scrub up as he stretches out gingerly on the examination bed. The good news is that, with his wife gone, he seems to have lost all his aggression and bravado. The bad news is that the more I see the more worried I become. Sunburn as harsh and extensive as this doesn't just hurt. It can lead to serious infections and even renal failure. There's even an outside chance it can kill.

'The skin's the biggest organ in the body. You've given yours quite a pounding, Mr Boyt,' I say as I try to work out what percentage of his body is affected. Too much is my first best guess. 'We're going to get some fluids into you

straight away because you're body's been losing them fast,'
I tell him. 'I'll give you something for the pain and I'm also
going to take a blood sample from you so we can see how
much salt you've got in your system. That will help tell us
how your kidneys are coping with what's going on.'

Getting the blood sample takes longer than it should. It
seems that Mr Boyt is not a fan of needles. Despite his pain
and precarious state he almost begs me not to get the syringe
close to him.

'I have to do this, Mr Boyt,' I tell him as I reach for his arm.
What I don't say is that there's a lot worse to come.

'Just close your eyes and let me do my job,' I say as I get
the first line into his arm. I hook him up to a bag of plasma
expanders and start it flowing. Then I get some IV morphine
and some ibuprofen to dull the pain of his flesh wounds. I'm
pulling on a sterile gown and getting a pile of specialised
burns dressings together for his back and legs when Rebecca
comes in with the test results.

'His urea is 24.5' she says, a worried look on her face.

That means he's lost a lot more fluid than we'd feared –
and he's in a lot more danger. I speed up the rate of the drip
and add some antibiotics to the mix. Rebecca starts to dress
and cover the worst burns while I make sure we can measure
exactly what's going on inside him. I'm going to put a central
line into his neck so we know exactly how much fluid is
going in. Then I'm going to catheter him so we can see how
much is coming out.

'No way, you can't do that to me!' he says when I explain
the process. But he's weakening, despite the fluids and the
medication we're getting into his blood stream. He's also
getting scared. He's finally woken up to the fact that he's on
the edge. I attach the equipment, then get pulse and blood

pressure monitors on him. Rebecca needs almost half an hour to finish protecting his skin.

'It's so badly damaged,' she whispers as I help out.

The weeping sores seem to be getting worse before our eyes. The skin is the body's barrier against the world. I've rarely seen it so comprehensively breached by the sun or so wide open to bacterial attack. I head back out to speak to his wife. She's reading a magazine.

'Is he sorted?' she asks, not sounding particularly bothered.

'He's stabilised,' I say. 'But I'm going to ask my senior colleague to come down and give us a second opinion on what happens next. We need to get your husband to a Burns Unit as fast as we can.'

All hell breaks loose when Edward confirms my opinion. Mr Boyt is groggy, unfocused and docile. Out in the waiting area his wife is not.

'So you want to boot us off the ship? For spending too much time in the sun? I can't believe you're telling me this and I don't see why you can't just look after him down here. What kind of doctors are you?'

'Mrs Boyt, your husband is seriously ill. This isn't just a bit of sunbathing. He's effectively got third degree burns over a very large part of his body. My colleagues and I are agreed that he needs specialist care. We've got a Burns Unit in Cairns on standby to provide it.'

'But you're all supposed to be doctors down here. It says Medical Centre on the door, so I don't understand why you can't take care of him. We've paid enough money for this cruise and we're entitled to help. You're here to work, not to

225

have a holiday. What are you all here for if you won't look
after my husband?'

'We're here for emergency care, Mrs Boyt and that's what
we're giving now. We're here to keep people safe when they're
on the ship. We can't do open-ended, ongoing care. If we
don't get your husband to hospital tomorrow morning it will
be nearly a week till we get a second chance. That's too long
and it's too dangerous.'

'Well what if we refuse to leave?'

'You won't be given a choice Mrs Boyt. That's not how it
is on cruise ships. If we say your husband has to be taken off
then he's taken off. Can I explain again how much danger
your husband is in? He's on the borderline for an emergency
evacuation and if his condition deteriorates he might still
need one. None of this is in dispute. It's about saving your
husband's life.'

She flounces around the waiting area as I run through her
husband's condition yet again. She threatens to sue anyone
and everyone over the dereliction of duty that's got us to
this point. She refuses to go back to her stateroom to collect
her things or to get ready to leave the ship in the morning.
Funnily enough, the only thing she doesn't do is ask to see
her husband.

'I don't need to see him. He's perfectly fine,' she says when
Rebecca offers to take her next door.

'He'd like to see you,' Rebecca says, though I doubt she
believes that any more than I do.

'The whole thing is ridiculous. Someone's going to pay for
this,' Mrs Boyt says as she finally walks into the passenger
ward. She doesn't soften even when she sees her husband
sedated, heavily bandaged and wired up to half a dozen
different pieces of equipment. 'They want us off the ship,' she

tells him. 'You've got twelve hours to pull yourself together. If you can't do it then our whole holiday is ruined.'

It's no surprise that Mr Boyt can't follow his wife's instructions and recover overnight. We've rehydrated him and we're trying to keep him infection-free but we can't risk keeping him on board for the long sail up towards Malaysia.

We're due in port at eight and I top up his painkillers at seven before we move him on to a trolley. He mutters and swears but at least has the good grace to thank us for taking it slowly when we do the lift. Underneath all the dressings his skin is still horribly raw. Every movement can open up new wounds and re-start the whole cycle of fluid-loss that we're fighting to stop.

Unfortunately his wife's mood hasn't improved as we wheel him through the ship towards the disembarkation point. She's not just furious about leaving the ship, she's got issues about the way we're doing it.

'Can someone please tell these people to go away? My husband is not some sort of freak show!' she screams at one point.

We're taking a short cut past some of the vast food storerooms. Most of the crew in that part of the ship are barred from entering the guest areas. Mr Boyt is probably the first passenger they've seen – and as he's half-naked, covered in bandages and attached to a mobile drip, he's certainly the most entertaining. Whole groups of onlookers gather to watch us wheel him by. Some tear past us or find other routes to get back ahead of us so they can have a second look.

Her mood doesn't improve when she realises they can't be taken to the shore straight away.

The ship is too big to get to the quayside in Cairns so we dock at a pontoon and transfer passengers to shore in a fleet of tenders. We've been told it's easier at this end and on shore if we wait for the crowds to thin before moving. Mrs Boyt doesn't like it at all.

'So you're telling me we have to wait for all the lard arses and old crows to head off on their excursions? Unbelievable,' she moans. 'I don't see why we should share a boat with them anyway. I don't see why we don't get sent something special from the coastguard. That's what we pay our taxes for.'

Rebecca tries to change the subject and pass the time by talking about other patients she's transferred from ships on tenders.

'The best place for this is Venice,' she says after a long silence. 'The last time I was there they sent one of those tiny vaporetto things for the patient. Inside it was a full-spec ambulance, but on the outside it looked like something out of a period drama. It was gorgeous, all polished wood and ancient coloured glass. We had flags flying on top of it and we whizzed up the canals like something out of a Bond movie. The hospital we went to looked like some kind of Doges Palace as well. It was like stepping back in time. The whole thing was just amazing.'

'Yeah, and because of your stupid rules we're missing out on the chance to see Venice at all,' Mrs Boyt replies.

We all put up with the silence after this and wait until one of the security officers comes over to say we're ready to roll. I wheel Roger's chair down the gangway towards the tender. The staff on board are young and seem to be in a hurry, which suits everyone just fine. They pretty much ignore Roger's moans as they help lift him on board. I sit next to him with his notes and hand them over to the paramedics on the quayside. A steward is wheeling two large suitcases off the tender. He loads them in the front of the ambulance as Mr Boyt is lifted into the back.

'I'll say goodbye and wish you both all the best now,' I say as Mrs Boyt sits on the jump seat next to her husband.

He seethes and doesn't say anything. Her last words are short and to the point.

'Yeah, whatever you say,' she mumbles as the ambulance doors close. Back on board the ship Rebecca is one of the first people I see.

'I want you to know I gave them a big wave when they left,' she tells me cheerfully. 'Well, it was sort of a wave. Although it only really involved one finger.'

# Part Four

# The South China Sea

# CHAPTER SEVENTEEN

'I'm here about my husband, Tom' she says, clearly nervous. Her name is Jody Howard. I'd say she's no more than twenty five. She's my final patient of the night and I take an immediate liking to her. It's obvious she's seriously worried about something. This seems to be the kind of conversation she would run a mile to avoid.

'So what exactly is the problem?'

There's a long silence as she gathers her thoughts. A couple of times she gets ready to speak, meets my eyes then checks herself and looks away. I shuffle some papers on my desk to try and give her the opening she needs. I've started rearranging my pot of pens before she's ready.

'We're competition winners,' she begins. 'We didn't pay for the cruise, we couldn't possibly have afforded it. We won it through a draw in a newspaper. Everything was included, with spending money and travel expenses thrown in. We're here from Sydney to Singapore. We get two nights in Raffles Hotel then they fly us home.'

'It sounds brilliant. Congratulations.'

She smiles weakly at me. 'Thank you. I was thrilled at first. We've had a tough few years. My husband's not been himself for quite some time. He's been so worried and business has been bad so he's had to work really hard. He gets angry and I've seen him shrink right back into himself. For a while I thought the cruise would bring the old Tom back to me. I thought it would give us time to be together, to forget about all our problems and to feel as if we're getting somewhere in life.'

'But it hasn't helped?'

There's another long silence as Jody gathers her thoughts.

'The whole thing has been bizarre. I just don't understand it.' She shakes her head and looks at her hands. 'He was angry on the first day, just seething about things the way he does. I think he was worried that everyone else would know we hadn't paid for the holiday and didn't fit in. He didn't want to talk to anyone because he said they'd all be snobs and stuffed shirts. We went out to the restaurants to sit with each other but we didn't talk to anyone else. He didn't even say anything to me at one meal. Not one word all night and I don't know why. I thought we'd done the wrong thing by coming. I thought we'd go stir crazy trapped in our cabin all day and that everything would get worse. Then I managed to get him to the bar on the front deck for a few late night drinks. It was our second night, or maybe our third. He liked it. It was the most wonderful thing to see him smile and not to have to worry about him for a change. I went to bed so happy that night.'

'And the next day?'

'It kept on getting better. He really cheered up. It was like he'd flicked a switch. I barely recognised him but it was wonderful. He was happy, doctor, genuinely happy for the first time in years. We had a nice lunch, we went to dinner that night and it was magical. We talked, we laughed, we even thought about going to one of the nightclubs. He was laughing at all the snobs and the stuffed shirts. He wasn't intimidated or angry. It was us against the world and we were going to be the winners. It was like we were kids again.'

'It sounds great. So what's happened since?'

There's another long pause. 'He's taken it to an extreme. He's got out of control. I didn't mind at first, even when he got really loud in the bars and at the talent show the other night. I wanted him to be happy and he was. But then he started buying everyone drinks. Last night he bought champagne for everyone in the bar – that was about thirty people, all of them strangers. This morning, when I told him we couldn't afford it and that I needed to know why he'd done it, he just stormed off. I thought he'd gone drinking, but it turned out he'd gone to one of the jewellery stores and he bought me this.'

She reaches into her bag and pulls out a pale blue Tiffany box. Inside is a silver necklace with a large hallmarked pendant.

'We can't possibly afford this. He knows we can't. I actually cried when he gave it to me and that set him off. It was like the last few days had never happened. He said I was calling him a loser and that I didn't have any faith in him and that I was dragging him down. He stormed out and I haven't seen him since. I'm going to take this back to the shop to see if they'll refund our credit card. But I think he must be on drugs. Can he have got drugs on board, doctor? Has someone sold him something?'

I think about the mystery guy who collapsed at the 'Love's Young Dream' party and all the others who'd probably taken drugs alongside him that night. Someone could have sold Jody's husband almost anything. But I doubt a passenger would start taking drugs for the first time on board. Something else must be going on. I ask a few more questions about her husband's past, his general health and his behaviour.

'Will he come and see me?' I ask.

Jody shakes her head. 'I can't see him doing that in a million years. He'd be furious if he knew I'd come here and said anything. We have to pay for all our spending on board. I'm already worried about explaining this appointment away when we get the bill. So what do you think is going on?'

I spend the next ten minutes talking her through my theory. I can't be sure without seeing and speaking to her husband, but it sounds like classic manic-depressive behaviour.

'It's called Bipolar Affective Disorder nowadays,' I explain. I don't point out how odd it seems that someone who may already have extreme feelings of worthlessness can now be branded as 'BAD'. Instead I try to explain where the mood swings can come from, what can trigger them and what can be done to bring things back to normal. 'It can be controlled with medication but it takes a while for the effects to kick in. And patients don't normally want to start treatment when they're on a high because at that point they don't see that they've got a problem. When you're having the time of your life handing out champagne in a bar you don't want some pill to take the fun away. That's why the treatment really does need the patient to fully understand what's going on. They need to want to sort this out. It works after people have hit rock bottom.'

'Can't I just give him the drugs without him knowing? I can put them in his food or something. Wouldn't that be the easiest way to do it?'

I shake my head. Funnily enough my mum did something like that for my dad once. She wanted to surprise him by booking a weekend in New York for their wedding anniversary. For a week beforehand she ground down an aspirin every morning and put it in his orange juice to try and protect him from DVT on the plane. But that's not going to work for Jody and Tom.

'We can't give the drugs without your husband's consent. He's not endangering himself or anyone else. Jody, this is going to be really hard, but if this doesn't right itself you're going to have to get your husband to accept that this isn't normal behaviour.'

Jody is about to speak when there's a knock at my door. I look up at the clock. We've overrun the normal appointment slot by at least fifteen minutes. But as Eileen opens the door I know straight away that this isn't the reason for the interruption. I can tell from her face that something's happened.

Eileen tries to be as polite as she can as she bundles Jody out into the waiting area. Then she turns to me.

'We've got a man, Mr Bhagwati, being brought up from the engine room. He has a bad hand injury. The people down there aren't very clear but it seems he's lost all or part of all four fingers. Dakila's gone down to help assess him and bring him up.'

I wash my hands, head into the Crew Ward and get ready for the main event. Two minutes later a gruesome, bloodied rescue party thunders down the corridor to our door. A group of guys in overalls and turbans are carrying the injured man. They're all shouting out instructions to each other as they manoeuvre him through the doors. But the man in their arms is silent. No cries, no moans, no complaints. If he's unconscious then we need to move fast. He can't be dead, can he?

'In here please.' I glove up as the patient is deposited on the consulting room bed. He's got his eyes open now so at least I know he's alive. I move towards him. He's got what look like two T-shirts wrapped around his left hand. That must explain why several of the men with him are bare-chested. In the corner of my eye I see one of the men pass over a bloody package made from another T-shirt. That must be the severed fingers.

Dakila starts putting a line into the man's arm and when Eileen's finished checking his blood pressure and other key indicators she heads out to get the drugs we need.

'Sir, how are you feeling?' The man doesn't reply, but his eyes flash to mine so I know he can hear me. 'Do you speak English?' He gives me a nod, but no words. 'OK, you might want to suck on this to dull some pain,' I say, passing over the 'gas-and-air' that's often given to women in labour. 'I'm going to take these off your hand now and see what we can do for you.' As I ease the material away it reveals the mangled remains of his hand. Blood oozes from the stumps – and all of a sudden a real jet fires out from one of them.

'Woah! A spurter! Can we get some artery forceps here?' I yell as I slap a temporary dressing on and hold tight. The man stays silent as I do it. He breathes in hard. At one point his eyes lock on to mine as if he's making some silent plea. But then they move beyond me. He's looking past our crowded consulting room walls and into another place far away.

Eileen gets the first bits of kit I need, then calls out some very worrying blood pressure and pulse figures. She heads out to get the drugs we need drawn up and I ask her to give them as soon as she's back. I also ask Dakila to speed up the original drip and get us some eye protection. I also need a few clues about when the accident happened so I know how much blood the patient has lost.

'They called straight away so it was less than ten minutes ago. But there's a lot of blood on the floor down there,' he says. I get him to test a sample in the blood-gas machine next door. It's not ideal, but it's the next best way to check blood loss. The result, which comes back in seconds, is yet more cause for concern. I've got a feeling that the man's going to need a transfusion. But before he does we've got to stem the flow and stop the bleeding.

'OK, I need the dressing trolley!' I yell. Dakila wheels it in. Laid out on the sterile field on top is a selection of swabs, antiseptic solutions, sterile scissors, artery clips and a syringe of local anaesthetic. Time to get to work.

I peel back the dressing with one hand while holding an artery clip in another. Once again a small fountain of blood spurts out with each beat of the man's heart. It's incredible how much power there is in an arterial bleed. It's the ultimate reminder that in cases like this you need to work very fast indeed.

'OK, here goes.' I focus on the blood's exact exit point, wait for a beat, then apply the clip. 'Gotcha!' The spurting stops. That's the first battle won. Now on to the next.

Edward has been called down and he arrives as I get to the final finger. It's been crushed rather than sliced off. It's oozing blood instead of spurting it across the room. 'Busy day, Doctor MacFarlane?' Edward asks, striding in. 'What have we got here?'

'Traumatic amputation. He's lost the two terminal phalanges on the index and middle finger and the terminal phalanx of the ring finger. There's a lot of other damage and some bad arterial bleeders but I've clipped them.'

There's a gleam of excitement in the older man's eye as I speak. Like every other doctor he can't resist the lure of an emergency.

'Well, this takes me back to the days when being a ship's surgeon meant just that,' he says. 'Now, let the dog see the rabbit.' I peel back some of the new dressings. 'Well, I don't think this man will be playing the piano any time soon,' Edward says as he pulls on a gown and gloves. 'Right, let's get some ring blocks in place. Let's do basic debridement and irrigation, then aim for primary closure.'

We work side-by-side for the next half-hour. We anaesthetise each finger in turn. We cut away the non-viable tissue and wash away the blood, dirt and grease. Then we close the skin over the exposed stumps of bone.

Eileen knocks on the door as we finish up. 'Sorry to disturb you, doctors. This gentleman has been getting very upset. I said he could speak to you now.'

One of the patient's colleagues steps nervously forward. He's one of the shirtless ones, the one who handed over the lost fingertips.

'You have the fingers and you can sew them back on, yes?' he asks. 'You can keep them in cold ice, yes? He can have his fingers back and it will be OK?' He starts nodding his head and smiling insistently as if sheer determination can make it happen.

I try not to take all his hope away. 'The fingers are on ice next door,' I say. 'We will do what we can. It was very good that you were able to save them. He will thank you for that. When we get him to hospital on land they will see what they can do.'

The man bows his head. There's no light at all in his eyes as he leaves. He too seems to be able to move to another place at will.

'It's very good that you've still got your thumb, sir. That's the hardest thing to live without,' Edward tells the patient as we start to bandage his hand.

There's no response and Edward fills the silence by talking about yet another case from yesteryear.

'Once upon a time I had a man very like you in my care who lost everything but his little finger. On land I believe they amputated one of his toes and grafted it on to his hand. That gave him a claw. It wasn't pretty, but it gave him options. You're better off than that dear man, my friend.' Edward smiles kindly at our patient. Mr Bhagwati looks away and closes his eyes.

Ten minutes have gone by since Edward and I finished working on Mr Bhagwati's hand. We've moved him to a clean bed in the Crew Ward. Now we're tackling his next problem. He looks glassy-eyed. His skin is clammy and dangerously pale. We've bulked his blood up with plasma expanders and his body's own defences have helped by pumping other fluids into his system. But fluid can't transport oxygen. He's needs more haemoglobin. If he doesn't pull out of his slump soon we're going to have to think about a blood transfusion.

'Well, gentlemen, I think we need to put out a call for blood just in case,' Edward says as Dakila and I stand at the patient's side. It's my first time preparing for something like this on board and it's a difficult prospect. We'll obviously match up the blood groups before proceeding. But we can't test blood for infections. We have to rely on the donors' self-declarations. And, of course, we have to find willing volunteers fast.

'Shall I try his colleagues before we put out a general call to the rest of the crew?' Dakila asks. 'I'll go down there and announce it. I'll tell anyone who's willing to come up here in half an hour. They were all upset about the accident. Hopefully at least one of them will want to help.'

He turns out to be wrong. When we open the Medical Centre door half an hour later some two dozen men are standing there. All of them are silent, waiting patiently with heads bowed. Each of them is ready to do whatever it takes to save their friend – and Eileen isn't the only one to have a tear in her eye as she welcomes them to the Centre. When the paperwork is done we identify several potential donors and Dakila starts to fill some blood bags in case Mr Bhagwati needs them. 'I'm only going to authorise this as a last resort,' Edward says grimly as we look for any signs of improvement in the patient's condition. We're getting within range of the boats and helicopters that can do an emergency evacuation and the captain is steaming ahead to get us to our next port as early as possible as well. Everyone is doing everything they can to help this man – and fortunately his own body has joined the fight. His blood pressure has picked itself up off the floor, his vital signs and his pulse are closer to where we want them to be. He's a fighter and he's even got a bit more colour in his cheeks.

'He's stabilised,' I tell Rebecca when she takes over from Dakila and starts watching the patient. I need to head back to my office with Mr Bhagwati's supervisor. Even the most minor crew injuries throw up a lot of paperwork. This one raises an awful lot more legal, insurance, and health and safety issues, so the documentation has to be perfect. The admin takes a good forty minutes to complete. From start to finish I've got one eye on the door. I'm ready to run if Mr Bhagwati's condition deteriorates and Rebecca needs help. But as it turns out I'm not needed.

'He's very resilient. He's dealing with the anaemia and I think he's going to be able to make it to port,' she says at the Crew-Ward door when I look in on them. 'Edward's been in and he's not going to risk transfusing him. I just wish the guy would say something. He understands me, but it's as if he can't bring himself to speak.'

We look across at the patient. The distant look is back in his eyes again. He's calm but there's something wrong. Suddenly I get an idea what it might be.

'Has he been to the loo?' I ask.

'I've asked him if he needs to but he doesn't say.'

I walk across to the man's bedside. This must be one of those cultural things where some men can't face showing weakness in front of women – and needing a bedpan is very much seen as a weakness.

'Mr Bhagwati, do you need to be taken to the toilet?' He flashes an anguished glance at Rebecca who diplomatically leaves the room. He looks back at me. As usual he doesn't speak but he nods so fast and so vigorously I can't stop myself from smiling. I offer him my shoulder, help him to stand and offer him a bottle. When I turn away he starts to use it. Five minutes later, back on his bed, he finally allows himself to sleep.

We watch over him and check his vital signs for the next nine hours. He's an emergency disembarkation in Manila and when its time for him to leave we put him in a wheelchair and push him through the corridors towards the usual exit point. That's where we get a final surprise. The same two dozen men who had lined up to give blood for their colleague are waiting to say goodbye. This time they aren't in their work clothes. They're not covered in grease and oil and sweat. They are all in their finest clothes. Washed clean, smart and silent, they stand together and make a guard of honour for him to pass between.

On the quayside I talk the local paramedics through his

situation very quickly, then step aside as they help him out of the chair and into the ambulance. As I start to wheel the chair back towards the gangway Mr Bhagwati uses his good hand to call me back to him. He speaks for the first time.

'Thank you,' he says. Just two words. Then the ambulance doors close and he's gone.

Eileen and I have got into the habit of visiting Mr and Mrs Baxter every other morning at coffee time. They're delightful company – but seem to be getting more fragile by the day. Mr Baxter is always immaculately turned out. I've not seen him wear the same tie twice. He's weak and his eyes are sunk deeply into his skull. But when the conversation comes to the thanks he wants to give in Singapore he comes alive. For a few lovely moments he seems fit and young again. Then the tiredness hits him. There's sadness in his eyes as he folds back within himself.

For her part Mrs Baxter could be the ultimate definition of the phrase 'living on her nerves'. I wonder when she last slept properly.

'Are you finding the room service meals all right?' Eileen asks at one point. 'You do know that if you want something different they'll make it up for you. You can order anything you want. We've got food stores the size of buses. If you want it we've probably got it. The boys will do it for you. We've made sure of that.'

Mrs Baxter gives her a grateful smile. 'We're managing just fine,' she says. 'We don't eat a great deal but the gentleman who brings the trays is very accommodating. He does seem to care as well. So many of you seem to care.'

Eileen and I barely speak as we head down the corridor. 'What do you think?' she asks when we get back to the Medical Centre.

'It's as if he's making it through on sheer strength of will. I've never seen someone so ill but so focused. Nearly two weeks down, two more to go. The poor man must be exhausted.'

'She's struggling as well, isn't she? She looks wiped out. She looks more on edge each time we see her. It can't help being in that room twenty-four hours a day. I wish she'd let us sit with him for an hour or so. I don't think she's set foot in a single part of the ship or spoken to any other guest. She needs a break and she needs a friend.'

I look across at Eileen. 'Do you know what? I think I know just the woman.'

It takes me quite a bit of looking but in the end I find her sitting in a sunny spot just by the golf nets. She's got a book in her lap but is paying more attention to the people practicing their swing in front of her. She looks relaxed and happy.

'Mrs Philip, I wonder if you could do me a bit of a favour?' I sit next to her and explain the Baxters' situation. 'As Mr Baxter finds it hard to leave their cabin I think his wife is feeling a little isolated. To be honest I also wonder if they're both not feeling a little claustrophobic cooped up in that room together all the time. I'm sure you remember my senior nurse Eileen? She feels that Mrs Baxter would benefit from having someone to talk to. Would it be very awkward for you to go around and introduce yourself to them?'

Mrs Philip smiles. 'Doctor, it is only young people who

think there is anything awkward about anything. The one benefit to being old is that you no longer worry about what other people think. Nor do you worry about convention. That allows me to do what I think is right. I am sure that Mr and Mrs Baxter will accept my visit in exactly the same spirit. I will call upon them this afternoon. If what you say about them is true, I have a feeling I will enjoy their company enormously.'

# CHAPTER EIGHTEEN

I used to fly into Hong Kong to do medical repatriations and I thought the view of the city was petty good when you got the train in from the airport. It's nothing compared to the one you get when you sail into the harbour at dawn. The skyscrapers seem to rise out of the sea. Most of them have still got their lights on and it's like a jagged staircase of back-lit glass. It feels as if we've got all 2,000 passengers on deck as we approach. The excitement and the energy is the same as it was in San Francisco and Sydney. This isn't just another vaguely interesting stop where people can stretch their legs and do even more tax-free shopping. It's a place everyone really wants to see.

The Captain comes on to the public address system as usual to talk through some of the city's delights. Cruise TV in the rooms and the daily newspapers have already given us plenty of information about the trips on offer and the places worth seeing. Some of the conversations I've heard recently suggest an awful lot of guests plan to take advantage of the lack of a baggage limit and get a lot of new clothes made and copied. After wearing the same three basic uniforms for two months now I'd wear almost anything a Hong Kong tailor ran up for me, just as long as it isn't white or short-sleeved and doesn't come with matching trousers.

Edward and Eileen are on shore leave so I'm in charge of the Medical Centre for the day.

'Try it for size, young man. One day all this may well be yours,' Edward had said grandly as he left.

I don't go quite as far as sitting in his chair but I do enjoy the feeling of control. I also enjoy dealing with some of my fellow officers for a change. At the start of the cruise I'd thought they might come under my jurisdiction as 'crew'. As it's turned out the few times the officers have needed help they've been seen by Edward. Today I put the Chief Engineer's mind at rest about a growth on his back – then hear his latest theories on the benefits of offshore tax planning. I also hear a bit more about Marianna Defoe's backstage demands when the Cruise Director comes in to get a top up of his blood pressure medication.

'I tell you what, if my blood pressure's high now you should have tested me when she was on board,' he says. 'If we book her again we'll have a mutiny backstage. Fly-on acts like her cause chaos. They turn up, they drive everyone nuts, then they're gone and the team has a collective nervous breakdown. And she really told you she was a close personal friend of mine? Not till the Pacific freezes over.'

When the CD has left I see one of the electricians who's pulled a muscle in his back and can barely walk. Then I arrange some blood tests for a diabetic chef who's eating far too many of his own cakes. Rebecca comes in when he lumbers out.

'Ben, I've had a strange phone call,' she says. 'It's an Australian woman who says her husband can't sleep. I said we can't do cabin calls for something like that and he'd need to come down to see us but she says he won't do it. She wants you to go and see him. She says you know her.'

'What's her name?' I ask, though I've already guessed.

'It's Jody Howard.'

Jody looks more worried than ever when I get to the couple's stateroom. It's small and doesn't have a balcony. Competition winners clearly get what's left when all the paying punters have been shown to their rooms.

'Thanks for coming. This is Tom,' she says, stepping aside so I can get into the room.

'Hello! Good to meet you! Great to see you!' the man says far too loudly. He grabs my hand and gives it a bone-crusher of a shake. His skin is pinched tightly over his cheekbones. There's a smile on his face but there's hysteria in his eyes.

'It's good to meet you too. I'm Doctor MacFarlane. How can I help?' I say, trying to talk the man down by being as businesslike as possible.

'It's nothing. Nothing at all. Just a problem sleeping. Can't stop thinking. Too much to do on board. Can't stay in here in case I miss anything. Driving the wife bananas. Been awake for seventy-two hours now and starting to feel it. Heart racing. Something's got to give.'

I sit on the edge of the bed opposite him. When I flash a quick glance at Jody I can see a stricken look on her face. I want to tell her to stop worrying because this is exactly how I want her husband to be. He can't get treatment unless he accepts his behaviour is abnormal. It looks as if he's starting to walk down the exact right road.

'You've been feeling this way for a while, Mr Howard?'

'Tom, call me Tom.' It's his turn to flash a look at his wife. 'I've been losing it for a while. Done a few stupid things.

Spent money I don't have. A bit worried about that now. The guy in the shop did well by us. Refunded my card. But I keep wanting to go back and buy more. I want to be out there, living it. Getting it all mixed up.'

We talk for a good half-hour. Jody, to her huge credit, had excused herself and left us on our own. I learn about the stress of Tom's failing business, the pressure he feels his family puts on him, the slights he thinks he has endured from his friends and neighbours.

'All I need is sleep. If I could just turn my brain off for ten minutes I'd be OK,' he declares at one point. But he keeps listening when I say there's a lot more to it than that. I talk him through the patterns of manic behaviour. I explain where the episodes can lead. I tell him how much damage he might do if he doesn't get help.

Jody is in the corridor when I leave.

'Is he OK?' she whispers.

'He should be. I've given him a bit of sedation and I've left a whole lot of information I printed off about depression and how to treat it. If he reads just one page it's a step in the right direction. I'll do whatever you need for the rest of your time on board but the real work can't start till Tom sees a doctor back at home. Are you ready for that?'

'I'm ready.'

'Then you'll make it. Now go in there and tell him everything's going to be OK.'

'Mrs Philip, how are you? Mrs Coates and Mr and Mrs Baxter? It's nice to see you all.'

We're a day out of Hong Kong and I'm walking through the

galleria on my way to the gym when I stumble across a very relaxed group of people.

Mrs Baxter in particular looks better than I've ever seen her. There's a touch of colour in her cheeks. She's sitting back a little in her chair rather than leaning forwards. For once her forehead isn't tied up in a knot of strain and when she smiles her eyes are no longer so scared.

I pull an empty chair across to the space Mrs Philip is indicating for me.

'This is our favourite place and the waitress knows us well. Her name is Kaisa and she's from Estonia,' she says. On cue Kaisa arrives with a fresh pot of tea and an extra cup and saucer for me. Mrs Coates, whose latest hair style is topped off with a jaunty purple beret, is talking about the show she had seen the previous evening. We chat about the new set of entertainers who have joined us for the next few weeks and about some of the celebrity guests she's met on previous voyages.

'Are we keeping you from your exercise?' she asks, looking at my gym bag when I've finished my tea.

'I suppose I ought to work off some of this good living,' I say.

As I stand up I realise that Mr Baxter has barely said a word. 'You all right, sir?' I ask just before leaving.

'Never better,' he replies, but his face is a dangerous shade of grey.

We are still three days and one more port from Singapore when Mr Baxter takes a turn for the worse. His wife calls the Centre and Eileen and I both go to their cabin. Mrs Philip is there to open the door. She won't meet our eyes.

'Hello Mr Baxter. We're just here to check all's well.' He just gives a weak smile as I approach. Mrs Baxter, sitting in a chair by the window, doesn't speak either. For once she's not looking at her husband. Maybe she's just too exhausted. I suddenly realise that we've all been obsessed about keeping her husband healthy. But what if she is the first to fall?

Eileen must have read my mind. She sits casually on the edge the coffee table so she can chat with Mrs Baxter while I put my medical bag down and take a look at her husband.

'Can I just take a quick listen to your chest, sir?' I say, putting my stethoscope to my ears. I can hardly miss the way he winces in pain as he unbuttons his shirt so I can pull it up at the back. He must be in far more pain than he's letting on. I listen in. The base of his remaining lung is full of crackles and there's not a lot of air shifting around. I pull down one of Mr Baxter's lower eyelids. The 'whites' of his eye are a telltale yellow. The secondaries in his liver must be impeding the flow of bile.

I smile and stand up. 'Sir, you impress me more each time I see you. You've perhaps got a bit of a chest infection but we can work on that with some antibiotics. Eileen can come up and administer them intravenously for a couple of days if you want. I think I'd also like to start you on some steroids. They should give you a bit of a boost as well.'

Eileen's at my side as I help Mr Baxter with his buttons. 'I'll pop back up later to give you your injection and bring the other tablets. It looks as if you're going to have a wonderful view of the sunset from here,' she says as we take our leave.

We head down to the Medical Centre in silence. There's a costume ball this evening and the lift is crowded. One woman is wearing a perfect flapper dress from the twenties. Another is a dead ringer for Fay Wray. There's laughter and a lovely relaxed sense of anticipation in the air.

'So now we add pneumonia to all his other challenges,' Eileen says very quietly when all the others get out and the lift goes further down. 'He should be tucked up in a hospice with a proper palliative care team. Oh Ben, I hope we're doing the right thing.'

We've agreed that we are and we've gone through the notes yet again when there's a knock at the Medical Centre door. It's Mrs Baxter.

'Don't worry, there's no change. Mrs Philip is still with him,' she says. 'I needed to speak to you both in private.' We all sit down. Romeo brought in new flowers earlier on in the day and the smell of pollen is almost overwhelming. 'Can you tell me what these antibiotics and steroids are for?' she asks.

I tell her. 'If we get your husband to hospital in Thailand they can manage his pneumonia and his pain,' I say. 'With good care they'll get him back to where he was a couple of days ago.'

There's a long silence before Mrs Baxter speaks. 'Doctor, I think you know that this isn't about pain. My husband will take any degree of pain. He has to make it to Singapore. If he doesn't then none of this has been worth doing. It has cost us both so much. But we have to see it through to the end. I need you to promise that he won't be forcibly removed from this ship to be treated elsewhere.'

'We only want what's in your husband's best interests,' I begin. She cuts me off mid-sentence.

'I will write a cheque for whatever is required,' she says. Her words come fast and there is steel in her voice. She's a different woman as she leans forward in front of us. She's on a mission of her own now. 'I will sign a document to remove you of all legal responsibility for whatever may happen to my husband or to myself. I have also thought of the wider implications of this. I don't want any other patient to suffer while you're looking after Arthur. If you need to be back here at any time I want you to assure me that you will put your other responsibilities first and leave us. I don't want you to visit our cabin if you are needed by someone else in another part of the ship. I will put that in writing as well. I'll put it all in writing. I just want my husband's wishes to come true.' She stands up and leaves the Centre without saying goodbye. Had she stayed I think we would have seen her cry.

Edward sits very still while Eileen and I tell him what we propose to do. He can overrule us and demand that Mr Baxter gets the treatment he needs on shore. He doesn't.

'Of course this man will pay his respects to his comrades. It's just two more days. We promised to get him to Singapore. We're not going back on that now.'

Dakila and Rebecca give up their shore leave in Thailand to take on extra cover so one of us can be in the Baxters' cabin at all times. We draw up a rota and talk through how we might deal with any of the complications Mr Baxter's condition might throw up. But with less than seventy-two hours to go it appears as if the main threat to his journey may come from elsewhere.

'Ben, we've got a bit of a problem. Edward's with the Baxters and there's a passenger I need you to see on his behalf.' Eileen has called me in my cabin. I look at my watch. We've got forty five minutes until surgery opens.

'I can do it now if you want. What's the problem?'

'It's a man with severe diarrhoea. He says he was previously fit and well, he's not immuno-suppressed, he's only forty six years old. It sounds as if it's something viral.'

There's no need for Eileen to say any more. We've gone two and a half months without much more than a hint of the dreaded noro or Norwalk virus. We've never come close to breaching any of the notifiable limits for cases of diarrhoea and vomiting, or 'D&V'. As we're less than forty-eight hours out of our last port we're still on heightened alert for the bugs. If there's any risk that they've snuck in from land then we pretty much go onto autopilot. We've been rehearsing our protocols and procedures every few weeks. If the alert levels rise too far we pretty much lock the ship down. At Code Red almost every member of the 1,000 strong crew will play some part in the fight-back procedure, even if it's only washing their hands a few more times every hour. In the meantime pre-arranged teams of workers will begin a forensic clean-down service. Every surface that is ever touched will be disinfected almost the moment the last person has passed it. Cleaning crews will practically follow passengers around the ship to wipe down anything they brush into. Any or all passengers can be quarantined in their cabins. We can close off single decks or whole sections of the ship. It's an exhaustive and exhausting operation. This would be the very worst time to have to trigger it.

'It's probably nothing. It will be a dicky tummy, nothing more,' I say as I grab my medical bag and head to the passenger's cabin. Eileen doesn't reply. I imagine that she's thinking the same three things as I am. Firstly, if we have a full-scale outbreak our arrival in Singapore might be delayed or postponed altogether. Such is the bad publicity over 'plague ships' that ports can refuse to let stricken vessels dock. Secondly, if we are called upon to bring in the 'deep clean and quarantine' procedures then we'll struggle to have someone with Mr Baxter at all times. Finally, and maybe most importantly, there's the thought that if there is a bad bug aboard then the weakest passengers will probably be hit the hardest. Keeping Mr Baxter safe might soon become a whole lot harder.

'Hello. You're Mr Hobbs?' A very pale, slightly embarrassed-looking man looks up from the double bed in the mid-size cabin a deck above my own. His eyes track me slowly as I step into the room wearing a plastic apron and pulling on latex gloves. If he wasn't so utterly wiped out he'd probably be terrified.

'I'm absolutely mortified by this. I've barely been to my doctors in years, I can't believe I've been hit like this halfway through a holiday,' he says when he's got used to my appearance. His wife, a pretty, sporty-looking lady in her late thirties gives a rueful nod of agreement.

'Andrew is never ill. I can't think when he last took a day off work. I've hardly ever seen him like this.'

I pull a chair over towards the patient's bed. 'It's just knocked me for six, taken everything out of me, and I mean that literally as well as metaphorically,' he says. 'It's been explosive. Subatomic at times, if you know what I mean. I literally feel as if nothing's left in me. It also feels as if it's never going to end. That's why I called you up here. I just thought I had to do something to get back on my feet.'

'It will end,' I say firmly. 'There's nothing worse than being in the middle of these things, especially when you're not used to them. But it's like banging your head against a brick wall. It's so good when it's over. Now, are you on any medication?' He's not, which is good news. If he's on antibiotics then it's more likely that he's got something like *clostridium difficile*.

That's something that can spread a lot faster and is likely to require isolation.

'Did you leave the ship in Bangkok?'

'We did our own tour. We've been before.'

'Did you eat or drink anything while you were there?'

'We had lunch. We stopped for a drink and a snack near the Temple of the Dawn as well.'

I'm saying a silent prayer of thanks as he talks. If he caught this bug from some badly cooked food off of the ship then I can relax a bit. The more symptoms he describes the more it sounds like simple case of viral gastroenteritis. When it comes to bugs like norovirus and Norwalk you're more worried about vomiting than diarrhoea, and this man's got the latter not the former. I still need to follow procedure, however, and record everything he has eaten and where in the past forty-eight hours. But when I review the information I think it's something we can contain.

Andrew finds the energy to ask a lot of questions when I've finished my assessment. Some people want to bury their heads in the sand when they're ill. He's in the opposite camp. He wants as many facts as possible. Is it really true that bugs are better off out than in? If I put more in at one end will it all come straight out the other? How can I sleep if I can't seem to control what my body wants to do? How will I know when I'm clear of this? I try to answer them as fully as possible. I remind him and his wife to wash their hands and keep out of public areas for as long as possible. I tell them someone may be back to fog their cabin with disinfectant the way cabin crews sometimes spray planes before landing.

'It's only a precaution and I'll be back after breakfast tomorrow to check you're OK as well. In the meantime just call the Medical Centre and let us know if you feel worse at any time.'

Back at my desk I type all the details in the D&V log. 'It's OK. It's a one off, an isolated case,' I tell Eileen when she comes in to ask. But a 2am cabin call suggests that I might be wrong.

'I've had diarrhoea and I've been vomiting ever since dinner,' the lady says dramatically when I meet her.

I hold back, for the moment, from telling her that gastric illnesses tend to have one symptom or the other. Rarely does the body need to expel from both ends. I'm thinking – hoping – that this is simply her way of exaggerating her discomfort and justifying this night-time cabin call.

'I need to be rehydrated,' she says, sitting up in bed. She clearly knows her medical procedures, but I'm becoming a tiny bit more hopeful that this is more about the drama than the actual symptoms.

'It would definitely be useful for you to drink some fluids. I've got some oral rehydration fluids in my bag and I can mix them up for you now. I can also give you an injection for the nausea if it's that bad.'

'I still won't be able to keep them down. I can't drink anything. I'll need a drip.' Her voice, as she makes the request, is strong.

'Mrs Phillingham, I think we should hold that back as a last resort. It's no fun having something put in your arm when you don't really need it.'

'When I had this in America I was put on a drip. I know what it's like to have one connected. I've got the same symptoms now and I know it's exactly what I need. My husband has packed me a few things and I can come down to the Medical Centre right now.'

I put my hand up to stop her getting out of bed. The last thing I want is for her to spread whatever she does have around the corridors.

'Mrs Phillingham, if you need treatment we'll treat you here. We've already considered quarantining one patient already this evening.' I try to bite the words back as soon as I say them. Mrs Phillingham is thrilled to hear she may be at the vanguard of an illness that is already sweeping the ship. She turns to her husband in triumph and he steps forward to speak to me.

'I feel that my wife needs to be rehydrated artificially. In fact I demand it.'

'You will be billed for this, Mr Phillingham. If it's something you are requesting and not something I'm recommending, then I very much doubt your travel insurer will refund any money.'

'The insurance paid for it in America,' his wife complains. 'How much will it cost here?'

I pick a random figure of several hundred dollars and try to sound convincing.

'That's an outrageous amount of money.'

'That's the way the tariffs are set on board. Now, I can just as easily give you some rehydration fluids and that anti-emetic shot.'

The couple calm down a little as I mix the drink. I ham it up, to be honest, to make them feel they're getting more than they are. I'm not sure why they'd think I really need to check my patient's pulse and temperature before handing her a drink but she seems to appreciate the gesture. I congratulate Mrs Phillingham on her bravery and her resilience and say I'll call as a matter of urgency first thing in the morning. She likes the sound of that even more.

'Do you mind if I wash my hands one more time before I leave?' I ask. I step back into the couple's bathroom. The lights are bright and my face looks pale and worried in the mirror. Six more hours until we dock in Singapore. Just six short hours and Mr Baxter will have made it.

By the time I get to the Medical Centre in the morning Dakila has taken over the watch slot with the Baxters and Edward is sitting in his consulting room drumming his fingers impatiently on his desk.

'How are they?' I ask. After the events of last night I've decided not to visit the couple, just in case. If there is a bug on board I won't be the one to take it to them just before they leave.

'They're putting on a brave face but the medications aren't working. His breathing is becoming more laboured. I was there until four this morning and I've added in another antibiotic. He was on back-to-back nebulisers most of the night. He became quite confused at times, due, I'm sure, to the low levels of oxygen in his blood. He's weakening, Doctor MacFarlane. But we're only hours away from Singapore now. I still say this man will make it.'

Neither of us can stop looking at the clock. If we had windows down here we would surely be able to see the island now. I wander back into the waiting area and try to read one of the newspaper printouts. As I do Eileen picks up the phone. Until now I don't think any of us wanted to tempt fate by thinking too much about the actual arrangements for the Baxters in Singapore. But with less than two hours to go Eileen has decided to get on the case. With a vengeance, as it turns out.

'I do not care what it costs. Can you hear me? Must I spell it out to you? I do not care what it costs,' she barks down the phone in one tense conversation with what I think is a taxi company. This is a new Eileen. I'm glad I've got the chance to hear her in action. She makes about half a dozen tense calls then flops down on the sofa alongside me.

'Everything's going to be fine,' she says. 'Now all we can do is wait.'

Edward has arranged a low-key emergency disembarkation for the couple. Eileen and Mrs Philip are to go with them as far as their taxi.

The captain himself makes an announcement over the ship-wide PA system as we approach Singapore. He explains who Mr Baxter is, where he had fought and why he is back here after all these years. He says that Mr Baxter is not well and has struggled to cope with the rigours of the journey. He says that Mr Baxter and his wife will be leaving the ship first using the main gangway. He asks for our understanding if our own port visits are momentarily delayed. He asks everyone to wish the couple God speed.

'Did you know that people in the galleria actually applauded?' One of the shoppies told me a few days later. 'It was like Diana's funeral. It was the most unusual captain's announcement I've ever heard. I don't mind saying I shed a very discrete tear.'

It also proves to be one of the most effective announcements of the voyage. I don't think I've ever seen a port visit quite like it. At every harbour the rush to leave defies belief. In popular ports all semblance of civilised queuing seems to disappear. The most upright of passengers play the dirtiest of tricks to ensure that they get ahead of the crowds.

Today, though, two thousand people seem to stand still as the Baxters prepare to leave. Only a few dozen are actually anywhere near the couple as they make their exit. None can really make any practical difference to the couple's departure. But still everyone waits until the captain comes back on the PA system to say that the couple have made it on to shore, are in their taxi and are on their way to pay their respects to the dead. There's applause across the whole ship. On the crew deck several officers salute, even though they didn't know and are unable to even see the man they chose to honour.

There is one thing more. It seems that this extraordinarily weakened man, with his extraordinarily strong wife, have somehow managed to leave the ship in style. Mrs Baxter is wearing a hat and a silk dress made of rich purples and mauves. She is carrying a small bouquet of white flowers that her room steward made up for her that morning. Her husband is in a wheelchair in full military uniform. He has a row of medals on his left chest. On his lap is a framed, black and white photograph of a group of long-dead friends.

# CHAPTER NINETEEN

'You know, last time I was in Kuala Lumpur I thought I'd been kidnapped,' I say.

We're all having dinner together as we approach the twenty-seventh port of our voyage.

'I was doing a simple fly-in job to pick someone up from the airport and we had so much time before the flight back that I thought I'd dash into town to take a look at some of the buildings. The cab driver quoted a decent price so off I went. About half an hour, maybe three quarters of an hour later we're still tanking along this vast eight-lane road to nowhere and I swear I thought he was taking me to Iraq or something. I don't think any airport in the world can be as far from its city as Kuala Lumpur. By the time we finally made it to the middle we had to speed all the way back to stop me from missing the flight. The driver thought I was out of my mind.'

'A lot of people think you're out of your mind, Ben,' says Dakila helpfully.

'Not least because you persist in thinking you will enjoy yourself more in a job on land,' adds Edward. 'So how is the job hunt going? Still tempted by the wilds of East London?'

'I'm still waiting to hear from them, to be honest,' I say,

trying not to sound too defensive. 'I've polished up my CV, I've worked on my covering letter and I'm ready to start applying when the next set of rotations come out in two weeks time. If all goes to plan I'll be doing the forms on the beach in Sharm el Sheikh.'

'So no chance of any distractions there,' says Eileen with a smile.

Only Rebecca stays quiet as the jokes build up. 'So where are you going next, my dear?' Edward asks her after a while.

She brightens up. 'I've got big plans. I've put in a bid to get on a South American tour. There's one that does Rio, Buenos Aires and goes right down to Tierra del Fuego. If I don't get it I'll happily do the Med for the summer because I fancy the idea of hanging out in the South of France or Capri for a while. I've also got a bit excited about doing Canada and Alaska. Plus, of course, I'm feeling a bit of a fraud for just joining this worldie halfway around. I think I ought to do the whole thing at some point.'

'Well this year there are some autumn departures on the worldies,' says Eileen, clearly thrilled to hear Rebecca's enthusiasm. 'It's a really interesting route as well, heading east and going via Cape Town and Tokyo. Frankly you've not done the world till you've done it backwards. I think there are some new ports on it as well. I can't say Guam sounds very nice but I shouldn't judge till I've explored it. There's a glorious little beach restaurant in Phuket I remember from a previous trip as well. Next time I do that route I'd like to find it again. You should join me. It's really just grilled fish with a little bit of lemongrass and a splash of lime, but it's divine.'

'I'd love to do that,' Rebecca says. 'I love eating on the edge of the sea with sand underneath my feet. Doesn't that sound

good?' she says, turning to me. I don't really say anything.
But I have to admit that it does.

Marcia looks like a tiny, frightened flower. She's immaculately
dressed. She sits upright and respectful in my consulting
room chair. And she doesn't say a word when I tell her she's
pregnant.

'Do you want to talk about what this means, about how
you're going to feel or what you should do next?' I ask.

Still she says nothing. She stays motionless in her chair,
hiding her feelings deep within herself and taking herself
far from this small, metal walled consulting room. I imagine
she's probably taking herself back in time as well. To the
time before this happened to her. I look at her file on my
screen. The crew notes tell me she works in the housekeeping
department and she's been with the company for three years.
She's from the Philippines, twenty two and, I'm guessing,
unmarried.

'You can come back any time if you need to talk about
this. To me, or to any of our nurses,' I say eventually. After
another few minutes of tense silence she stands up, gives me
what is almost a bow of thanks, then walks softly away. I get
the feeling I won't ever see her again.

I'm wrong.

'Hello Marcia, how are you feeling today?' Once again she
sits still on my consulting room chair and says nothing. I try
to make sure I'm looking as open and friendly as possible
but it doesn't do any good. Marcia just sits alongside me,
occasionally twisting her hands together in her lap, never
once meeting my eye.

'We've got plenty of time to talk, Marcia, There's no-one outside today so there's no rush at all. I'll help you with anything that I can.'

Still she sits in silence. I turn away and pretend to sort some papers on my desk, wondering if that will give her the opening she needs to speak. It doesn't. I ask if she would rather speak to one of the female nurses. That doesn't make any difference either. I think back suddenly to the first day I met Edward when he'd said part of my job on board was to be a counsellor. This looks like one of those moments. I talk a bit longer but when I pause Marcia stands up. There's anguish in her eyes as she nods her head and all but creeps out of the room.

The next day, at exactly the same time, she's back. The chambermaids work long, difficult hours and I'm guessing this must be one of her few daily breaks. Her face is as pale and impassive as before.

'How are you feeling in the mornings, Marcia? It can't be easy doing the beds and the rooms if you're feeling sick.' Her eyes blink fast, but still she doesn't say a word. I'm thinking of all the ways I can help her and cursing myself for not being able to break through. I decide to take a new tack.

'I'm going to just talk through a few things, to explain how you're going to feel and what it all means. You can stop me and ask any questions whenever you want. OK, you're likely to get morning sickness, if you're not already getting it. It doesn't just hit you in the mornings so don't worry if you get it at other times. This kind of sickness is perfectly normal and it won't harm you or your baby. It's usually worse in the first few months but some mothers do feel it for a lot longer. We'll just have to wait and see how it is for you.

'If you're worried about work I'd say you should have no problem carrying on with your job for many months yet. I'd just want you to take care that you don't get too tired or do anything too physical. Get as much rest as you can and eat sensibly. If you want me to I can find out if you could maybe get given some other duties in a few months' time if you're struggling.' The wringing of the hands in her lap is getting more pronounced. I carry on talking as I try to work out what that might mean. 'You'll want an ultrasound scan on land at around twelve to fourteen weeks so it will help to get more of an idea of when you think you became pregnant?' She's still giving nothing away and all of a sudden something else occurs to me. 'Marcia have you told anyone at home about this? You can call someone from here, if you want. The phone here works anywhere in the world.' I pull it across towards her side of the desk. 'I'll leave you for a moment. Do call anyone if it will help.'

I step outside. Eileen looks up from her desk and I put my finger on my lips. I stand behind my door for a few minutes. Marcia isn't talking to anyone and her silence suggests she isn't about to start. I go back in.

'Come back at another time if that's easier. Bring a phone number and you can make a call from here any time you want.' Still she says nothing. This time there's not just anguish in her eyes as she flees the Medical Centre. There are tears.

I'm ready for Marcia the following evening but she doesn't turn up. She's not there the next morning either. I mention her to Eileen when we lock the surgery doors after clinic and she shrugs.

'All we can hope is that she heads home after her next tour, gets accepted by her family and has a healthy baby,' she says.

'You think that's likely?'

'It's possible. One of the alternatives is that she finds some abortion clinic in Europe or tries to do a DIY termination in her cabin. It wouldn't be the first time we've had to deal with the aftermath of something like that. They're some of the saddest scenes I've ever witnessed on board. I wouldn't wish them on anyone.'

I head back to my room and try to focus on a pile of outstanding insurance forms. It's hard, because Marcia's face keeps popping up in my mind. She's so tiny, she works so hard and she needs so much help. But one of the secret skills of medicine is the ability to let go. You can't live every patient's life. You can't solve every problem. The ship sails on and by the time we approach the Gulf of Oman I've managed to persuade myself that her story will end happily.

'No news will be good news,' Eileen keeps telling me. 'If we never see her again that means she's getting through this safely. We can check the crew records when we get to Southampton. If she's still working then she must still be OK. All we can do is wait.'

Edward is pretending to sulk as we have lunch outside Dubai. To be fair, he has good reason to. Dakila and I have been taking the mickey out of him relentlessly for the past twelve hours.

'So which building is your apartment in?' Dakila asks in our latest onslaught. 'Is it that one, the older, shabby block just behind the new, shiny one that's stolen all the sea views?'

'Gentlemen, I think I shall dine on my own tonight. If you're not very careful I may also pull rank and cancel your shore leave for the rest of the trip.'

Fortunately he doesn't follow through. I've got the afternoon and evening off and join Gavin and Monique on a whistle-stop city tour followed by an amazing dinner on the edge of Dubai Creek. They've both been to Dubai before and say it grows exponentially every time. Gavin takes a photo of a 'To Let' sign on one of the building sites. I'm supposed to show it to Edward and say I managed to track down his apartment but in the end I think he's probably suffered enough.

Back on board the others have had a quiet clinic. The phones don't ring once all night – but we all wake up grumpy the next morning.

'You get so used to the engine noise and the motion when we're at sea that you can't sleep properly when you're in port. You wait till your first night back on land. You won't sleep a wink. You might even feel sick,' Eileen tells me at breakfast.

We try to come up with a few juvenile Medical School jokes about lack-of-motion sickness and head down to what proves to be another wonderfully quiet clinic. When it's done I head up to the spa to do its latest health and safety check.

'Any excuse for you to go in the ladies dressing room,' Monique says as she cordons it off so I can check for hazards and rank its cleanliness. Next up I do a legionnaires' check on the hot tubs and spa area. Monique says she'll pay my bar bill if I mark the spa down as unsafe and give her two days off while it's deep cleaned. As usual I tell her I'm still holding out for my first Rolex.

An hour later I've hopefully shaken off the smell of chlorine and I'm hosting a table at a lunch for guests. We've got an array of officers present but Edward and I seem to be most in demand. Almost everyone we speak to has a symptom they'd like to discuss with us.

'Sometimes I feel tired, doctor,' is one of the first that comes my way.

'I get this stomach-ache every few months. What do you think it is?' comes next, shortly followed by: 'Doctors at home in Newcastle say my sister has kidney stones. Do you think they've got it right?' When we meet up afterwards it seems that Edward faced a similar set of questions.

'It's the nature of cruising,' he tells me. 'At the start of the voyage everyone wants to sit next to the Captain or the Chief Engineer. But after three months they run out of things to ask them. No-one ever runs out of things to ask a doctor.'

Back in my cabin after dinner I turn on my computer and catch up on some emails home. For some reason nothing I write comes out properly. It doesn't seem right to tell Cassie how much I'm looking forward to seeing her – but then to go on about how good it's going to be on the reefs of Sharm el Sheikh in three days time. Instead I run through some of the crazy things I was asked over lunch and list some of the injuries our middle-aged, middle-management team got when they challenged some of our much fitter maintenance crew to a football game on shore this afternoon.

'Wish you could do this job too. Wish you were here,' I type at the end of the email. Then I head off to have a drink with the others. I don't know why but England suddenly feels even further away than ever.

# Part Five

# The Red Sea to the Mediterranean

# CHAPTER TWENTY

'Ben, I need your help. We're being blackmailed.' Eileen calls me over at the end of our final evening clinic on the Red Sea. We've done a long five-day sail towards the Suez Canal and we're due in Sharm el Sheikh tomorrow morning at eight where I'm due a half-day off to do some diving. I seem to remember that I once had a plan to fill in job application forms at this point in the cruise. Maybe I'll do that another time.

'Who's blackmailing us?' I ask. 'Surely not little Marti?'

The woman at Eileen's side is Marti Eden, a petite former ballet dancer from Rotherham who has worked in various entertainment and excursions departments for about ten years. Dakila and I had helped her get all her tour guests on the right buses back in Barbados and I went on an excursion with her in Costa Rica. She's like a stand-up comedian on the tours and the guests adore her.

'Less of the little, if you don't mind,' she says in an accent no amount of world travel seems to fade. 'Anyway, I wouldn't call it blackmail. It's just a little gentle persuasion.'

'We forgot that Kiri had signed up to do an excursion to the pyramids in two days time,' Eileen explains. 'I'm on shore leave and I'm not giving it up. No-one else wants to do the excursion and I've said she'll have to manage without us.'

'And I said that was absolutely fine,' Marti tells me. 'I just made the point that if you didn't help out I couldn't guarantee that all my guests wouldn't have ice in their drinks just before coming back on board. I'm not a doctor. I've no idea what the implications of that would be for the Medical Centre once we're back at sea.'

'Like I said: blackmail,' repeats Eileen.

'So, Ben, can I put you down for my pyramids trip?' Marti asks. 'I'll let you choose your own camel.'

I didn't take much persuading, to be honest. I had a brilliant half-day off in Sharm where the diving was as good as Eileen said it would be. Now, one day later, I'm off the ship again, earning a bit of extra cash and get to see the Sphinx. Plus it's always fun to see Marti at work. She's a commission and tips queen. Rumour has it she easily out-earns Edward and might rank with the art auctioneer and possibly makes more than the captain.

'It's simple. The bigger the laughs, the bigger the tips,' is her theory. 'Remember the more facts and local colour you can throw in to the announcements the better – but it doesn't really matter if you just make it all up. When we were in the Bahamas last year I asked a lady at the end of the tour if she'd enjoyed Grand Cayman. "Grand Cayman? I thought it was the Grand Canyon," she said. How exactly you can mix up those two I don't know. I spent all of last night mugging up on the Pyramids but half the group will probably think we're at Pompeii, so I doubt it will make the slightest difference.'

Fortunately my role won't require me to tell any tall stories. Unfortunately I'm also barred from accepting any tips. When the day comes I'm really here just to carry a first-aid kit and make sure Marti doesn't lose anyone.

'Now, ladies and gentlemen, we're going to see plenty of ancient relics today – and no, I don't mean the other passengers,' she begins, to groans from everyone who's heard that one a thousand times before.

She gets us all off the ship and on to the coach where we edge through Cairo's crazy traffic, shuffle round the obligatory parchment factory and get surrounded by swarms of children every time we leave the bubble of our air-conditioned bus. We do a whistle-stop tour of the Museum of Egyptian Antiquities to see Tutankhamen, head back into the sunshine to take pictures on the banks of the Nile, then head over to Giza for the main event.

'Now, it's last call for the camel rides, ladies and gentlemen. Anyone else want to sign up? It's much more fun than walking and the camels will stop right in front of the Sphinx for photos. If you're going to have your picture taken in front of the pyramids, then trust me you want to be on a camel for the full Agatha Christie look.' Marti is on the microphone at the front of the bus. She wants her commission so much it almost hurts.

'Ben, do you mind going with the first group?' She asks. We're knee deep in dust as Marti and the locals line us up with our rides. Around three dozen of us have opted to go on the camels and there's a lot of laughter as we're all jerked upwards.

'I'll go wherever and whenever my camel takes me,' I say. With a sudden lurch my camel hurtles to the front of the pack just as Marti had asked. 'Hold on tight everyone,' I shout back at the group, very aware that it's my job to pick up the pieces if anything goes wrong. Fortunately nothing does.

My advance party of ten are led jerkily around the perimeter area of the Giza complex. More than half of the group have been to the pyramids before but nothing ever really dulls their impact.

'If you pay a little extra they'll sort something out with the guards so you can actually climb one of the small ones,' one of the passengers shouts out. But the Egyptian sun is unseasonably hot today and no-one tests the theory.

'OK everyone, if you want to pass me your cameras I'll do the honours,' I say when we're as close as we can get to the Sphinx.

I've clambered off my mount and have a bit of fun pretending I'm from either *Heat* or *Country Life* magazine depending on the age of my subjects. I repeat the process with the next wave of guests, then wait for Marti and the stragglers. The first of that final group certainly looks ready for a good picture. He's way ahead of the others and he's no longer alone on his camel. Two young lads have joined him – one sitting in front, one behind. They're kicking hard and are all swaying drunkenly as the camel strides forward.

'That would make a great picture. Have you got a camera?' I yell as the trio approach. Then I try to swallow the words back. All of a sudden it's clear that this isn't a bit of fun for someone's family album. Something's gone wrong.

I can feel sweat start to run down my back as I rush towards the camel.

'Are you OK up there?' I yell. But I don't expect a reply. Our guest is clearly unconscious. I've got a terrible feeling he might be dead.

The two local boys look panic-stricken. I wonder suddenly if they saw what happened to him. Did they think that by supporting him they could turn back time? Or did they think they could change what had happened by ignoring it?

'We need to get him down. Somebody get him off the camel!' I'm shouting the words at anyone who will listen. The boys probably don't speak much English, but it has to be clear what I need them to do. Fortunately they do it. They get the camel to jerk itself down on to its front knees and I reach out and grab our passenger as he falls. He must weigh about seventeen stone and it's not easy to manoeuvre him on to his back on the hot, dry dust.

'Can you hear me?' I shout at my patient. I've got my hand on his neck feeling for a carotid pulse. I've got my ear against his mouth listening for any sound of breathing while I watch his chest of any movement. I draw a blank on all counts. Deep down I know the man's dead. But as his heart may only have stopped beating a few minutes ago I cling to the chance I can bring him back.

'I need someone to find Marti and call an ambulance!' I shout at the other passengers. Then I turn to the man on the ground. 'Come on sir, I'm not losing you without a fight,' I tell him. Then I bring my first down hard on his chest, pinch his nose, pull his head back, check his mouth is clear of debris then deliver the regulation three short breaths into his lungs. First task done, I begin the cycles of chest compressions and mouth-to-mouth breathing to try to revive him.

'Come on! Come back to me,' I tell him between breaths. 'One sign. Just give me one sign.' He doesn't but I'm suddenly more determined than ever to try and save him. 'Come on sir! I am not giving up on you,' I say, gasping for breath. Sweat is dripping off my face and sticking my shirt to my back now.

This whole area, one of the world's busiest tourist sites, seems empty and silent all of a sudden. Then the camel carrying the man's wife comes into view. The world suddenly starts to get very noisy indeed.

'What's happening? That's my husband! What's happened to him?'

The woman is so desperate to get off her camel that she stumbles and falls as it kneels down. Her whole body seems to disappear in a cloud of red dust and she is coated in it when she picks herself up off the ground and throws herself across to me. Tears are already streaking down her cheeks and blood from a cut just below her right cheekbone is starting to mix in them.

'I'm Doctor MacFarlane, I'm the ship's doctor,' I say, pumping the man's chest. I'm sure I've gone far beyond the moment we can save him. But I know I can't stop trying now his wife his here. She has to see that we've done everything that we can.

'I don't know your name,' I say after the next three breaths.

'I'm Antonia Howard. This is my husband Timothy.' She says kneeling on the ground and reaching out for him. 'He was laughing so much. He was laughing when the camel stood up with him. He was happy. What's happened to him?'

She knows the answer, of course.

'I think your husband had a heart attack. I think it would have happened very suddenly.' I look over her shoulders to the rest of the group, searching for Marti and desperately hoping I'll see someone who can help. I do.

'I'm an ex-policeman. I can take over from you,' a smart,

grey-haired man says as he comes alongside me. I nod my thanks, finish my next three breaths then let him start on the chest compressions.

'Mrs Howard, we're doing all we can,' I say to her. She's still on her knees in the dust and I try to help her to her feet. She shakes herself free. He face is flushed and she looks as if she's going to hit me.

'This isn't happening,' she says. 'He isn't dead. He can't be dead. This is my husband. You have to do more than this!' She falls back to the floor and grabs her husband's shoulders as the fellow guest works on his chest. I pull her away and she turns on me. She lets out a cry of awful anguish and starts to strike my shoulders with her fists.

'Antonia, darling, come here my dear.' One of the other guests pushes past me and takes the blows. She's a much older woman in flowing cotton trousers and a soft, peach coloured blouse. She grabs Mrs Howard's wrists then wraps her into her arms. 'Antonia, he's being cared for. We have to let them do their work,' this good Samaritan says. Mrs Howard sinks to her knees, taking the other lady with her. A third passenger joins them in the dust as Mrs Howard's sobs get louder. She too puts her arms around her friend.

'An ambulance is on its way. Marti has called it,' she says. 'They'll have proper equipment on that. Timothy would have wanted you to stay strong for him. Try to do that for him, my dear. Come here. Let me hold you.'

I leave the three women on the ground and take over the CPR. The cycle of breaths and chest compressions would be exhausting even without the heat and dust of our surroundings.

It's made so much worse by the fact that the odds of us saving this man are lengthening fast. I can't tell his wife, but I think it would be too late to save him, even if the right equipment arrived now.

'Come on sir, we're not giving up on you,' I say between breaths. But I'm talking to his wife now, as much as to him.

The ex-policeman takes over from me again as Marti comes forward.

'They say the ambulance will be here in minutes. I've called the ship as well,' she says. Then she pulls closer. 'Would he have felt anything?' she whispers, already using the past tense.

'Maybe he had one moment of pain. But it must have happened so quickly. That's the only good thing about this.' I'm about to say more when someone tugs on my arm. It's one of the boys who'd been on the camel with Mr Howard. He's being pushed forward by one of the older camel leaders.

'Everything OK, yes? This man, he is OK, yes?' the boy asks. He's trying to smile but his face is pinched with worry.

I shake my head. 'No. He's not OK,' I say. The boy's face crumples and he bites his lip so hard it looks as if it might bleed. I put my hand on his shoulder and give it a squeeze. 'You did a good thing,' I say. I doubt I'll be understood but I want to at least try. I don't think that we could have saved Mr Howard even if we'd been standing next to him when the attack hit. The two boys stopped the man from falling to the ground. So at least Mrs Howard will have a peaceful-looking body to mourn in the hospital.

We hear the ambulance long before it arrives, the siren a slash of modernity cutting through the ancient landscape. The paramedics leap out but there's very little they can do.

We move Mr Howard into the back of the ambulance and connect the ECG machine.

The screen shows nothing. No electrical activity in his heart. No chance to save him. The ex-copper and I have been carrying out artificial breathing and cardiac compressions for thirty long, hot minutes. This is that awful moment when you need to call a halt.

There's a timeless silence as I do so. It hovers over us all as we cover Mr Howard's body with a sheet. The two ladies with his wife try to join her in the ambulance but there's no room. Marti leads them away, then darts back to speak to me in the front seat.

'The poor, poor woman. Tell her that we're all thinking of her,' she whispers. 'But Ben, we've got an evening sail. We leave at nine. You know you can't be late. The ship won't wait for you. Whatever state this lady is in, you need to be back on board.'

I can hear Mrs Howard sobbing in the back of the ambulance as we jerk and start through the snarling Cairo traffic. She's silent when her husband's body is wheeled out into the searing white lights of the hospital. Suddenly everything is clinical, serious and real. The doctor who takes charge is calm and businesslike. He's in his early thirties, speaks decent English and takes the time to put Mrs Howard's mind at rest over the way her husband died.

'No pain. Very fast. He did not feel any pain,' he tells her, one hand on her arm, as she stares unheeding into the distance. She looks cold in the air-conditioned air. She's lost and alone – and in the back of my mind I know it's only going to get worse.

'Mrs Howard I need to talk to you about what happens next.' I've waited as long as I can. Now, sitting on a row of metal chairs in a noisy hospital corridor, I need to tell her that I'm leaving.

She looks at me blindly. 'I don't understand,' she says when I've finished. 'Please, doctor, please. You can't leave me here on my own. You have to get my husband and I back on board the ship. We need to be with English people. We've got friends on board. We can't stay here.'

'Mrs Howard I am so very sorry. We're not able to take your husband back on to the ship.'

'But you are! You've got places for bodies. I've read that in the papers. I know that's true about cruise ships. You have got somewhere for him.'

'We do have a morgue but it has to be for people who pass away while they're on the boat. I will make a call to check but I don't think there's anything we can do when something like this happens on land. I'm so sorry, Mrs Howard.' I'm kicking myself for not checking this beforehand. I move out of her earshot and ring the Medical Centre. After explaining the situation to Eileen, she puts me through to Edward. He confirms my fears.

'The body has to stay where it is. The authorities will need to examine it and confirm the cause of death before they issue a death certificate. We can do most things here but we can't do a postmortem examination. Even if we stored the body on board there would be all the issues of exporting a corpse from one country and importing it into another. There's too much red tape and bureaucracy to go through. We can't do it. Cairo wouldn't allow it, the captain won't allow it – and it will create more problems than it's worth for the guest when she gets back to Britain.

This is how it is. It isn't an area where there's any leeway or discretion.'

'So what happens next?'

Edward puts Eileen back on the line. 'Guest relations are packing up the couple's cabin right now. They'll deliver everything to our agents in Cairo and then on to wherever the lady chooses to stay. Our agent can liaise with everyone. Apparently they've been going the extra mile in guest relations already. They've called her family in England and spoken to her travel insurer. They've called the British Embassy and found her an interpreter she can call in case anything else crops up. You can tell her all of this so she knows she's not on her own. But we can't take the body on board. And Ben, it's getting late. You need to be back here.'

I look at my watch one last time. I've had a taxi waiting for me just outside the hospital for half an hour. Now I have to get into it. How strange that one of the most difficult goodbye's I can remember will be with a lady whose name I've only just learned. I put my phone back in my pocket and turn to her.

'Mrs Howard, Antonia, I'm afraid I've had it confirmed that your husband's body has to stay here. The official procedure will have to take over.' I give her the details of all the people who are helping her and tell her she should call me in the Medical Centre if any other hurdles are put in front of her. Then I stand up. I shake her hand with awful finality. 'Mrs Howard I am so very sorry. But I have to leave.'

I missed the massive barbecues on the passenger and crew decks as the ship sailed through the Suez Canal. I'm not really in the mood for any of the late-night parties we've got going on in different parts of the ship either. Instead I wash away Cairo's dust in a long, hot shower and leave my dirty uniform in the corner of the room. Albert takes it away for cleaning when he brings me some dinner. I eat out on my balcony while flicking through a newspaper printout from the Medical Centre. As the time difference is in my favour I ring Cassie rather than just emailing her at midnight. I realise, as we speak, that I should have been doing this far more often over the past four months.

'You know what? It really is good to hear your voice,' I say halfway through the conversation. It's good to hear her laugh as well. She takes my mind off the events in Egypt by talking about some of the stupid things that happen at Medical School. She makes me smile by describing the tropical medicine unit she's just done where everyone was grossed out by stories of tumbu flies, geography worms, dung beetles, flesh flies and all the other creatures that do awful things in embarrassing places.

'Are you sure your flatmates won't mind if I come to stay for a full month?' I ask a bit later on when we're talking about our plans for the future.

'If they do I'll put a flesh fly in their beds,' she says. 'I'll see you soon and I can't wait.'

I spend a long time staring at the sky on my balcony when I've hung up. Then I sleep like a baby. When I wake up the sun is poking through some clouds and everything feels strangely exciting. I look at the map I keep on my desk and check our exact position on Cruise TV. I step out on to my balcony. We've travelled such a long way and seen so much of the world. Now, suddenly, we're in the Mediterranean. We're on our way home.

# CHAPTER TWENTY ONE

'So this is it, Ben. The end of the adventure. A week and a half more and it's all over. You walk down the gangway in Southampton and head off to an ordinary job in an ordinary hospital in some ordinary city. A year or so down the line you've moved up a grade, you've got a couple more qualifications under your belt and you're ready to focus on your pension pot for the next thirty years. Sound appealing?' Rebecca smiles at me as we share a team breakfast on the crew deck.

The Mediterranean feels good. We don't have the wonderful high temperatures we enjoyed back in Australia. There are none of the wild seas we saw in the Atlantic. Instead there's that comfortable feeling that you belong. It feels as if we're being given the space to recharge our batteries before heading off on another voyage into the unknown. Rebecca's still talking about doing South America. Dakila has been angling for the Med, followed by another worldie. Eileen, I think, is going just for the worldie. Before I left my cabin this morning I did look at a few more route maps online. It always surprises me how many places you can visit in this job. I forget that however much you travel there is always so much more to see.

'I've totally lost track of what sounds appealing and what doesn't anymore,' I say when I snap back to attention. 'But I think I can see what everyone means about cruise crews becoming institutionalised. I'm not sure I remember the days of the week, let alone how to pay a bill or where to buy a pint of milk. I've no idea how to get home from Southampton. And I've only been on board for three and a bit months.'

'So what does Cassie think about you coming back?' Eileen asks.

As usual, the mention of Cassie's name makes me smile.

'Amazingly enough, she's looking forward to seeing me,' I say. I look over at Edward and Dakila. 'I think I might still need a bit of advice from you two on surviving long absences. But I think we're over the worst.'

Eileen gives a mischievous smile. 'I'm very pleased to hear it,' she says with a twinkle in her eye. 'And remember, if you do one more tour of duty you'll be able to get Cassie to join you. It's only a few pounds a day to have a partner on board after your second four-month contract. All you have to do is sign up, Ben. You know it makes sense.'

Dakila helps me change the subject before dashing off to join Marti in the galleria. He's earning a last bit of extra money accompanying one of her final excursions. Eileen is going on a private tour of the Parthenon and follows soon afterwards. The rest of us talk shop again as we head back down to the Medical Centre.

'Don't expect an easy day,' Edward warns as we get the rooms ready for morning surgery. 'A lot of the crew won't have easy access to a free doctor for at least a month after we get to Southampton. They'll be taking advantage of this place while they can. Passengers who've got a bit of spending money left over might also pop in to sort out some final niggles before they're thrown back on to the good old NHS at home. Now let's open the gates and let the barbarians in.'

My clinic is always different when Eileen isn't on board to triage patients for me. Sometimes I like it this way. The people with the more minor problems can often be the most interesting. They're also people I might not otherwise meet. Today I get to chat about Ukrainian politics with one of the deck staff who has got an infected cut on his hand, I find out a bit more about some celebrity passengers from a very indiscrete butler with conjunctivitis and I catch up on life at home with a military historian. He's been flown out to give a series of lectures and hasn't packed enough statins to last the voyage. Towards the end of the clinic I even share a few laughs with one poor man from the security staff whose whole stomach is covered in angry red welts.

'I wanted to look good for the wife back at home, so I bought this cream off a woman in Egypt. She said it would get rid of my beer belly,' he admits ruefully.

'It's certainly hidden your beer belly,' I say.

I take a closer look, give him some legitimate creams to calm the skin down, and ask him to come back if it's not cleared up in a couple of days. He groans when I prescribe more time in the crew gym and less in the crew mess if he truly wants to impress his wife in Southampton. The fun ends, though, with one of my final patients of the morning. He's in his early fifties and looks to be the saddest man in the world.

He's Chinese and his dark, hollow eyes seem lidded with a whole lifetime of sorrows. He gives a half-nod, half-bow of greeting as he takes his seat alongside my desk. But his face is grim and tired and he can't seem to bring himself to smile. Like so many of the crew members I see, it is clear he wishes he is anywhere but here. Seeing a doctor is regarded as a sign of weakness in a world that only values the strong. I'm guessing that he's one of the people Edward was talking about earlier. This may be his last chance to see a doctor in some time. I wonder how long he's waited before coming here. I don't yet know him but I find myself desperately hoping I can help.

'What brings you here today, sir?' I ask, trying to lift his spirits.

The man holds out his left hand and winces as he tries to rotate his wrist. The soft tissues around it are swollen. The muscles of his hand have largely wasted away and his fingers are contorted into the shapes known as swan-neck deformities. Mr Lei grimaces again as he tries to clench his fist.

'That looks painful. Is it the same with your other hand, Mr Lei?'

His eyes darken. He lifts up his right arm and winces yet again. I'm remembering his slow walk into my surgery. I'm guessing he has pain in plenty of other joints as well.

'Have you had this problem for long?'

'Many years,' he says, just as I'd expected.

'Has it been getting worse recently?'

It has, of course. I assume he is only here today because it's become intolerable. I examine him carefully, document his deformities and the range of movement he displays at each joint. This has to be rheumatoid arthritis, which can strike at any age and slowly destroys the membranes that stop one bone grinding against another. Painkillers can control the symptoms but don't prevent the ongoing destruction. If you've got enough money, or the right insurance, you can use the latest drugs that can slow or halt the process. But I've got a horrible feeling they will be out of this quiet, proud man's reach.

I look at him. I admire the dignity he's showing. His hands, his arms, his neck and his whole body are in such pain. The bottom line is that he shouldn't be working. The reality is that he has to.

'My friends, they do some work for me when I have to stop,' he says at one point.

He has a faraway look in his eyes. Is it shame, embarrassment – or fear? He's almost completed this tour of duty. Is he terrified that he won't be offered another? I ask him what medication he's using now. He's not taking anything and I look at him in amazement. His threshold for pain must be extraordinarily high.

'I'll prescribe you something that will help you right away,' I say and write out the note. When I've finished he bows his head in thanks and then, with a look of infinite embarrassment and regret, he hands over two very tired-looking ten-dollar bills. I don't know why but I almost feel tears welling up in my eyes as I see them. Is this why he waited so long to ask for help? Did he think the doctors want backhanders like everyone else on board? Was he waiting all this time to save what he hopes will be enough?

'Mr Lei, please keep your money. Your medication will be free and I'm here to help you whenever you need it,' I say firmly. I want to shake his hand as he leaves but I'm afraid it might break. Instead I pass over his prescription and give him

my version of a salute. He bows his head again and leaves
with dignity.

I spend the afternoon doing a bit of research to see if there's
any other way I can help Mr Lei when my phone rings. It's
Dakila.

'Ben, we've had an incident on the tour,' he says. 'Someone
tried to grab a passenger's handbag. She got dragged along
a bit.'

'Dragged along?'

'It was someone on a bike.'

'So how's the passenger?'

'Not good. She's hurt her wrist and upper arm quite badly.
She's got some deep cuts and grazes on her legs and she's
pretty shaken up. I said I'd take her to hospital for a check-up
but she refused. She's worried that she'll be kept in overnight
and won't be able to finish the cruise. She's with her husband,
she's on a worldie and she wants to do the whole trip.'

'Are we sure she didn't bang her head?' If so then she'll
need a CT brain scan and we can't risk having her in our care.

'Amazingly enough she managed to stay on her feet all
the way through it. I saw it happen from the other end of the
street. She's a tough cookie. I'd say she's OK to come back on
board.'

I think it through for a moment. 'Well, if you're sure she's
only got superficial injuries, then it's fine to send her over
here,' I say.

'Good. Because I put her in a taxi ten minutes ago. She and
her husband should be with you any minute now.'

I unlock the Medical Centre doors, call up the guest's

details on the computer system then sit back to read the newspaper front pages while I wait for her to arrive. My patient is a stout, short-haired lady with a determined look in her eyes. I wonder, briefly, why the mugger picked her. She doesn't look like an easy target. I can't say I'm surprised that she fought back.

'I gather you've been in the wars, Mrs Henderson.'

'Well I didn't let myself get beaten. I've still got my camera, my purse and most of my dignity.'

'Now, dear, we can never be certain that anyone was trying to take those things from you,' her husband chides. He's shorter, slimmer and seems a lot more cautious than his wife. If I was a mugger I think I might have grabbed his bag first. 'I like to think well of people,' he says as I bring my focus back to our conversation. 'I'd like to believe that the strap of my wife's bag simply got caught on the boy's handlebars by accident.'

'Do you also believe that he accidentally pedalled away as fast as his legs would carry him afterwards?' his wife asks tartly. 'My husband thinks too well of people. In his world there is always a lot of light. In the real world I think things are a little darker.'

I check again that Mrs Henderson didn't injure her head. She gets a bit fed up by the questions, to be honest, but I don't want to take chances. After that I examine the rest of her. Her wrist took the brunt of her fall and is almost certainly fractured. She's got heaving bruising on her upper arm, what look like some broken ribs and a particularly nasty gash over her right shin.

'You know it would probably have been more sensible to follow my colleague's advice and go to a local hospital with all this. These injuries could have been a lot more serious,' I say.

Mrs Henderson shakes her head firmly. 'This is probably

our one and only world cruise, doctor. We've done three and a half months so far. Our whole family is going to be in Southampton to welcome us home.'

'We're not supposed to know that, my dear,' her husband interrupts.

'Well, we simply can't give up now,' she says. 'Will you please patch me up and let me stay?'

I look at the clock over the door. 'I think I'm going to have to because we sail soon. But I think you're actually going to be fine – and I totally understand why you've come back on board. Doing three months on a five-star ocean liner then flying home from Athens on a no-frills airline would be pretty grim. Follow me. I'll start off with some X-rays, then I'll clean all this up in time for dinner.'

Evening clinic is about to begin by the time the Hendersons are ready to leave – and we've got a visitor in the waiting area who knows them well.

'I met this couple at my photography class,' Mrs Philip says once they've greeted each other. 'We took a tour of the Royal Palace together in Phnom Penh. Frances helped me cross the roads there. I heard you'd had a spot of bother this afternoon, my dear. But if Doctor MacFarlane has looked after you, then I'm sure you'll be fine.'

I tell her to stop before I blush. Or at least to say those things when the Captain is listening. I step back a bit and look at Mrs Philip as the others leave. It's amazing to see this tanned, confident figure and think back to that distracted, distressed old lady in the pink nightdress I'd met at the start of the cruise.

Her smiles disappear the moment the Hendersons leave. She steps into my room, sits down and I get a terrible feeling I know what might be coming.

'I'm not here for an appointment. I'm here to pass on some news, some sad news,' she says softly. 'I've just spoken to Mrs Baxter on the phone. Arthur passed away last night in their hotel room in Singapore.'

'I'm so sorry to hear that. How is she coping?'

'She's upset and exhausted, of course. But in a strange way I wonder if she's not pleased. He's not in pain any more.'

'He also died in the same city as his friends and comrades. There must be some comfort in that.'

Mrs Philip has written out some contact details for Mrs Baxter in Australia and I put the note aside so we can send a message and some flowers on her return.

'I'm going to visit her in the autumn,' she says as she stands up to leave the Medical Centre. 'It will be spring there and Joan says I'll enjoy it. I wanted to thank you for introducing us, doctor. She's turned out to be a wonderful friend.'

'As have you, Mrs Philip,' I say with even more feeling. 'As have you.'

I'm on deck at seven the following morning watching the ship ease into our berth in Venice. Ronald Knightly – Mr Zip Wire – comes darting over as I take a few photos.

'I've been looking for you, young man. I've found something that could be very much to your advantage if you're going ashore today,' he says with a huge smile on his face. He reaches into his pocket for a tatty little piece of paper. 'It's a list of genuine extracts from real-life phrase books from around the world. I thought the one from the Italian phrase book might spice up your afternoon.'

He passes over the piece of paper.

'Togliti I vestiti! Sono un medico', it says. Translation: 'Take your clothes off! I am a doctor.'

'Not bad, is it?' he says. 'You can keep it if you want. Just don't forget to tell me how you get on!'

We chat for a bit longer, then he heads off to find his wife and I dash inside to collect Mrs Henderson. We've made an appointment for an orthopaedic consultation in a local hospital. I want to hear the results from her doctor first-hand just in case there are any hidden nasties. It turns out that there aren't. The doctors are as good as I'd hoped. On board we have a top secret, unofficial and probably heavily libellous list of comments about the various hospitals, clinics and individual workers that guests have come into contact with over the years. The hospital in Venice gets some very good reviews – just as well as it probably sees more damaged cruise-ship passengers than almost anywhere else in the Med.

The couple invite me to join them for lunch when we've been given the all clear. We find a place with a wooden pontoon overlooking some stunningly decrepit buildings. It's nice to be the only English-speaking people in the place.

'To the successful completion of your cruise,' I say when our wine arrives.

'To winning the lottery and being able to afford another one,' says Mrs Henderson. When our food arrives we spend a lazy hour talking through the highlights of the voyage. The couple particularly liked San Francisco and New Zealand. Mr Henderson liked the Panama and Suez Canals while his wife liked the beaches in Thailand and the snorkelling in Sharm el

Sheikh. She also likes the change of pace in Venice, though her husband has his doubts.

'It's nothing about Venice *per se*,' he says defensively. 'I simply feel there is something intellectually irrational about coming here as part of a four-month world cruise. It's one of the rare moments when we are not on the boat, yet here we are still surrounded by water. Venice is a quite inappropriate place for a cruise liner to dock. Don't you think we have simply swapped a giant metal ship for a much older version made of marble and stone?'

'Darling, you think too much,' is his wife's typically forthright answer.

It's the penultimate night of the cruise and Edward has invited us all to the Officers' Dining Room for a farewell dinner. It's not somewhere the rest of us use more than once or twice a week. I'm not keen because it always seems so much stuffier and more formal than our other dining rooms. Tonight, though, it's got real atmosphere. Edward is in his element and table-hops like a minor celebrity. He's clearly adored by his waiter, an older, quieter version of Romeo, and spends ages discussing the food and wine before ordering: 'the usual, my good man, bring me the usual.'

It's doubling up as a mini-retirement party, though, as we're still not supposed to know Edward's plans, we're trying not to mention this out-loud – some more successfully than others.

'Did Maureen not want to join you on your last cruise? I mean on these last few weeks of this last, I mean, latest cruise?' a flustered Eileen asks at one point.

For his part Edward just smiles – and bats the attention back on to me.

'I feel the bigger question is whether or not this is young Ben's last cruise and who he would choose to have at his side if it is,' he says, archly. I look around the table. Who can I bat this on to now? In desperation I ask Eileen if she's had any news from Kiri. Fortunately she has and I get a few moments out of the spotlight.

'She emailed me last night. Kieran's got problems with his visa but she's got a locum job at a private clinic and is making enough for both of them. They're researching the bar scene, which I think means drinking a lot and staying out very late. The good news is that she still seems utterly excited about it all. She says she's certain that she's done the right thing.'

'Ten dollars says they'll both be back on board this time next year,' says Dakila. 'Which brings us right back to you, Ben, because I don't think you answered Edward's question. Will you be back on board for another cruise in two months time? Or have you received a formal offer from the good doctors of Stratford?'

'The good doctors of Stratford seem to have gone very quiet of late,' I admit. 'I'm becoming a little concerned about what Edward wrote on my reference.'

'I told the truth. I said that in my experience they would be very lucky to get this doctor to work for them. Could they have taken that the wrong way?' he asks with a twinkle in his eye.

A long dinner turns into a long night in the Officers' Bar. Once more Edward is a clear favourite of the staff. One of the waiters makes sure we get a table near a window. He brings our drinks and serves them with little bowls of nuts and olives.

'It's all a little different to the Crew Bar all of you unaccountably prefer,' Edward says as we settle back into our chairs. 'I don't know how you can sit in a room without windows. This is so much more civilised.'

'Is that Gibraltar?' Rebecca asks as we peer out to the starboard side.

'If it is I'm very glad we're not stopping. I certainly hope we leave it behind soon,' says Eileen.

I look at her. 'What's wrong with Gibraltar? I thought you'd like a little bit of Britain on your travels.'

'It's not the place, it's the monkeys. Edward, don't you remember? A few trips ago we had that dear old passenger who did a bit of shopping on shore leave. A group of monkeys decided there was food in her bag and they went for it. Well, they went for her, to be exact.'

'So what happened?'

'They jumped on her shoulders, grabbed her hair, most of which was false, and bit and scratched every bit of flesh they could find. She had to go to hospital on the Rock and then get rushed back to us in time to sail. She had lacerations right over her scalp and face. We had to research the rabies and herpes risk and the poor love needed an injection in her backside. She stayed in her cabin wearing a bandana for nearly a week. It wasn't till we got to Istanbul that she could wear her wigs again. Those monkeys can be a terror.'

'I've got other bad memories of this stretch of water as well,' Edward adds as we gaze on out into the night. He turns to Eileen. 'Do you remember burials at sea?'

'I certainly do. It's a shame we're not allowed to do them any more.'

'The ceremonies could be unutterably moving,' Edward continues. 'I saw my first one when I was about your age, Ben. A passenger had specifically come on our cruise to die – something else you can't really do any more. He was in his late eighties and had been suffering from asbestosis for years. He'd been given a matter of weeks to live and had paid for an eastbound transatlantic cruise with the express intention of passing away in the middle of the Atlantic, the one place in the world he loved the most. We said goodbye to that gentleman at sunset. We gathered on the aft deck when everyone else was at dinner. The captain said a few words. The body was wrapped in an old sail, just as he had requested. The body slid down slowly into the water and was gone. We threw flowers and waited in silence until the light began to fade.

'At other burials over the years crew members asked to be wrapped in the flag of their country when they left the ship for the last time. Colleagues who are normally barred from the passenger decks are allowed to gather to pay their respects. Sometimes a few scrape together a few instruments and play the relevant national anthem. Tears fall, even if you don't know the man in question. I very much regret the passing of that tradition. If I were to die at my post that's how I would like to be buried.'

'I'm not sure Maureen or the children would approve,' Eileen says.

'Well I certainly don't want to do what everyone does today – sneaking ashes on board in sandwich boxes, then scattering them over the railings where they just blow back in on someone's balcony or end up floating in the pool. Anyway,

I haven't told you why this particular patch of sea has bad memories for me.'

We all sit back and wait for the story. As we do so I realise that I'm going to miss Edward's tales of yesteryear. I like having this link to the past. I also like socialising with my colleagues rather than just commuting home at the end of a shift. An inner city A&E is going to be a culture shock in every way.

'It was a dear lady who had been cruising for many years. She was practically a permanent passenger. She passed away in the night just outside of Rome, I believe. A few days later, just about here, we were due to hold the ceremony at dusk. She had many friends and there was a large crowd on the deck for the service. But what none of us knew was that a crew member had accidentally pressed the lever and released the body in the afternoon.'

'So what did you do?'

'We had a marvellously moving ceremony, just as the dear lady would have wanted. The Captain said a few words. Some of the lady's friends said a few words. We sang a Welsh hymn. What we thought was the lady's body was covered by a Welsh flag. We all threw white flowers as it slipped off the deck and disappeared beneath the waves.'

'So what was really underneath the flag?'

'A sack of potatoes.'

The night ended up being one of the latest of the whole cruise, which turned out to be bad news as we had one of the most mind-numbingly boring days ahead.

'It's admin time,' Eileen says, passing round the coffee first thing. 'As soon as clinic is over we need to get going. This whole place has to be turned upside down. If you thought you could wind-down you were wrong. The cruise isn't over yet.'

We barely come up for air for the next eight hours. Eileen even gets Romeo to bring us sandwiches at lunchtime so we can eat while we work. We take turns stock-taking, working on the inventory, checking every piece of equipment and double checking all the paperwork. All our passenger and crew files need to be in order. Records of every consultation, treatment, and health and safety issue have to be in the right places.

'Head Office may never look at any of this. But if they do, then you can bet that the one fact they need is the one thing we've missed. So let's not miss anything,' Eileen says as she puts another pot of coffee on and rallies us to keep going through the afternoon.

At one point I sit back in my consulting room chair and take a break to check my emails. I've got one from Jody Howard who tells me that Tom has seen a doctor in Melbourne and is working out a drugs regime to treat what's now been officially diagnosed as bipolar disorder.

'We're going to be OK. I'm going to get the old Tom back. Thank you, thank you, thank you,' is how she signs off the message. I fire off a quick, happy reply.

There's also good news of sorts from the crew welfare department. I asked them to check Marcia's records and it seems she's worked the full tour without any unauthorised time off. If she's still pregnant then that must mean she's doing OK. Maybe, after a while, I'll stop worrying about her. I thank the welfare people for the information, log off my computer, sip my coffee and look around. It's good to get a bit of closure on some of the things that have happened in this little metal room. I'm going to miss it, I know. I get a weird, teenage urge to carve a secret message inside a desk drawer for its next occupant. But then I hear Eileen approach and snap back to work.

Evening clinic is a nice break from the paperwork. Very few passengers come to see Edward but I get plenty of last minute crew members. One of the window cleaners has waited until now to ask about a problem 'down there' as he puts it, while one of the bar managers is suffering a brutal flare-up of colitis. The only person I don't help is the dancer who claims he needs some controlled medication to dull the pain of a previously undisclosed knee injury. What he really wants, of course, is something to sell when we're on land.

When the last patient has left I help Eileen lock up and we dash upstairs to change for our last big dinner. A whole flurry of formal events, masked balls and celebratory parties are going on across the ship to mark the end of the voyage. The worldies in particular have got something to shout about. They've done something like 35,000 nautical miles, visited two dozen countries and toured about thirty different towns, cities and islands.

'Apparently we've also got through something like 1.8 million eggs, 120 tonnes of potatoes, 400,000 pints of milk and 5,000 bottles of gin,' says the passenger next to me as we wait for the master of ceremonies to announce the arrival of the captain. 'Not to mention 500 gallons of ice cream a week.'

The clouds are low but there's a nice bit of sunshine poking through them as we finally approach Southampton the next morning.

'We haven't cured cancer or walked on the moon but we have achieved something,' Mrs Coates declares from under her latest jaunty beret. 'We've been around the world and back. How many people can say that?'

We wish each other well in case we don't see each other again in the chaos of disembarkation. 'Oh, please don't cry,' I say when she's reached up and pecked me on the cheek.

'I can't help it. I always cry at the end of a voyage. I wonder how I'll ever manage without all the people I've met. I wonder how I'll settle down to ordinary life and how I'll ever be able to afford this again. Thank you for being a good friend,' she says. Then she hurries along the deck and disappears inside.

I follow more slowly. In my cabin Albert has stacked up my luggage and the room looks horribly unfamiliar. I've left him what I hope is a good tip. Earlier on Edward told us how much we're all getting as our share of the surgery profits and we've left Romeo a nice slice of the cash as well.

Now all I have to do is head upstairs and wait for the chance to leave. Some of the old-timers are moaning about the delays and the ever-increasing amount of admin we have to go through before we can walk down the gangway. As it's my first time I've no idea what to expect. And, as I'm strangely reticent about leaving the ship, I'm quite happy to stand back and let others face the formalities ahead of me.

Edward is suddenly at my side as I watch some crew luggage being opened by the security staff.

'It's really most unfair that it's the crew they're searching,' he booms. 'The passengers are the worst and always have been. You know when the original Queen Mary completed her inaugural transatlantic voyage to New York in 1936? Not a single ash tray was left on board. Not one. And that was in the good old days.'

He's still alongside me when we've shuffled to the front of the crowd and are finally stepping out into the sunshine.

'It has been an absolute pleasure, young man and I do hope we stay in touch,' he says when we're back on solid ground. 'I've enjoyed working with you and I look forward to finding out what your future holds.'

'So do I,' I admit.

'Dare I suggest one more cruise before you make up your mind?' he asks as he spots his wife and shakes my hand one last time.

I look over at him and smile.

'Maybe one.'

# AUTHOR'S NOTE

I have so many people to thank for the technical details and anecdotes that went into this book. At sea they include Leo, Jane, Pedro, Sarah, Ieuan, Gretchen, Steve and Graham, while on land my thanks go to Janice, Richard and Gareth. Special thanks go to Neil Simpson, a talented ghost-writer, who was able to take my thoughts, memories and experiences and turn them into such a great narrative. On the publishing front I want to thank Ciara Foley and Heather Rainbow, my editors at Hodder & Stoughton who worked so hard on this project and on my first book *Holiday SOS*. Their experience and effort helped transform the written words into a fully fledged book. I'm so pleased to have had them both on my side. Many others at Hodder have helped too – in particular I want to thank Katie Davison, Rowena Webb, Kerry Hood, Lucy Hale and Jason Bartholomew. Finally, thanks to my agents Andrew Lownie and Meg Davies who continue to work hard to promote the books and develop the SOS concept.

I am constantly aware of the importance of patient confidentiality so all the names and many of the identifying details of the events in this book have been changed. Furthermore, since I wanted *Cruise Ship SOS* to read like a novel rather than a medical textbook or a traditional memoir

I have combined a lifetime of experiences into a single, fictional round the world cruise. That said, I wouldn't be at all surprised if the exact scenarios my colleagues and I have faced aren't happening again right now on a ship somewhere on the high seas.

Cruise liners are getting bigger every year. With more than 6,000 people on board you can be sure of two things. Firstly, that the medical team will be very busy people. Secondly, that they'll do everything in their power to make sure the guests and crew are treated with dignity and receive the highest standards of modern medical care. I love medicine, I love travel and I love the camaraderie you experience working as part of a medical team overseas. I hope I've captured all three passions in this book. I wish everyone reading it many years of safe and happy holidays!

Ben MacFarlane, London, Spring 2010

If you enjoyed *Cruise Ship SOS*, follow Doctor Ben MacFarlane
on his adventures as a repatriation doctor in

ISBN 978 0 340 91976 7
Price £7.99